TOM BRUCE

Loss and
Anticipatory Grief

Loss and Anticipatory Grief

Edited by

Therese A. Rando
Therese A. Rando Associates, Ltd.

Foreword by

Robert Fulton

Lexington Books
D.C. Heath and Company/Lexington, Massachusetts/Toronto

Library of Congress Cataloging-in-Publication Data

Loss and anticipatory grief.

    Includes index.
    1. Grief. 2. Death—Psychological aspects. 3. Terminal care—Psychological aspects.
4. Bereavement—Psychological aspects. I. Rando, Therese A.
BF575.G7L67   1986   155.9'37   85-45082
ISBN 0-669-11144-9

Published simultaneously in Canada
Printed in the United States of America
Casebound International Standard Book Number: 0-669-11144-9
Library of Congress Catalog Card Number: 85-45082

The paper used in this publication meets the minimum requirements of American National
Standard for Information Sciences—Permanence of Paper for Printed Library Materials,
ANSI Z39.48-1984.

The last numbers on the right below indicate the number and date of printing.

10 9 8 7 6 5 4 3 2 1

95 94 93 92 91 90 89 88 87 86

*This book is dedicated with deepest love
to the memory, spirit, and character of
A.J. Nookie,
who gave new meaning to the word "tenacious."*

Contents

Foreword

Robert Fulton, PhD
Professor of Sociology
Director, Center for Death
  Education and Research
University of Minnesota

". . . he's a human being and a terrible thing is happening to him. So attention must be paid. He's not to be allowed to fall into his grave like an old dog. Attention, attention must be finally paid to such a person."

With this impassioned plea, Linda, Willy Loman's long-suffering wife in Arthur Miller's *Death of a Salesman*, attempts to reawaken filial love and respect for Willy in their disaffected son, Biff. This classic American drama was performed for the first time in New York city in the winter of 1949, before a galvanized audience. It deservedly earned Miller the Pulitzer Prize for drama that year, as it brilliantly heralded the nascent problem of aging in America.

Such a call to action: to respond to a person in need, ill, or confronted by death with care, comfort, and relief, is as ancient and universal as it is inspiring. History records the compassionate acts of mercy of St. Bridget of Ireland during the fifth century, a time otherwise marked by savage warfare and brutal atrocities as well as the Hospitaller Knights of St. John and their selfless courage at the time of the crusades. More familiar to us all, perhaps, is Father Damien's work among the lepers of Molokai, or the ministrations of the Quaker Elizabeth Fry to patients and their families in England during the last century. Contemporaneously, we are witness to Mother Theresa's dedication to the "untouchables" of Calcutta, as well as to the example of caring exemplified by St. Christopher's of Sydenham, England, the modern hospice founded by Dame Cicely Saunders in 1967.

Such concern for those in distress testifies not only to our common humanity, but also reminds us of our shared fate. In the Western world the impulse to succor those in want can be traced to the Parable of the Good Samaritan, the Seven Acts of Mercy, and, ultimately, to the love of Christ.

We know—we have always known—that human beings die and that all relationships end in separation. Nations and peoples, however, experience dying and death differently. As with an individual, a nation's culture and history provide a unique context for the inevitable encounter with death. The focus of concern at any given time, however, will vary. For example, in the United States, the "death awareness" movement over the past three decades brought attention to the manner in which individuals and institutions had come to deny both the prospect and reality of death. The practice of death avoidance was shattered, however, by the publication of Elisabeth Kübler-Ross's book, *On Death and Dying,* in 1969. The book not only exposed many of the problems of the dying in America's health care system, but it also helped illuminate problems that the denial of death presented to caregivers themselves in public institutions.

The issues associated with dying and death in the United States today, however, have taken on new significance as the circumstances of life have changed. Progress in medical science and the general enhancement of life since the turn of the century, for example, have greatly increased the proportion of elderly persons in society. The consequence of this development is that death is now primarily the experience of the aged.

The context in which dying and death are experienced in the United States has also undergone a significant change. The overwhelming majority of deaths now take place outside the home in either a hospital or nursing home setting. The trend, moreover, toward increased hospitalization and institutionalization of the chronically ill or dying patient can be expected to continue.

These changes that are overtaking the United States and, indeed, the modern industrialized world are also having a direct and frequently deleterious effect on family relations. Today's elderly, whether they live in Stockholm, London, Tokyo, or New York, are increasingly retired from work, and often live physically as well as psychologically removed from their children and grandchildren. Geographical and social mobility, moreover, frequently deprive the elderly of traditional family and community assistance.

Family relations have also been directly affected by contemporary mortality and the new social patterns and attitudes related to dying and death that are emerging. Prolonged separation of the elderly due to hospitalization or residential change serves to reduce family and friendship contacts and strain long-standing social and emotional commitments. With a sense of having "lived out one's life," the death of an elderly person need not affect the emotional life of his or her family to the same degree it once might have. This does not mean, of course, that when an elderly parent or relative dies, grief is absent. Rather, the character, degree, or extent of a survivor's grief appears to depend upon many factors, not the least of which is the nature and intensity of the social bond itself.

The experience of grief and its consequences is the subject of this collection of readings edited by Therese A. Rando. It is her purpose to bring to the professional and lay public alike a set of guidelines, based on her experience and research as a clinical psychologist, for therapeutic intervention on behalf of grieving survivors. More particularly, she and her colleagues address the phenomenon of anticipatory grief, that is, a grief reaction, first identified by

Lindemann of Harvard Medical School, that can be experienced prior to an actual death. It is Dr. Rando's thesis and the main thrust of these collected essays that therapeutic intervention on the part of skilled caregivers can facilitate the grief work of survivors prior to the death, as well as potentially provide a more positive post-mortem bereavement experience. As she states in her introductory essay,

> It is well known that the experience of terminal illness—that period of time in which anticipatory grief occurs—has a profound influence on postdeath bereavement. To the extent that healthy behavior, interaction and processes can be promoted during this time, the individual's postdeath mourning can be made relatively better than it would be if the experience lacked the therapeutic benefits of appropriate anticipatory grief.

The theme of utilizing the forewarning of a loss in a positive and creative way is carried throughout the book. The general argument presented is that premature detachment from the dying person, poor communication, lack of appropriate acts, and failure to close the relationship predispose the survivor to a poor bereavement outcome.

Therapeutic intervention, it is argued on the other hand, can help prevent problems in mourning from occurring. Importantly, it is also recognized that the dying person him- or herself can experience anticipatory grief and that such intervention may be the most important thing that can be offered to the patient by those involved.

The collection of readings is organized under five general headings: I. General Perspectives on Anticipatory Grief; II. Anticipatory Grief and the Principals Involved; III. Clinical Interventions in Anticipatory Grief; IV. Developmental Issues in Anticipatory Grief; and V. Practical Considerations in Anticipatory Grief. Within such an organized cachement, Dr. Rando introduces the book with an historical account of the concept of anticipatory grief, its several perspectives, and the psychodynamic processes that are involved, as well as outlines the problems and prospects associated with this sometimes controversial concept.

Vanderlyn R. Pine, in his essay, "An Agenda for Adaptive Anticipation of Bereavement," clarifies many of the issues surrounding the definition of anticipatory grief, locates it within a general framework of grief, and points to its practical application. In doing so, he reminds us that the "anticipation of bereavement" will elicit different grief reactions and that grief itself must be understood as spanning a broad continuum of potential reactions.

J. Eugene Knott and Eugenia Wild poignantly sensitize the reader to the dilemmas and difficulties to be confronted in living with a loved one diagnosed with cancer. They emphasize what needs to be stressed again and again—that knowledge or forewarning of a death may not be recognized by the different parties concerned. Denial, hope, or one's faith may all play a part in shielding the dying patient and/or the survivors from an inevitable death.

Of particular importance is a point that several of the authors make: that the major reason for interest in the phenomenon of anticipatory grief is the fact that, as a result of medical advances, terminally ill patients, adults as well as children, are living longer and longer with their illnesses. Consequently, the danger of decathecting too soon is ever present, threatening to envelope everyone involved in an exquisitely painful experience.

Therese A. Rando, in her central contribution to the book, "Understanding and Facilitating Anticipatory Grief in the Loved Ones of the Dying," amplifies on the theme of the significance of the larger social group's involvement in a person's dying and in doing so brings a family systems approach to the challenges and tasks of forewarning. In discussing the changes that have occurred in the past six or seven decades in American social life, she makes clear how uniquely vulnerable the American family is to loss.

After outlining the complicated issues involved in contemporary dying, Dr. Rando offers the reader guidelines for clinical therapy intervention that are calculated to serve the patient in achieving an appropriate death and the survivor in achieving an acceptable resolution of loss.

Marion A. Humphrey, a clinical nurse, invites the reader to recognize the impact that anticipatory grief has on the caregiver as well as on the patient or the family member. She felicitously outlines the adaptational tasks which are required by the several parties and the specific intervention strategies that are seen as facilitating healthy grief work. (As an aside, I am struck by a thought that her chapter stimulated in me, namely, how far we have come in our views on dying and death, and how different our perspective is regarding what issues are important to address. For more than two millenia, such sacred texts as the *I Ching,* the *Tibetan Book of the Dead* and the *Egyptian Book of the Dead,* as well as the more recent Ars Moriendi literature of the West, served humankind as fundamental guidebooks for the safe passage of the human soul into the next world. Today, however, in our secular and psychologically oriented world, our focus now is primarily on the need to comfort the dying person and to offer therapeutic assistance to his or her presumably grieving survivors. While this is not the place to explore the ramifications of such a religio-philosophical shift in our attitudes and reactions toward dying and death, it nevertheless needs to be recognized and taken into account in any discussion concerning the components of the grief reaction.)

This thought remains with me in the various essays subsumed under the headings "Clinical Interventions in Anticipatory Grief," and "Developmental Issues in Anticipatory Grief." The basic themes are forewarning of loss, facilitating the grief of the survivor, and the therapeutic value of pre-mortem grief. Hulen S. Kornfeld and Richard W. Boerstler recommend meditation for those who are dying. It is their thesis that the meditation process is a useful way to help stabilize vital signs through autonomic nervous system response. Taught to the patient's survivors, it permits them to engage in a positive caring act, while sharing with the patient the benefit of calm bodies and minds. A derivative of this method is that in assisting the patient in "letting go," closure among the patient and his family and friends is also potentiated.

The value of forewarning of loss is stressed in several of the other essays. Not only is it seen by Janice DeFrances Van Dexter as a critical strategy in the classroom, allowing the teacher to intervene in a benign way on behalf of a child whose parent or sibling may be dying, but such forewarning is also recognized by Mary Elizabeth Mancini as valuable in sensitizing emergency room personnel to the special needs of a survivor of a sudden death. She recommends guidelines for therapeutic communication between caregivers and the families of sudden death victims. Skill in delivering bad news, preparation of the body for viewing, facilitating the venting of emotions, and sensitive assistance to the survivors during the viewing of the body, are not only ways in which the survivors are aided, but also, in the programmed and orderly management of such moments, caregivers themselves are cared for. Concern for the caregivers is also echoed in David M. LaGreca's careful delineation of anticipatory grief from the clergy perspective. Among other points in this essay, he accurately depicts the caregiver as a catalyst who can both change and be changed in the anticipatory grief situation.

Forewarning of loss is also taken up by N. Claire Kowalski in her essays, "The Older Person's Anticipation of Her Own Death" and "Anticipating the Death of an Elderly Parent." In her review of the life of an older person and in her discussion of the various theories of psychological development as they relate to aging, she bumps up against the fact that life is, indeed, idiosyncratic: that individuals will deal with their dying and their deaths in the same unique, if not perverse, ways as they have dealt with all the other aspects of their lives—theories of psychological development notwithstanding. While she is correct in observing that few elderly people admit fear of their own deaths and that others express an ambivalence toward their mortality, those of us who have worked with the dying know that there are others, young as well as old, who positively anticipate their dying and warmly embrace the prospect of their own deaths. There is no question, however, that for the dying person and his or her survivors, the forewarning of death can ease the process of dying itself as well as the psychological and social consequences of the death.

This is seen most clearly in the last section of the book, "Practical Considerations in Anticipatory Grief." Here discussion is given over to such mundane, but nevertheless important, issues as prearrangement of funerals and financial planning for the terminally ill. Howard C. Raether offers practical advice for the reader and points out a fact that has also been stressed by Dr. Rando and others. Namely, that the dying person him- or herself has the potential to experience anticipatory grief, and that the consequences may be either positive or negative. It is his observation that, while many terminally ill individuals may be significantly helped by taking control and prearranging their own funerals, a surviving spouse, on the other hand, may feel slighted by such action, or even profoundly injured. In this, as in many other aspects of the subject, a subject which involves human relationships and potentially profound emotions, one must conclude that "it depends."

Perhaps more clear cut is the importance of forewarning as it relates to financial planning for the terminally ill. James Blackerby and Edwin Steward point out the critical value of rational action at a time when the dying patient is possibly suffering a major emotional upheaval. The organization of one's financial affairs to relieve the burdens on the surviving spouse and other beneficiaries can therefore be seen as a significant contribution to the mental well-being of the patient, as well as to significant others during this critical time. This section also includes a discussion by Dennis A. Robbins on the legal and ethical issues in terminal illness care for patients, families, caregivers, and institutions. Somewhat tangential to the thrust of the other papers, it nevertheless offers the reader a brief but excellent overview of the emergent dilemmas presently confronting us as a result of medical science's ability to prolong life by such means as the respirator, the organ transplant, radiation, and chemotherapy. Robbins is correct. Since the development of the kidney machine in Seattle, Washington, in 1954 and the subsequent passage of the Uniform Anatomical Gift Act, we have been witness to a brave new world in which the impulse to live or prolong life has come into direct conflict with our traditional concepts of life and death, selfhood, and privacy, to say nothing of the rights of the survivor.

Out of order in my discussion of the various chapters of the book, but certainly not out of place, is Stanley M. Aronson's essay, "A Physician's Acquaintance With Grief." In his essay he reminds us that one's grief is a solitary passion in which one despairs that life can provide nothing to replace the person who has died. A caring physician, he asserts, must not only provide solace to the grieving person, but his own personal sadness must also be tempered by his knowledge that life is ultimately stronger than grief. Contemporary Western medicine, he observes, has refined, albeit imperfectly, the art of predicting the future, and a physician must come to accept anticipatory grief as a near constant companion as he goes about his professional duties. The truth, he states, must be unfolded slowly, however—otherwise much harm may be done. He quotes Emily Dickinson: "the truth must dazzle gradually, or else every man be blinded." Herein lies, I think, the importance of the experience of forewarning and the value of the concept of anticipatory grief. It is to

Dr. Rando's credit that she has orchestrated this collection of readings so that we may better understand the powerful luminosity of death and that we not be blinded by our grief.

Acknowledgments

There are a variety of individuals who deserve explicit appreciation for their direct or indirect influence on the content and production process of this book. I mention them here in a small attempt to publicly recognize the significance of their contributions.

First, I must thank those who contributed chapters to this book. United in a desire to explicate the experiences and needs of the dying patient, family member, and caregiver, these professionals have thoughtfully and, in many cases, uniquely examined anticipatory grief. From this they have generated specific and important interventions designed to promote the healthiest possible navigation through this complex experience. I am particularly grateful to Robert Fulton, PhD, who has taken the time to review the manuscript and write its foreword. Since he is the individual most consistently identified with promoting discussion of anticipatory grief, I am honored that he has lent his careful consideration to this work. Appreciative mention must also be made of the Forum for Death Education and Counseling. This organization's local chapter offered the March 1984 conference on anticipatory grief which helped spawn ideas for specific chapters of this book through its workshops and attempts to raise public consciousness about meeting the needs of those involved in the anticipatory grief experience.

It is imperative that I acknowledge, albeit anonymously, the hundreds of patients, families, caregivers, and friends who since 1970 have taught me about the benefits and detriments of anticipatory grief. I can promise them that what they have conveyed to me will continue to be utilized to promote healthy life and death in those with whom I come in contact. I thank them all for what they have taught me through their own lives and deaths, and will forever be awed by the intimate privilege of sharing these with them.

Three people deserve particular mention for their influence on this work. All three have contributed significantly to this volume in terms of specific chapters, but merit additional identification here for their personal impact on me. Since 1975 long-term friend and associate Marion A. Humphrey, RN, MA, CS, has been offering me unparalleled and unique insights into the dying experience from the individual perspectives of all involved. I can think of no one who posesses a better grasp of how best to intervene to promote a truly appropriate death. J. Eugene Knott, PhD, mentor and friend, deserves, as he will forever, specific testimony for his special role as supporter, advisor, and confidant in my thanatological pursuits. I only wish that he could have been spared the personal ordeal that taught him so much about anticipatory grief. And last, but in no way least, I must express deep gratitude to my colleague and friend, Vanderlyn R. Pine, PhD, who has been distinctly instrumental in encouraging new analyses of the theories and explanations of experiences of grief, dying, and death that previously have been far too frequently accepted without critical examination. He has modeled, stimulated, and supported an attitude of inquiry and a sociohistorical perspective which has set in motion attempts at new understandings of these phenomena, out of which will spring new and, I believe, ultimately more useful clinical interventions for the benefit of those we seek to serve.

This is also the point at which I finally have the opportunity to publicly thank those relatives who contributed to this book by lovingly intervening in my life in ways and at times that helped me to overcome my own personal tragedies related to this topic. They attempted to step into the breach to soften the blows experienced by the two nieces and one nephew who struggled so intensely to cope with the devastating sequelae of deaths and griefs which had lacked the optimum benefits of anticipatory grief. On behalf of Beth, Randy, and myself, I offer heartfelt gratitude for the familial support of Mr. and Mrs. Joseph D. Morris, Miss Rita E. Rando, Mr. and Mrs. Robert Tesoro, and Mr. and Mrs. Joseph Franco.

At Lexington Books, I wish to extend my appreciation to Margaret Zusky, who most diligently pursued this project, and the other staff involved: Karen Maloney, Karen Storz, and Martha Cleary. I must also thank Jodi Pollock for her capable and concerned secreterial assistance during part of the preparation of this book.

Without a doubt, this book would never have been possible without the professional, as well as personal, support of my administrative assistant, Barbara A. Tremaine-Vargas. In countless ways she enables me to function in my myriad roles. Whatever professional successes I have enjoyed in the past four-and-a-half years are due in no small part to her competent and efficient coordination of my business life.

And the most special acknowledgment of all goes to my best friend, Anthony.

Introduction

T hink smarter, not harder." As a youngster I was given this advice and have found it practical and pertinent to all areas of life. I believe it aptly calls for what is lacking in clinical thanatology today. As a field, we have rushed to minister to the dying, the bereaved, and their caregivers, armed with best intentions and deep commitment. However, in our zeal to assuage the pain of loss, whether before or after death, we have too often been guilty of insufficient circumspection, of jumping too readily to incorporate into our armamentarium untested theory, insufficiently supported clinical observation, and unreliable data. To be sure, the reasons for this are understandable. Our goals are noble: we want to cure and we want to palliate. Nevertheless, in the mid-1980s the time has come for us to stop and look more deeply and critically at the information on which we base our interventions. "Thinking harder" by struggling to empiricize every investigation, often losing rich clinical data, or rushing to apply all theories to all persons will not be useful unless we have "thought smarter" and been more clear on what we are doing, why we are doing it, and what the effects are.

It is in response to these contentions that the essays in *Loss and Anticipatory Grief* have been compiled. Anticipatory grief is a topic whose time has come. Significant sociocultural and technological changes have combined with changing medical realities to spawn the current concerns with illness, loss, and death and their various psychological, social, physiological, spiritual, economic, governmental, and practical sequelae. While the topic has been up on the thanatological table for discussion since Erich Lindemann's brief introduction of it in 1944, has benefitted significantly from Robert Fulton's various analyses of it since 1971, and has been addressed in passing by a few others since then, anticipatory grief has not been given the attention due to such a critical area. It is quite unique in its availability as an area that, by definition, offers opportunity for primary prevention. As noted repeatedly throughout this book, interventions at this point can prevent problems from developing; later interventions can only try to remedy difficulties that have already occurred.

This book has been written in an attempt to carefully and comprehensively examine the multidimensional phenomenon of anticipatory grief and to delineate the specific and practical interventions that can maximize its positive benefits and minimize its liabilities. Following the foreword contributed by Robert Fulton, PhD, the fifteen chapters of this book fall within five sections:

General Perspectives on Anticipatory Grief: Anticipatory Grief and the Principals Involved; Clinical Interventions in Anticipatory Grief; Developmental Issues in Anticipatory Grief; and Practical Considerations in Anticipatory Grief. Each chapter, while reflecting sound comprehension of the pertinent theoretical and empirical literature, has been written to be clinically practical. Each author not only describes the salient issues, questions, and dilemmas relevant to his or her topic, but offers concrete interventions to enable the reader to extract pragmatic clinical strategies to utilize in working with individuals experiencing anticipatory grief.

I believe that the clinician, the academician, and the researcher will each find new information in this compendium. It is my hope that this will enhance the "thinking smarter" process mentioned above, and in doing so will benefit not only the dying and bereaved, but the entire field as well.

Part I
General Perspectives on Anticipatory Grief

1

A Comprehensive Analysis of Anticipatory Grief: Perspectives, Processes, Promises, and Problems

Therese A. Rando

Very similar to the hotly contested "Can children mourn?" controversy has been the recent thanatological debate about the nature of anticipatory grief.* Since the concept was first introduced without extensive elaboration or fanfare by Erich Lindemann at the close of his classic 1944 article, "Symptomatology and Management of Acute Grief," the phenomenon has been of interest to individuals working with the dying, their loved ones, those already bereaved, and their caregivers.

In his article, Lindemann had described the pathognomonic characteristics of grief and delineated the tasks of "grief work." These are: emancipation from the bondage to the deceased (or, to use the psychoanalytic term, "decathexis"—the withdrawal of emotional investment in the deceased and the detaching and modifying of emotional ties so that new relationships can be established), readjustment to the environment in which the deceased is missing, and the formation of new relationships.

However, Lindemann had also noted that the *threat* of death or separation could itself initiate a bereavement reaction. He cited the case of the person who is so concerned with adjustment after the potential death of a loved one that all the phases of grief are undergone: specifically "depression, heightened preoccupation with the departed, a review of all the forms of death which might befall him, and anticipation of the modes of readjustment which might be necessitated by it" (pp. 147–148). However, as Lindemann points out, such advance preparation is not without some cost. While it can serve as a safeguard should the death actually occur, it may inhibit continued involvement if the death does not occur and the loved one returns to be reunited. Lindemann

---

This chapter is dedicated in loving memory to Gavin Everett Knott, whose years of living with leukemia made anticipatory grief a familiar companion to so many.

*Although some authors differentiate the terms "grief" and "mourning," in this chapter they are used interchangeably to refer to the intrapsychic processes prompted by either a tangible (physical) or psychosocial (symbolic) loss and manifested in the psychological, social, and somatic realms.

illustrated this phenomenon with the example of the soldier who returned from the battlefront and complained that his wife did not love him anymore and had demanded an immediate divorce. Lindemann interpreted this action as constituting the effects of grief work done too effectively. In this case, the woman had emotionally emancipated herself (decathected) so completely that she no longer had emotional investment in her husband and the ensuing readjustment demanded that she direct herself towards new involvements and interactions.

Since that time, numerous researchers, clinicians, and theorists have articulated the costs and the benefits of anticipatory grief. This has resulted in an accumulation of seemingly contradictory information. However, closer inspection reveals that the discord is more apparent than real. Nevertheless, a critical therapeutic point stemming from this cannot be overstated. It is imperative to recognize that—as in the controversy pertaining to whether or not children can legitimately mourn like adults—the clinical issue is that an experience is occurring which requires attention. Whether or not children are engaged in the same intrapsychic processes as adults is a moot question when it comes to practical matters. The fact is that the children *are* in pain and require intervention, notwithstanding the terms used or processes hypothesized. The same can be extrapolated to anticipatory grief. There is an experience going on that demands attention. The fact that there is semantic argument over what to call that experience is irrelevant to its existence and to the necessity of assistance.

The purpose of this chapter is to offer a new and comprehensive analysis of anticipatory grief. Its premise is that anticipatory grief is a more complex and multidimensional set of processes than heretofore outlined. A justification for its study is offered, followed by a review of the literature and a discussion of the reasons for the many discrepancies and contradictory findings that exist. The main emphasis of the chapter is to offer substantive clinical data to discern both what anticipatory grief is not and what it is. The final section provides a delineation of the numerous component processes that comprise this significant phenomenon.

Justification for the Study of Anticipatory Grief

The primary justification for the study of anticipatory grief lies in its unique ability to provide an arena for primary prevention. In the field of grief and bereavement, the focus of intervention is usually on assisting the survivor to cope with a fait accompli, and there is nothing that he or she can do to alter the situation; that is, the loved one is already deceased. Treatment consists of helping the individual pick up the pieces after the fact. It is in the area of anticipatory grief that the caregiver has the golden opportunity to use primary prevention strategies and to make therapeutic interventions that may facilitate appropriate grief work and a more positive bereavement experience for the survivor-to-be. It is well known that the experience of terminal illness—that period of time in which anticipatory grief occurs—has a profound influence on postdeath bereavement. To the extent that healthy behavior, interaction, and processes can be promoted during this time, the individual's postdeath mourning can be made relatively better than it would be if the experience lacked the therapeutic benefits of appropriate anticipatory grief.

The basis for more in-depth investigation into the experience of anticipatory grief arises from the important need to capitalize on this therapeutic opportunity and use it to the individual's healthiest advantage. Unfinished business, premature detachment, poor communication and interaction with the patient during the illness, and lack of appropriate anticipation all predispose the griever to poor bereavement outcomes. Consequently, it is critical that anticipatory grief, which under appropriate conditions can supplant these problems, be recognized as a legitimate and unique phenomenon for intervention. Interventions made at this point can prevent problems in mourning from developing; later interventions can only attempt to remedy difficulties that already have occurred.

For the dying person, who also experiences a variety of anticipatory grief, therapeutic intervention in and support of the process of anticipatory grief constitutes the most important actions that can be taken.

As the quality of terminal illnesses change due to recent advances in medical technology, the interim between diagnosis and death is lengthening. Termed the "living–dying interval" (Pattison, 1977, 1978), this period of time brings to the dying patient and his or her loved ones a number of problems that originate from the chronic nature of most diseases. These include, among others, numerous remissions and relapses, with myriad psychological reactions to each; lengthened periods of anticipatory grief; increased financial, social, physical, and emotional pressures; long-term family disruption; progressive decline of the patient and emotional responses of loved ones to this decline; longer periods of uncertainty; intensive treatment regimens and their side effects; and dilemmas about decision making and treatment choices. In most cases, dying is a gradual process. Few become bedridden or die immediately as was the norm in the past. During times of remission, terminally ill patients still want to work, play, relate to others, and be involved in social activities. They still want and need honest communication and interaction. However, interspersed with these times are those of relapse—graphic reminders of what is to come. It is often a depleting experience for everyone involved. The uncertainty of some situations, the certainty of others; the inconsistency of the illness or its relentless and persistent consistency; the steady debilitation or the up-and-down nature of the loss of control; the wish that the end would come, and the fear that it will all are examples of the pressures that place uncommon stress and demands on the dying person and the concerned others involved with him or her. As a result, the period of time within which anticipatory grief exists has become more complex and burdensome. Although it offers more time for preparation, the other side of the double-edged sword also slices: the extra time is often filled with the painful witnessing of progressive debilitation over which there may be no control. For this reason, to assist those who must struggle through such an extraordinary process as dying due to a terminal illness, it is imperative to examine the phonomenon of anticipatory grief, which both strongly influences and is influenced by this process.

Contradictory Research: Review of Literature and Reasons for Discrepancies

Much of the clinical research points to the adaptational value and positive effects on the postdeath grief experience of having some advanced warning and the opportunity to experience moderate amounts of anticipatory grief prior to a death (Ball, 1976–1977; Binger et al., 1969; Burton, 1974; Chodoff, Friedman, and Hamburg, 1964; Friedman, 1967; Friedman et al., 1963; Fulton and Fulton, 1971; Futterman, Hoffman, and Sabshin, 1972; Glick, Weiss, and Parkes, 1974; Goldberg, 1973; Natterson and Knudson, 1960; Parkes, 1972, 1975; Parkes and Weiss, 1983; Raphael and Maddison, 1976; Rees and Lutkins, 1967; Richmond and Waisman, 1955; Vachon et al., 1976; Vachon et al., 1982; and Wiener, 1970).

Others have found a period of anticipation to be unrelated to postdeath grief experience (Benfield, Leib, and Reuter, 1976; Bornstein et al., 1973; Clayton, Desmarais and Winokur, 1968; Gerber et al., 1975; Kennell, Slyter, and Klaus, 1970; Maddison and Viola, 1968; Maddison and Walker, 1967; Parkes, 1970; Schwab et al., 1975; and Wolff et al., 1964).

Despite not finding an overall correlation between anticipation and postdeath grief, both Gerber et al. (1975) and Schwab et al. (1975) did find that in their respective populations the longest, most extended illnesses were related to poor adjustment subsequent to the death. This corresponds with the findings of Hamovitch (1964) and Maddison (1968) and with some of the findings of Rando (1983) and Sanders (1982–1983). The latter two each discovered that both the shortest and longest periods of anticipation were associated with poorer outcome, as compared to a medium length of time of anticipation.

Finally, there are those who caution more specifically than others that a period of anticipatory grief can lead to premature detachment, which can deprive the patient and family of the possibilities still remaining in the relationship, and end in actual or emotional abandonment of the patient (Levitz, 1977; Lindemann, 1944; Peretz, 1970; Rosenbaum, 1944; and Travis, 1976).

There are a number of reasons why inconsistency is so prevalent in the writings and research devoted to anticipatory grief. Chief among these is the erroneous practice of conceptually confusing forewarning of loss with anticipatory grief (Fulton and Gottesman, 1980; Siegel and Weinstein, 1983). It is clinically clear, and has been made as apparent empirically, that individuals may be well aware of the impending loss but not grieve in anticipation (Clayton et al., 1973), or they may have been explicitly informed of the fatal diagnosis but refused to believe it, or ignored it, or misunderstood the warnings (Parkes, 1970; Vachon et al., 1977). Consequently, neither anticipatory grief nor awareness of impending death can be assumed to exist merely based on the length of time the decedent was ill prior to the death or on the delivery of a fatal diagnosis by a physician.

In their insightful article, Siegel and Weinstein (1983) posit other explanations for the contradictory research findings. Among these they note that the many factors associated with a protracted illness, such as social isolation, physical exhaustion, emotional anguish, and depletion of emotional and financial resources, may artificially inflate postdeath symptoms and be so strongly associated with poor bereavement outcome that they overshadow or cancel out the gains provided by a period of anticipation. Alternatively, they cite poor research designs with serious methodological weaknesses that are often predicated on popular but untested assumptions as contributing to the diverse findings. Fulton and Gottesman (1980) explicate several of these assumptions that appear to have arisen from traditional psychoanalytic perspectives on grief and that fail to give due consideration to either the sociopsychological or sociocultural aspects of grief. These include the assumptions that all those in a particular state of bereavement experience a comparable volume of grief and that once grief is begun the grief reaction is dissipated in a continuous and irreversible path toward resolution. Both of these erroneous assumptions indicate a failure to examine carefully the phenomenon of anticipatory grief on Fulton and Gottesman's requisite three levels of analysis. On the psychological level, one must take into account the particular coping abilities, beliefs, feelings, and other psychological characteristics of the persons involved. On the interpersonal level, the type of relationship that is being grieved, the manner in which the principals deal with or deny their grief, and the type of support they receive for coping with it will profoundly affect its experience. Finally, on the sociocultural level, anticipatory grief will be influenced by the presence or absence of norms, roles, and rituals for the grievers.

There are still other dimensions confounding the anticipatory grief literature. Differences in methodologies of the studies and significant variations among subject populations preclude important comparisons and limit generalizability. Both Raphael (1983) and Bowlby (1980) point out that in a number of studies the severe reactions that occurred after a sudden bereavement were generated because the deaths were not only sudden, but untimely (that is, the deceased were younger than in studies where sudden death had less of a traumatic impact) or traumatic (that is, involving violence, accidents, mutilation, and so forth.) For example, in the Gerber et al. (1975) study, in which the deaths were of elderly persons who succumbed to an illness, sudden death was found to be unrelated to an increase in bereavement symptomatology as contrasted to the findings of Glick, Weiss, and Parkes (1974), who investigated reactions to the deaths of younger individuals, many of whom died from traumatic events. The sudden death of an elderly individual under natural circumstances, of course, would be expected to elicit different reactions than the sudden and violent death of a younger person; however, such important variations have heretofore been insufficiently accounted for in the literature.

The lack of a precise and consistent definition of anticipatory grief has impaired the generalizability of findings. Fulton and Gottesman (1980) point out how inadequate operational definitions limit the validity of the studies. To my knowledge, only one empirical study (Rando, 1983, discussed below) has attempted to operationalize the concept of anticipatory grief through specific behaviors as opposed to inference of its existence from observation, length of illness, self-assessment, or report of physical or psychiatric symptoms, most usually those of depression. These problems with definition and measurement, combined with the conceptual confusion of anticipatory grief with forewarning of loss or length of illness, contribute to the inconclusive research findings on the topic.

What Anticipatory Grief Is Not

The preceding section discusses anticipatory grief being confused with forewarning of loss or length of illness. Anticipatory grief cannot be assumed to be present merely because a warning or terminal illness diagnosis has been given or a sufficient length of time has elapsed from onset of illness until actual death. There are several other assumptions that tend to accrue to anticipatory grief that appear to stimulate the controversy surrounding its adaptive value and therapeutic desirability.

One of the major misconceptions is that anticipatory grief is merely conventional, that is, postdeath, grief begun earlier. A corollary fallacy is that there is a fixed volume of grief to be experienced and that the amount of grief experienced in anticipation of the loss will decrease by a corresponding quantity the remaining grief that will need to be experienced after the death.

If the above notions were true, one would expect that the grief following unanticipated loss would mirror that following anticipated loss, although it would be presumed to last longer since none had been dissipated prior to the death. Notable among researchers in this area are Glick, Weiss, and Parkes (1974) and Parkes and Weiss (1983) who provide rich clinical data that document that grief following unanticipated bereavement differs in both form and duration from anticipated grief. This is not because a period of anticipation necessarily lessens the grief. Rather it is due to the fact that unanticipated loss so overwhelms the adaptive capacities of the individual and so seriously injures his or her functioning that uncomplicated recovery can no longer be expected. Because the adaptive capacities are enormously and severely assaulted, the mourners are often unable to grasp the full implications of their loss. They frequently suffer extreme feelings of bewilderment, anxiety, self-reproach, and depression that render them unable to function normally. They are stunned and cannot fully comprehend what has happened. They are hit without warning from "out of the blue" and lose their security and confidence, with many never able to regain it again and always waiting for another major loss to befall. Despite intellectual recognition of the death, there is difficulty in accepting the loss which may continue to seem inexplicable. The world is without order and, like the loss, does not make sense. Grief symptomatology persists longer than usual. For example, in contrast to those who had experienced anticipated deaths, it was found that widows without time for anticipation of the death failed to move toward remarriage. They appeared to be unwilling to risk future unanticipated loss for themselves or their children. Nevertheless, the grief was as deep among those who anticipated the death of their husbands as among those who did not. Thus, in unanticipated loss, grief was not augmented, but the capacity to cope was diminished. In this regard, the value of a period of anticipation is that it allows for less of an assault on the mourner by providing an opportunity for emotional preparation for the loss. In contrast to the unanticipated loss, when expected death comes its occurrence will make sense because it will be seen as the result of a predicted process (Parkes and Weiss, 1983).

Others cite important differences between anticipatory grief and conventional (postdeath) grief. Aldrich (1974) noted that although some parallels are apparent between the two types of grief, there are several important dissimilarities. These are found in ambivalence, denial, hope, endpoints, and acceleration.

Ambivalence is viewed as having a special impact on anticipatory grief because the target of ambivalent feelings, that is, the dying patient, is not only still alive but is potentially vulnerable, balanced between life and death. This vulnerability makes any hostility or death wish appear particularly potent and dangerous and may contribute to the clinical impression that anticipatory grief appears to be more readily denied than conventional grief. On the part of the dying patient, anticipatory grief may also tend to be denied, not only because of the extent of the anticipated losses but because of the normal ambivalence he or she may feel about the fact that he or she is dying and not someone else.

Hope is ever present as long as there is some life left. There can always be some action that could conceivably delay the loss or prevent its occurrence. Of course, this is missing in conventional postdeath grief where the loss has already and irreversibly occurred. This potential for action can be both positive and negative in anticipatory grief since, for the anticipatory griever with unacceptable ambivalence, guilt about that ambivalence can be increased by committing what may be interpreted as errors of omission or commission in patient care. Concerns about one's behavior influencing the timing or extent of the loss would be absent for the individual whose loved one has already died, since nothing could change the irrevocable fact that the loss has already transpired.

The endpoints of anticipatory and conventional grief are markedly different. Anticipatory grief has a definitive end. It ceases with the death of the patient and, although grief will continue thereafter, it will no longer be anticipatory grief. In contrast, conventional grief may theoretically continue on indefinitely as is evidenced by mourners in chronic grief. The acceleration of both types of grief differ as well. Conventional grief ordinarily diminishes as time passes. In opposition to the theoretical expectation that anticipatory grief would accelerate as the loss approaches, clinical observation reveals that it is influenced by ego defenses and that probably the balance between denial (which presumably would forestall anticipatory grief work) and acceptance (which presumably would facilitate anticipatory grief work) explains why anticipatory grief does not necessarily increase as the loss grows nearer.

In conclusion, Aldrich (1974) feels that a period of anticipation can provide an individual with a positive opportunity to grieve in advance of the loss; however, the very same period can also complicate the working-through process by giving the hostile component of ambivalence a more realistically destructive potential.

Other investigations have revealed fundamental physiological differences between anticipatory and conventional grief. In 1972 Hofer et al. replicated their earlier findings (Wolff et al., 1964) that indicated through urinary 17–hydroxycorticosteroid excretion rates that what is normally construed as the anticipatory grief experience is significantly different from the postdeath grief experience. Further corroboration of the pre- and postdeath variation of physiological indices, which are known to both influence and be influenced by psychological states and responses to stress, has been supplied by Schleifer et al. (1983). Relative to predeath levels, they found suppression of mitogen-induced lymphocyte stimulation in widowers following the deaths of their spouses. This suppression of immunity following the death of a spouse is viewed as a possible causal factor associated with the increase in morbidity and mortality commonly witnessed after bereavement. Taken together these studies suggest that despite similarities of anticipatory and postdeath grief the experiences are sufficiently dissimilar so as to generate disparate physiological responses.

Another of the principal areas of dispute regarding anticipatory grief centers around the degree to which decathexis and preparation for life after the death of the loved one can and should occur. Since this will be discussed in depth below in order to lay the groundwork for a more complete and accurate perspective on anticipatory grief, suffice it to note here that the process of anticipatory grief *does not* automatically have to result in premature detachment from the dying person. Nor is it valid to assume that the process is unable to be initiated simply because the death has not yet taken place. Such an assumption is erroneously based on the belief that *only* the ultimate and final loss signified by the patient's death is what has prompted the anticipatory grief.

Finally, a common, but nevertheless fallacious, notion is that when a person is anticipating a death, and is not denying its advance, that individual is also engaging in anticipatory grief. The existence of this phenomenon cannot be presumed merely because the mourner is aware of impending death (Clayton et al., 1973; Parkes, 1970; Fulton and Gottesman, 1980; Parkes and Weiss, 1983; and Vachon et al., 1977.) As will be addressed below, the process of anticipatory grief is predicated on an active psychosocial process that is undertaken by the mourner. It does not necessarily occur by itself as a result of knowledge of anticipated loss. Reacting to the pain of a loved one's terminal illness and impending death is part of anticipatory grief, but by itself is not a sufficient condition to meet the experience of anticipatory grief that involves the process of active mourning. Anticipatory grief can take place on an unconscious level, where the mourner is not aware of the process at a particular time, but this is to be differentiated from the absence of the process going on at all at any level.

What Anticipatory Grief Is

Before specifically delineating the multidimensional aspects of anticipatory grief, it is important to respond to the assertions in the literature that such a phenomenon is an impossibility. Chief among the proponents of this viewpoint are Glick, Weiss, and Parkes (1974), Parkes and Weiss (1983), and Silverman (1974). Although all of these individuals believe that a period of anticipation can be useful, they do not feel that the benefits derive from what has traditionally been termed "anticipatory grief." I contend that such postures appear to be based on the connotations involved in the term "anticipatory grief," and that the adherence to such a position that anticipatory grief is impossible reflects an action similar to throwing the baby out the bath water.

It is important to realize that these thanatologists are not minimizing the critical value of a period of preparation. They agree that forewarning of loss allows for certain kinds of anticipatory preparations that can be therapeutic: learning to live with the prospect of loss so that when it does occur it is at least not unexpected, nor conducive to the deleterious experience of unanticipated bereavement; making plans for the future to the extent that such plans are not felt as betrayals of the dying loved one; and readying the assumptions regarding one's reality for examination and change. Parkes and Weiss (1983) point out that these preparations all contribute to help the loss, once it finally arrives, make sense as the end result of an understood, although hated, process. However, these same researchers believe that anticipatory grief per se rarely happens, and they maintain that this is only proper. They support this conviction by noting that (1) the periods of acceptance and recovery usually witnessed after the period of searching in early postdeath grief are rarely found before actual death no matter how early the forewarning; (2) grief implies that there has been a loss and that to accept a loved one's loss while he or she is still alive leaves the bereaved-to-be vulnerable to later self-accusation for having partially abandoned the dying patient; (3) grief presupposes decathexis, which is quite difficult no matter what the understanding of the future might be, with the bonds of attachment and love not being so tractable to the demands of expediency and, in fact, resisting detachment; and (4) anticipation of loss frequently intensifies attachment.

Silverman (1974) also puts heavy weight on the fact that widows usually remain involved with their terminally ill husbands until the time of death. Her data suggest that it would have been dysfunctional for these women to have commenced grieving in advance of their husbands' deaths and that they could begin to mourn only after the loss, that is, the actual death, took place. She feels that confronting the reality of the death, coming to terms with the changes it would cause, and real grieving can only eventuate after the husband's death. She views any efforts to have helped the widow and her husband cope with the problems of illness and ultimate death, to grieve in advance, or to aim for open discussions about the impending death as inappropriate. While he lives, it is the wife's reality to care for him and the *appropriate* goal to deal with during the terminal stage of an illness is to maximize the possibility for whatever living is possible during that period. Further, Silverman asserts that the shock, emptiness, reluctance to face widowhood, and loneliness are parts of a process that cannot truly be encountered until the husband is no longer there to interact with. Anything prior to this is a rehearsal and not the real thing. "Some people even talk about the coming death, but this is not grieving in advance. Engagements are not marriages." (Silverman, 1974, p. 330)

I am firmly convinced that both the Parkes and Weiss and Silverman perspectives fall victim to at least two major misconceptions. The first derives from an overfocus on the ultimate loss of death, with a consequent disregard of, or at the very least a lack of sufficient appreciation of, the other more minor (as compared to the major loss of death) losses inherent in a fatal diagnosis and a terminal illness. These include, for example, the loss of previous functioning, health, abilities, and body parts; the loss of the future that had been planned with and for the loved one; the loss of the hopes, dreams, and expectations that had been invested in the relationship and in the loved one; the loss of security, predictability, and control; and the loss of the notion of personal invulnerability. As will be discussed in further detail below, it is evident that there are three time foci for the losses that occur: past, present, and future. This means that anticipatory grief is not solely relegated to the loss that has yet to occur, that is, the actual death. The phenomenon of anticipatory grief is not composed exclusively of grief over losses that are being anticipated but in fact encompasses grief for losses that have already befallen or are currently being experienced.

The second major misinterpretation concerning anticipatory grief is that it necessarily involves a major decathexis from the dying individual. Although it certainly can eventuate in this, anticipatory grief need not automatically come to this conclusion. Unfortunately, this expectation has been incorrectly derived from Lindemann's example (1944) of the soldier with a failure on the part of his readers to appreciate that this was an extreme case. Premature detachment from one not yet dead is a dramatic example of a component of the process that has been misdirected. Indeed, some decathexis must occur. However, it is not decathexis from the actual person that is to be undertaken, but rather decathexis from the hopes, dreams, and expectations of a long-term future with that person and for that person. The future can be grieved without relinquishing the present! Continued involvement with the dying person and the goal of max-imizing the possibility for whatever living is possible is not inconsistent with nor precluded by the experience of anticipatory grief. This is evident in the observations of Futterman, Hoffman, and Sabshin (1972), who reported on the grief of bereaved parents during the terminal illness and after the death of their child. The researchers observed that although anticipatory mourning had been engaged in prior to the death, at the time of the child's actual death mourning was rarely completed and significant work remained to be accom-plished. They also reported that although some signs of detachment were evi-dent, parents had maintained care of their child's physical and emotional needs, thus melding both anticipatory grief and the care of their child. The research-ers saw detachment and provision of care and love as not being mutually ex-clusive, since parents were able to integrate both coping processes. They wrote about anticipatory grief and its effects before, at, and after the child's death:

> Presence of grieving at this time [of actual death] testified to the significant emotional investment in the child that had been maintained through the en-tire illness, while the [relatively more] limited intensity and duration of post-bereavement turmoil testified to the work accomplished in anticipatory mourn-ing. (Futterman, Hoffman, and Sabshin, 1972, p. 267)

Basically, the term "anticipatory grief" is a misnomer. It is a misnomer because "anticipatory" suggests that one is grieving solely for anticipated as opposed to past and current losses and because "grief" implies (to some) the necessity of complete decathexis from the dying person as opposed to one's hopes for and with that person in the future. This is not to dispute that many have erroneously interpreted anticipatory grief as being a process that fully reconciles the bereaved-to-be with what they will have to contend with subsequent to the death. In attempts to clarify this mistaken idea, Silverman (1974) is absolutely correct: a rehearsal is not the real thing. However, just because anticipatory grief is not exactly like postdeath grief, which it never could be since the death has not yet transpired, does not mean it is not grief. Parkes and Weiss (1983) are equally correct: there is rarely the same acceptance and recovery witnessed in anticipatory grief as in postdeath grief. Why should there be? Losses are still in the process of being experienced, so they cannot yet be resolved. However, this lack of resolution, obviously precluded by the fact that hope still exists and the final irreversible separation has not yet occurred, does not mean that grieving is not taking place. In point of fact, some of the losses attendant to the terminal illness may have indeed already been accepted and resolution may have been attained for them, even though the major loss of the death of the loved one neither has been accepted nor resolved. They are also correct in their observation that anticipation of loss frequently increases attachment. Again, this does not obviate a grief process, since anticipatory grief need not mean withdrawal from the dying loved one. Finally, they continue to be correct with their assertion that as a result of omissions or commissions, thoughts, and feelings during this time period, the bereaved-to-be are vulnerable to later self-accusation. However, these are realities that are part and parcel of the anticipatory grief experience, illustrating some of its limitations and possible dangers. They are not reasons why anticipatory grief is either extremely rare or impossible.

Multidimensional Nature of Anticipatory Grief

One of the reasons for the discrepancies in the thinking about anticipatory grief is that there is frequently a failure to appreciate the complexity of the phenomenon. Anticipatory grief is not a unitary concept that remains unaffected over person, place, time, and experience. Rather, it is multidimensional: defining itself across two perspectives, three time foci, and three classes of influencing variables.

Two Perspectives of Anticipatory Grief

There are two distinct perspectives from which anticipatory grief may be experienced and viewed. The first is that of the dying patient, which hereafter will be referred to as "patient anticipatory grief." The second perspective is that of others who are emotionally involved in some way with the dying person, which, for the sake of convenience and simplicity, will be referred to as "family anticipatory grief," despite the fact that it *also* encompasses the anticipatory grief experienced by friends, acquaintances, coworkers, others who have concern about or interest in the patient (for example, the students of a teacher, the fans of an actor, the readers of a novelist, the citizens of a politician's district, and so forth), and caregivers.

Three Time Foci of Anticipatory Grief

In contrast to the implications inherent in the term "anticipatory," which suggest that it is solely a future loss that is being grieved, there are, in fact, three time foci toward which anticipatory grief directs itself: past, present, and future. As suggested above, this is one of the reasons why the term "anticipatory grief" is a misnomer. In the experience of grief undertaken between the receipt of knowledge of fatal diagnosis and the actual death, that period traditionally seen as encompassing the time of anticipatory grief, the grief that is experienced actually is stimulated by losses that have already occurred in the past and those that are currently occurring, as well as those that are to come.

Even in the face of an ongoing terminal illness, there are losses that have already occurred which must be mourned. For example, in nursing her husband through his final bout with cancer, it is not uncommon for a wife to grieve over the vibrant and healthy man she has already *lost* to cancer and to mourn their altered relationship, lifestyle, and their dreams for the future that will never be realized. It will not be unusual for her to remember the activities they shared when he was well; to recall how, in contrast to how he currently is, he was strong and independent; to grieve over the fact that so many limitations have been placed on their lives and interfered with their plans; and to mourn for all that has already been taken away by the illness. Each of these losses is a fait accompli—and this is what is meant by anticipatory grief entailing mourning over losses in the past. This past may be recent, as in the case of the altered lifestyle, or in the more distant past, as in the lost opportunities that are regretted in light of the limited time left. In both cases, paying attention to these past losses does not mean that the wife is not still fully involved with her husband in his present state. In fact, because of her concern for her remaining time with him, and out of her desire to protect him, the wife may not even address these losses. She may work to keep them out of her own conscious awareness and push them aside to deal with after the death. If she does feel grief over them, it might not be evidenced, just like grief after a death might not be visibly manifested, or it, too, may be denied or put aside. However, despite what is done with it, the situation calls for some grief response because losses have transpired. This is true notwithstanding the fact that the subject content of the loss may pertain to the future, in terms of the hopes, expectations, dreams, and plans held for it. Whether or not these losses are grieved or even acknowledged is not the issue in this discussion. The issue is that even in the shadow of the ultimate loss of death, there are other losses that have already occurred that necessitate a grief process.

In addition, this woman experiences conditions which stimulate grief in the present. She witnesses the ongoing losses of progressive debilitation, increasing dependence, continual uncertainty, decreasing control, and so forth. A fundamental part of her grief is grief for what is currently being lost and for the future that is being eroded. This is different from grief about what *will happen* in the future. Rather it pertains to grief over what is slipping away from her right now, for the sense of having her loved one being taken from her, and for what the increasing awareness of her husband's impending death means at this very moment in time.

This woman also grieves for future losses yet to come. Not only is her husband's ultimate death mourned, but also the losses that will arise before his death. This may entail mourning in advance for such things as the fact that she and her husband will not be able to take their annual vacation to the Bahamas this year or that she knows he will lose his mobility and become bedridden. Such grieving is not limited exclusively to losses that happen prior to the death. It may also focus on those losses that will or might ensue in the future after the death, as a consequence of it: the loneliness, the insecurity, the social discomfort, the assaulted identity, the economic uncertainty, the lifestyle alterations, the fact that he will not be present to walk their daughter down the aisle on her wedding day, among others.

It is absolutely critical to recognize that a major component of anticipatory grief is the mourning of the absence of the loved one in the future. Although the true reality of this absence cannot completely be realized until the death has occurred and the person is no longer available for interaction, it is possible to get a small, but important, indication of what this will be like through extrapolation of present experiences that foreshadow the permanent absence in the future. During the illness, experiences such as when the wife is forced to attend a social function alone, or the children must accommodate themselves to their father missing their award ceremonies, or the family must become accustomed to a reduced income not only reinforce the current reality but portend a small bit of what the world will be like after the death. In miniscule ways these can help the family prepare for the new world that will exist after the father's death. They *do not* mean that there is not continued investment in the father in the present, only that there are starting to be precursors of the ultimate loss that is drawing closer.

Ideally, any decathexis that occurs in anticipatory grief is not from the dying patient in the present but from that image of the dying person as a living individual who will be (physically) present (in the manner in which the griever is accustomed to relating to the patient) in the griever's future after the death. There should be continued involvement with the patient in the here-and-now, despite the decreased emotional investment in the hopes, dreams, and expectations of a future that formerly included the patient. Emotional energy gradually must be withdrawn (decathected) from the notion of the dying person being available for interaction in the postdeath future, from the conception of the patient as a person in and with a future beyond the terminal illness.

As noted above, such decathexis is possible without sacrificing ongoing involvement with the patient in the present. When premature detachment has occurred in the relationships between the dying and their loved ones, when Lindemann's example of the soldier's wife who grieved her husband's potential loss so effectively that she no longer was attached to or invested in him becomes a reality in a terminal illness, then anticipatory grief has gone awry. It has not facilitated the finishing of unfinished business, nor promoted whatever continued involvement remains possible—two of the primary objectives of anticipatory grief (Rando, 1984.)

Three Classes of Variables Influencing Anticipatory Grief

Anticipatory grief has diverse complexions and myriad hues. Not dissimilar from conventional postdeath grief, an individual's anticipatory grief experience is idiosyncratic, determined by a unique combination of psychological, social, and physiological factors. These are delineated below, adapted and synthesized from the writings of Rando (1984). All grief, whether anticipatory or conventional postdeath, can be appropriately understood and evaluated only in light of these individual variables.

Psychological Factors. Psychological factors that influence a person's anticipatory grief fall into three categories. First are those characteristics pertaining to the nature and meaning of the person and relationship to be lost. These include (1) the unique nature and meaning of the specific loss to be experienced; (2) the qualities of the relationship to be lost; (3) the roles that the dying person has occupied in the family or social system of the griever; (4) the characteristics of the dying patient; (5) the amount of unfinished business between the griever and the dying patient; (6) the griever's perception of the dying patient's fulfillment in life; and (7) the number, type, and quality of secondary losses that result from the terminal illness and that will be caused after the death.

In the second category are the personal characteristics of the griever. These include (1) the griever's coping behaviors, personality, and mental health; (2) the griever's level of maturity and intelligence; (3) the griever's past experience with illness, loss, and death; (4) the griever's social, cultural, ethnic, and religious–philosophical background; (5) the griever's sex-role conditioning; (6) the griever's age; (7) the presence of concurrent stresses or crises in the griever's life; (8) the griever's lifestyle; and (9) the griever's sense of fulfillment in life.

The final category of psychological factors are those characteristics that pertain to the illness and type of death with which the griever must contend.

These include (1) the griever's specific fears about illness, dying, and death; (2) the griever's previous experiences with and personal expectations about illness, dying, and death; (3) the griever's knowledge about the illness; (4) the personal meaning of the specific illness to the griever; (5) the type, frequency, and intensity of the griever's involvement in the patient's care and treatment; (6) the griever's perception of the timeliness of the illness and impending death; (7) the griever's perception of the preventability of the illness; (8) the length of the illness; (9) the nature of the illness (death trajectory, problems of the particular illness, treatment regimen and side effects, amount of pain, degree of deterioration, rate of progression, number and rate of secondary losses); (10) the quality of the patient's life after the diagnosis; (11) the location of the patient (home, hospital, nursing home, relative's house); and (12) the griever's evaluation of the care, treatment, and resources that the patient is provided and to which he or she has access.

Social Factors. The social factors that influence a person's anticipatory grief are also separated into three categories. These social dimensions encourage or discourage anticipatory grief, help define the psychosocial context in which it takes place, and serve to create some of the secondary losses that will be sustained. In the first category are the characteristics of the patient's knowledge and response to the illness and ultimate death. These will have an impact on the griever since they determine the experience to which he or she must react. These include (1) the patient's subjective experience of the illness (course of illness, treatment regimen and side effects, amount of pain, degree of deterioration, rate of progression, number and rate of secondary losses, proximity to death); (2) the patient's attitude toward and responses to the illness and its ramifications (physically, emotionally, cognitively, philosophically, behaviorally, socially, spiritually); (3) the personal meaning of the specific illness and its location to the patient; (4) the patient's feelings, fears, and expectations about the illness, dying, and death; (5) the degree of the patient's knowledge of the illness and its ramifications; (6) the patient's comfort in expressing thoughts, feelings, and needs and the style and extent of that communication; (7) the patient's feelings of being supported, understood, and helped by others; (8) the patient's satisfaction with treatment; (9) the degree of the patient's acceptance of or resignation to impending death; and (10) the patient's will to live.

The second category of social factors are those that are characteristic of the family and its members' responses to the illness and impending death. These include (1) the family constellation (makeup of family, developmental stage, familial subsystems, specific roles of family members and appropriateness of roles); (2) the specific characteristics of this family system (degree of flexibility, communication style, rules, norms, expectations, values, beliefs, type and quality of interrelationships, socialization patterns, family strengths and vulnerabilities, family resources, established patterns of transaction and interaction, habitual methods of problem resolution, anticipated immediate and long-range needs of the family, quality of communication with caregivers); (3) current family awareness of and understanding about the illness and its implications; (4) family members' specific feelings, thoughts, and fears about the patient's particular illness, dying, and death; (5) the number and type of roles the patient filled in the family and the degree of role reorganization required to ensure the roles are fulfilled; (6) the role changes and psychosocial transitions that are undergone by the griever as a result of family reorganization in the face of the patient's illness and impending death; (7) the degree of strain that the illness and the family members' responses to it puts on the family system; (8) the family's participation in the patient's care; (9) the extent and quality of the family's communication about the illness; (10) the relationship of each family member with the patient since the diagnosis; (11) the presence of family rules, norms, values, styles, and past experiences that might inhibit grief or interfere with a therapeutic relationship with the dying patient; and (12) the total impact on the family system of the sum (although the whole is more than the sum of its parts) of each family member's unique constellation of individual anticipatory grief-influencing variables.

The third category of factors comprising the social variables influencing a person's anticipatory grief experience are general socioeconomic and environmental factors. These include (1) types of relationships and communication with caregivers; (2) quality and quantity of the griever's social support system (degree of acceptance, support, security, and assistance of its members, quality of communication with its members, and degree of access the griever has to it during the illness); (3) the griever's sociocultural, ethnic, and religious–philosophical background; (4) the griever's and patient's financial resources and their expected stability; (5) the educational, economic, and occupational status of the griever; (6) the degree of access to quality medical treatment and caregiving intervention for patient and griever; and (7) family and community rituals for illness, dying, and death.

Physiological Factors. The third class of variables influencing an individual's anticipatory grief experience are the physiological factors. These include (1) the griever's physical health; (2) the amount of the griever's energy depletion; (3) the amount of rest, sleep, and exercise available to and engaged in by the griever; (4) the griever's use of drugs, alcohol, cigarettes, food, and caffeine; and (5) the griever's nutrition.

The Notion of an Optimum Amount of Anticipatory Grief

Recent research has elucidated what the wise and observant clinician has known for years: there can be too much of a good thing! In findings that may account for the contradictory results of previous studies, Rando (1983) and Sanders

(1982–1983) both found that there appeared to be optimum lengths of time for a terminal illness as it impacted on the survivor's postdeath adjustment. Illnesses that were sudden or too short, as well as those that were too long, predisposed survivors to poorer outcomes.

In the Rando (1983) study, which investigated grief and adaptation of parents whose children had died from cancer, those parents whose child had died from an illness that was less than six months or more than eighteen months in duration appeared to be least prepared for the death, with those parents experiencing the longer illnesses being the least prepared of all and reporting the poorest subsequent adjustment. In contrast, those whose children had had illnesses in the interim ranges (from six months to eighteen months in length) were most prepared at the time of death and adjusted most satisfactorily following it. There was clear evidence of a pattern suggesting that as the length of illness increases, the percentage of parents with higher indices of postdeath anger and hostility and abnormal grief increases.

Rando's study advanced the notion that when the illness was too short parents were unable to adequately prepare themselves. When the illness was too long (in this case, longer than eighteen months), the experience and stress associated with it appeared to exacerbate disturbed reactions following the death, increased the intensity of feelings of anger and hostility, and acted to militate against adequate preparation when death finally came following such a long course, one presumably filled with remissions as well as relapses. The possibility of parental denial of death arising since the child had survived so long with the disease is an important one, as is the hypothesis that the parents became conditioned to expect that their child would survive despite the odds because it had happened consistently in the past. An alternate and not incompatible consideration is that the long and arduous experience of such a lengthy illness sapped the parents of their abilities to cope as effectively as desired, compromising their capability to be appropriately prepared at the time of death and to adjust afterward. The anger and hostility and the abnormal grief, which steadily intensified as the length of the illnesses increased, also may have precluded better therapeutic readiness and subsequent adjustment for these parents.

Rando's conclusions (1983) about the impact of the length of illness have been supported by Sanders (1982–1983), who discovered that survivors of death from a short-term chronic illness (less than six months in duration) fared better afterward than those from either a sudden death or a long-term chronic illness. Interestingly, the short-term illness group had been similar in levels of postdeath grief symptomatology to the sudden and long-term illness group when initially interviewed. It was only on follow-up eighteen months later that the short-term group was observed to be less symptomatic. This prompts the need to recognize that even relative comparisons of types of death, as well as evaluations of adjustment to bereavement, depend on the length of time since the death. This must necessarily be considered in evaluating research findings and designing appropriate research methodologies.

In an attempt to be more specific about the experience of anticipatory grief and not to rely solely on the assumption of its existence based only on the length of the terminal illness, Rando (1983) also operationalized anticipatory grief, the first study to do so. A parent's anticipatory grief score was determined by the numerical sum of the behaviors he or she reported to have engaged in during the child's terminal illness. These behaviors included (1) discussing with someone the possibility that their child would die; (2) grieving in anticipation of the loss of their child; (3) thinking what the future would be like without their child; (4) acknowledging the fact that their child was going to die; (5) discussing their child's dying with the child; (6) planning the type of death they wanted for their child; (7) making funeral preparations; and (8) starting to partially disengage themselves emotionally from their child.

Two associations were found to be statistically significant. Anticipatory grief was found to be positively associated with preparedness at death, with parental preparation increasing directly as the amount of anticipatory grief increased. A stronger level of statistical significance described the association between anticipatory grief and abnormal grief after the death. The more anticipatory grief behaviors engaged in prior to the death, the less abnormal grief was present following the death.

Several findings argued for the therapeutic effects of avoiding too little or too much anticipatory grief. There appeared to be an optimum amount of anticipatory grief as related to parental participation during the child's hospitalizations and the indices of anger and hostility and loss of emotional control. Parents reporting low and high amounts of anticipatory grief behaviors were found to have engaged in fewer participation behaviors during the illness, with the greatest number of low participators found among those who were also low in anticipatory grief. Low participation is related to individuals obsessed with more external problems (Hamovitch, 1964), which would most probably preclude adaptative anticipatory grief. Too much anticipatory grief appeared to compromise the parents' ability to continue interacting with their child, giving support to the concerns of those who warn about premature detachment secondary to the decathexis that can occur if anticipatory grief goes awry. Additionally, the low and high anticipatory grief groups contained higher percentages of parents with high scores on measures of anger and hostility and loss of emotional control. The medium amount of anticipatory grief behaviors appeared to be most therapeutic and facilitative of appropriate participation with the child during the illness, parental preparation at the child's death, and better subsequent adjustment after the death.

Several other patterns implied the relative importance of anticipatory grief. Although not statistically significant, there was a strong suggestion that psychosocial support during the child's terminal illness was related to the experience of anticipatory grief. Parents who were low on support during the child's illness tended to have engaged in fewer anticipatory grief behaviors. This suggests that anticipatory grief may be assisted by, or possibly requires, the support of others.

Individuals who were low in subsequent adjustment after the death tended to have engaged in fewer anticipatory grief behaviors prior to the death. As the amount of anticipatory grief behaviors increased, so did the percentages of parents with high subsequent adjustment. This finding provides more evidence for the assertion that anticipatory grief may facilitate postdeath grief and that the absence of it predisposes one to poorer bereavement outcomes.

The notion of an optimum amount of anticipatory grief is important for both the clinician and the researcher to maintain. Too much or too little anticipatory grief is nontherapeutic and appears to be related to poorer bereavement outcome. It may also explain the inconsistencies in some of the studies in this area. These studies are usually analyzed in a unidirectional way, only dichotomously examining the length of the illness (which, as noted previously, is insufficient in itself since it does not necessarily guarantee the actual experience of anticipatory grief) as related to the chosen outcome measures and failing to observe the pattern evident when discriminating among low, medium, and high amounts of anticipatory grief and lengths of illness. Such discrimination allows for the evolution of a more precise relationship among the variables that may be precluded by (1) collapsing the data into two categories (short- and long-term illness); and (2) drawing conclusions based on this arrangement of the data without recognizing that such categorization inherently is biased if some of those in the short-term illnesses are too short and some of those in the long-term illnesses too long. In such cases, the positive benefits of anticipatory grief may be obscured since they may be overshadowed or cancelled out by the negative effects of too much or too little anticipatory grief.

Clearly, further research is mandated to determine what constitutes appropriate and optimum amounts of anticipatory grief and to identify, differentiate, and predict what will be most therapeutic for different individuals in different situations. Although it is relatively simple to perceive a total nonexistence of anticipatory grief, it is more complicated to attempt to discern what the delimitation points are of what constitutes too much anticipatory grief or the upper limits of almost but not quite enough anticipatory grief. Because of this ambiguity, only the condition of an insufficient amount of anticipatory grief (taking into consideration the idiosyncratic influencing variables) should serve as a factor indicating high risk. At this juncture, lacking further research, it would be imprudent to advise individuals not to engage in anticipatory grief behaviors out of fear that they would surpass the optimum amount. Notwithstanding this, the concept of "optimum amount" is quite important to bear in mind clinically.

Costs of Anticipatory Grief

Although anticipatory grief possesses the potential to offer therapeutic benefits to the dying patient and concerned others, it is not without its problems. These are addressed here in the hopes of not only providing a balanced perspective but of identifying those areas in which moderation should be sought or support should be tendered because of the increased vulnerability the anticipatory grief may cause.

Whereas anticipatory grief can serve to bring people together and to heighten emotional attachment, too much of it or inappropriate application of its processes can result in premature detachment from the dying person (see above). Also, as noted above, immoderate amounts of anticipatory grief can compromise the griever's participation during the patient's hospitalizations, preparation at time of death, and subsequent adjustment following death (Rando, 1983). Rosenblatt (1983) has suggested that long-term anticipation of loss may appear at times to lead to less grief because the emotional exhaustion following the prolonged illness may lead to temporary numbness, to temporary suppression of grief after the loss, or even to relief that the long and excruciating struggle is over. This latter point is reminiscent of the concerns articulated by Aldrich (1974) in which anticipatory grief is regarded as possibly complicating the working-through process since it provides destructive potential for the hostile component of ambivalence, despite offering an opportunity to experience some grief in advance of the loss.

Rosenblatt (1983) offers clear evidence as to how anticipatory grief can make postdeath grief more problematic. He notes that anticipation can lead to enhancement of postdeath grief if it increases one's involvement in the care of the dying person and then that care makes the loss hurt more or leaves one with more memories and emotional involvement to disengage from after the loss. He also found that coresidence has an effect on anticipatory grief and that home care for the dying may make anticipatory grief more difficult. In such cases, where the survivors-to-be are living with the dying patient, anticipatory grief work may not occur, or if it does, it may be offset by the acquisition of additional memories, ideas, and behavior links that will require decathexis after the death. He points out that even if one has experienced some anticipatory grief, following long periods of hope and uncertainty and the struggle that ensues in support of that hope, one's efforts may seem invalidated by the actual death and this can intensify the grief experience. Also, a daily routine that centers on the dying patient and then is shattered by the death mandates the development of a new pattern of life, with such changes in routine and roles possibly augmenting the grief to be experienced following the death. In contrast, when the survivor-to-be and the dying person did not live together and the survivor-to-be had no involvement in the care of the dying patient, the longer the period of anticipation the less the grief after the death, at least within the first year of bereavement. Obviously, this has profound implications for the families of home-care hospice patients and for those who make their living caring for the dying!

Despite asserting benefits of anticipatory grief and a period of anticipatory socialization into the bereaved role, Gerber (1974) cautions that the period of anticipatory grief may contain the seeds of future problems because of the emotional strain of waiting for the death to occur, the poorly defined set of bereaved role expectations, and the drastic change in lifestyle brought about by the permanent loss. More specific concerns have been delineated by Fulton and Fulton (1971), who observed that a period of anticipation may reduce the amount of public mourning grievers display, putting them in difficult situations as they are expected by others, as well as themselves, to show emotions that have already been worked through during the anticipatory grief process. This can cause guilt or shame on the part of the mourners, stimulated by their own reactions to their less-than-expected feelings and the disapproval of others. A period of anticipatory grief may also make survivors feel that funeral rituals are unnecessary, taking away the opportunity to experience the social confirmation and support afforded by such rituals. And, very importantly, anticipatory grief was seen by Fulton and Fulton as possibly being less than therapeutic as it affects the dying patient, since he or she may be responded to negatively, if at all, by some survivors-to-be who have already decathected significantly. They conclude by perceptively synthesizing the costs and benefits of anticipatory grief and underscoring the two-edged effect with which anticipatory grief confronts us: "It possesses the capacity to enhance our lives and secure our well-being, while possessing at the same time the power to undermine our fragile existence and rupture our tenuous social bonds" (Fulton and Fulton, 1971, p. 99).

Definition and Component Processes of Anticipatory Grief

Anticipatory grief is the phenomenon encompassing the processes of mourning, coping, interaction, planning, and psychosocial reorganization that are stimulated and begun in part in response to the awareness of the impending loss of a loved one and the recognition of associated losses in the past, present, and future. It is seldom explicitly recognized, but the truly therapeutic experience of anticipatory grief mandates a delicate balance among the mutually conflicting demands of simultaneously holding onto, letting go of, and drawing closer to the dying patient.

By definition, the griever is pulled in opposing directions. He or she moves toward the dying patient as a consequence of his or her acting to direct increased attention, energy, and behavior toward the patient. At the same time, the status quo is maintained as ongoing involvement with the patient continues. Directly coinciding with this, however, the griever is starting to move away from the dying patient in terms of beginning to decathect from the image of that patient as someone who will be present in the future and from the hopes, dreams, and expectations for that patient and their relationship in the future. A critically important task in anticipatory grief is to balance these incompatible demands and cope with the stress their incongruence generates. It is no wonder that many grievers feel somewhat immobilized. They are subject to such conflicting pulls (moving closer to the patient, staying the same with the patient, moving away from the patient) all occurring at once, that they can get stuck in the middle just like anyone else who is being pulled in contradictory directions. Fortunately, these demands can be responded to in different ways, so that moving toward the patient can occur behaviorally and socially and moving away (in terms of decathexis) can occur intrapsychically and not be evidenced as premature detachment. (See chapter 7 for a fuller discussion of this subject.) Notwithstanding this, the competing demands are a major problematic issue in anticipatory grief.

It must be remembered that anticipatory grief takes time to unfold and develop. It is a process, not an all-or-nothing thing. Time and the experience of repeated frustration of the need to see the loved one improve are critical in confronting and displacing the normal need to deny what is happening. They gradually result in the progressive deepening of awareness that is necessary in order to experience optimum amounts of anticipatory grief in the manner most consistent with therapeutic benefit for patient and family.

Critical Situational Factors. Variables that influence anticipatory grief were addressed above. Three of these situational factors are highlighted in greater depth here because of their significant impact on the anticipatory grief that is experienced at any given time. In order to fully appreciate the dying patient and the family's experience of anticipatory grief analyzed below, it is necessary to know (1) at what point the patient and family are in the illness trajectory; (2) the amount of time since the diagnosis; and (3) the circumstances that have transpired since the diagnosis, including the patient's attitude and approach to life. It would be grossly inappropriate to compare the anticipatory grief of a patient who is newly diagnosed with a terminal illness to that of one who has been able for the last fourteen months to resume the majority of functioning in the absence of a relapse or to the anticipatory grief of one who is on his or her deathbed. Students of anticipatory grief must have a perspective on the topic that affords them sufficient realization of the impacts of the illness changes and fluctuations over time and how these influence the anticipatory grief experience. As just one example, coping mechanisms will be expected to change over time, depending on the phase of the illness:

During the acute crisis stage of dying, more primitive and immature coping mechanisms are commonly utilized. . . . For the most part, as I see people, the dying person and their family quickly discard these primitive responses, and move on to more mature coping mechanisms. . . . The living–dying interval is a time of repetitive stress. The dying person is also physically sick, and that drains one's psychic energy. . . . [During this time period] there is a general trend for the dying to use the ego-coping mechanisms along a developmental sequence. . . . Finally, when we come to the terminal phase of dying, we may expect the typical coping mechanisms to recede, and be replaced by isolating mechanisms, withdrawal, and increasing detachment. (Pattison, 1978, pp. 159–161)

The quality of the patient's life after diagnosis is a critical determinant of the anticipatory grief experience. This does not depend solely on the phase of the terminal illness or the patient's physical condition. Frequently, patients are dissimilar in their psychological and philosophical approach to life after diagnosis, as are their families, and these different approaches help account for the diverse experiences of patients and families. For example, some patients concentrate as much as possible on the business of living despite their terminal illness. If fortunate, they have an illness, a trajectory, and a family and social system that can support this attitude. Others more readily embrace the sick role immediately. Still others intermingle and balance to varying degrees the demands of ongoing living with those of anticipatory grieving, whereas some others focus exclusively on death, and their anticipatory grief leaves no time to enjoy the vital time that remains. Whatever the disposition, it will significantly affect the life of the patient and the family and consequently their anticipatory grief. This must be kept in mind, along with the phase of the illness, the time the patient and family have had to adapt to it, and the experiences they have undergone during this time, when considering the appropriateness of a particular patient and family addressing the components of anticipatory grief discussed below. For instance, it would be expected that the family of an end-stage cancer patient would be involved with more of these components than the family of a patient in remission; although this is a generalization and may not hold true in a specific case given the particular circumstances. Suffice it to say, it will be important to remember that these components of anticipatory grief will not necessarily all be pertinent to patients and families at the same time, nor do they all occur, or all occur simultaneously.

The Dying Patient's Anticipatory Grief

For the dying patient, becoming aware of having a terminal illness means confronting the fact that life, as it has been known, is now limited. The patient must reorient or maintain life, values, goals, and beliefs to accommodate this realization. The knowledge of impending death precipitates a crisis for the patient in that (1) it poses a problem that by definition is insolvable in the immediate future and to which the patient can only surrender; (2) it taxes the patient's psychological resources since it is beyond his or her traditional problem-solving methods and he or she has no previous experience to draw from; (3) the situation is perceived as a threat or danger to the life goals of the person; (4) it stimulates a crisis period during which there is mobilization of either integrative or disintegrative mechanisms characterized by a tension that mounts to a peak, then falls; and (5) it awakens unresolved key problems from near and distant past, including problems of dependency, passivity, narcissism, identity, and others (Pattison, 1978).

Anyone forced to cope with a terminal illness is confronted with the need to address a series of tasks (Kalish, 1970). Most if not all of these tasks only serve to remind the patient more acutely that time is limited and death is impending. Depending on the denial and coping mechanisms of the dying patient, these may or may not be addressed, either in part or total. These significant and critical tasks outline and comprise the anticipatory grief experience for the dying patient. The tasks the dying patient must attend to include (1) arranging a variety of affairs, for example, getting the will in order, leaving messages for friends, making funeral arrangements, providing for the welfare of survivors, and so forth; (2) undertaking the task of coping with loss, both of loved ones and the self; (3) seeing to future medical care needs; (4) planning the future through such specific actions as allocating whatever time, energy, and financial resources remain; (5) anticipating future pain and discomfort and facing possible loss of various forms of sensory, motor, or cognitive abilities; (6) coping effectively with the loss of self and identity and with the death encounter; (7) deciding whether to attempt to slow down or speed up the dying process; and (8) dealing with numerous psychosocial problems engendered by the illness and impending death.

The anticipatory grief of the dying patient is in many respects similar to that of the loved ones who are also grieving the patient's forthcoming death and the other losses associated with it. From the past, grief over previous losses and remembered omissions or commissions tend to emerge. In the present, the dying person must relinquish many of the physical, behavioral, and psychosocial capabilities and attributes that formerly both defined his or her identity to self and to others and that characterized his or her relationships with these others. The dying person may be treated differently now that he or she is terminally ill. Former roles and responsibilities may have to be reassigned to others. He or she may unfortunately experience the gradual decathexis of loved ones, some of whom may start to invest in others. Unfinished business may further complicate the entire process. In addition, the dying patient grieves in anticipation of the future losses that will befall before death (for example, the loss of control, independence, security, dreams and hopes, and myriad psychological, physical, and cognitive abilities), as well as those that occur by virtue of the death itself (for example, the loss of future existence, the ability to complete plans and projects, significant others, the world, and the self), and those that will occur to beloved survivors after the patient's death (for example, loss of companionship, guidance, financial security, and so forth).

In their anticipatory grief, dying patients struggle with many of the same feelings as grievers in conventional, postdeath mourning. (Since a full explanation of these is beyond the scope of this chapter, the reader is referred to Rando [1984] for a complete discussion of grief processes and interventions). Similar processes of grief must occur, since both groups of individuals are responding to loss. Although for the dying there will not be a period of reestablishment as for postdeath mourners, for many there may be a state of realization or resolution (similar to, but not as idealistic as, Kübler-Ross's state of acceptance [1969]) that can be reached. There will necessarily be a need to gradually become accustomed to the reality, identify losses, express feelings and thoughts, incorporate an altered sense of self, review life, finish unfinished business, and say goodbye. They, too, require permission to grieve from their loved ones and caregivers and must be assisted in doing this without incurring feelings of shame or guilt.

Emotions may be similar to those experienced by the postdeath mourner, but for the dying patient these will usually, and understandably, be felt more intensely given the inherent nature of the total extent of the loss of self, world, and everything and everyone in it. Frequently, there is a more dramatic loss of self-esteem than is typically seen in postdeath grief, and this has resulted from the vicissitudes of the terminal illness. Additionally, the dying patient may *die* more than once. As noted by Sudnow (1967), each dying individual actually undergoes four types of death: social death, psychological death, biological death, and physiological death. Often aspects of the first two types are experienced, noted, and grieved by the dying person.

Repeated loss of control is encountered throughout the illness. Society is poorly equipped to handle this and stresses independence, effectiveness, and power—all of which are in short supply for the dying patient, thereby increasing his or her losses, embarrassment, and sense of estrangement and alienation. By definition, the impingement of a terminal illness on an individual robs him or her of some measure of control, and the progressive losses that emanate from it continue to so rob the patient. Whereas in conventional mourning secondary losses will accrue, they will at some point diminish in number in contrast to the dying patient, for whom they will only increase. These realities, plus those intrinsic to pain, facing the unknown, and the ultimate experience of permanent separation and death, combine to intensify the emotions of anxiety, depression, sorrow, anguish, sadness, anger, hostility, frustration, guilt, and shame that most mourners must confront. Unfortunately, psychological coping with these emotions and other stresses in terminal illness is made additionally difficult because the illness itself and its physical sequelae deplete the patient of the energy required to maintain appropriate coping mechanisms, the patient lacks the previous experience with death to assist in the adaptation to it, and there is no expectation of pleasurable results in the future, which is normally required for healthy adaptation (Verwoerdt, 1966).

The Family's Anticipatory Grief

Family anticipatory grief (which in this chapter also encompasses the grief of others who have some involvement with the dying patient) is a phenomenon entailing three categories of interrelated processes that facilitate one another: (1) individual intrapsychic processes, (2) interactional processes with the dying patient, and (3) familial and social processes.

Components of the Three Interrelated Processes of Anticipatory Grief

I. **Individual Intrapsychic Processes**
   Awareness and gradual accommodation to the threat
   Affective processes
   Cognitive processes
   Planning for the future

II. **Interactional Processes with the Dying Patient**
   Directing attention, energy, and behavior toward the dying patient
   Resolution of personal relationship with the dying patient
   Helping the dying patient

III. **Familial and Social Processes**

Ideally, anticipatory grief that is therapeutic in nature will prompt appropriate engagement in each of these three sets of processes. The following delineation of their components is based in part on the writings of Cohen and Cohen (1981), Fulton and Fulton (1971), Futterman and Hoffman (1973), Futterman, Hoffman, and Sabshin (1972), Gerber (1974); Lebow (1976), McCollum and Schwartz (1972), Parkes and Weiss (1983), and Rando (1984). It is a listing of processes that *ideally* occur in anticipatory grief. Departure from these on the part of any family member reflects the fact that human beings do not always approximate ideal behaviors, as well as the fact that idiosyncratic variables have potent effects that impact on the ability to experience anticipatory grief in this ideal fashion. (See chapter 7 for specific treatment intervention strategies to promote ideal anticipatory grief as much as possible.)

Individual Intrapsychic Processes

In the individual intrapsychic realm, the family member experiences four interrelated subprocesses of anticipatory grief. These include awareness and gradual accommodation to the threat, affective processes, cognitive processes, and planning for the future. They overlap and are not exclusive of one another. Each is listed with its components.

Awareness and Gradual Accommodation to the Threat

Developing a progressively deepening awareness of the seriousness of the illness and its implications through the dawning realization that certain hopes about recovery or stabilization are not being actualized.

Gradually absorbing and coming to terms with the reality of the impending loss over time.

Rehearsing the death and its consequences with attempts to adjust in part.

Becoming partially socialized into the bereaved role through this time of anticipatory bereavement (Gerber, 1974).

Affective Processes

Confronting the need to manage the stress of and emotional reactions to the experience and incompatible demands of terminal illness.

Mourning past, present, and future losses attendant to the terminal illness and death and the unrelated losses that have been revived in this loss situation. This also means experiencing, managing, and coping with associated emotions and reactions such as shock, denial, depression, anguish, sorrow, anxiety, fear, anger, frustration, resentment, ambivalence, jealousy, despair, guilt, shame, helplessness, hopelessness, confusion, regression, uncertainty, numbness, vulnerability, hypervigilance, insecurity, exhaustion, and depletion, along with their social and physiological counterparts.

Experiencing and coping with the separation anxiety and fear elicited by the threat of permanent loss.

Gradually decathecting from the image of the dying person in the postdeath future and from the hopes, dreams, wishes, expectations, and plans that accompanied it.

Recognizing one's separateness from the dying patient and learning to tolerate the awareness that the patient will die while the griever continues to exist.

Maintaining some confidence in the face of the profound threat, which includes mastery operations such as information seeking and participation in care, as well as strategies for maintenance of emotional and interpersonal equilibrium, affirmation of life and its meaning, and processes of reorganization, such as revising values, goals, and philosophy of life in light of the loved one's illness and death (Futterman and Hoffman, 1973).

Cognitive Processes

Experiencing heightened preoccupation with and concern for the terminally ill patient.

Starting to slowly incorporate changes in one's identity, roles, experiences, beliefs, assumptions, and expectations that reflect the current reality and will begin to prepare the griever for the reality that will exist after the death in a world without the loved one.

Striving, through all the senses, to take in the loved one in order to emblazen these perceptions in the mind and the senses for the purpose of constructing a mental and sensory composite image of the loved one to endure after death.

Reviewing the past and attending carefully to the present in order to crystallize memories to keep after the death.

Bargaining with God or fate for a reprieve, for more time, or for a different illness experience.

Recollecting previous losses, griefs, periods of vulnerability, and other related experiences that have been revived by this loss.

Contemplating one's own death.

Developing a philosophy about how to cope with the patient's remaining time; for example, should there be pressure exerted to experience and squeeze as much out of remaining life as possible? Or, should a more natural and passive attitude be undertaken in which one takes what comes without the stressful burden of rushing to make all the last times memorable and meaningful?

Planning for the Future

Considering what the future will be like without the loved one and experiencing associated reactions to it.

Anticipating and planning for future losses and changes, both before and after the death.

Anticipating and planning for practical and social considerations that need to be addressed both before and after the death.

Interactional Processes with the Dying Patient

Anticipatory grief engenders numerous interpersonal processes involving the dying patient. This is quite critical to the concept and invalidates the belief that anticipatory grief necessarily must lead to premature detachment from the patient, cause the relationship with him or her to deteriorate, or predispose the survivor to guilt after the death. In point of fact, all of the processes here imply continued involvement with the dying patient, with some actually serving to intensify the attachment and improve the relationship as compared to what existed before the awareness of limited time. Moreover, although some may construe anticipatory grief and continued involvement as seemingly opposite processes, this is quite untrue. Indeed, it is only by preparing for the ultimate loss of their loved one through anticipatory grief that family members will become aware of any unfinished business remaining with the dying patient. And, it is only by interacting with the dying patient that family members will be able to finish their unfinished business with him or her, which itself is a crucial part of anticipatory grief. In this regard, anticipatory grief facilitates both the identification of unfinished business and the development of ways to achieve closure. There are three interrelated subprocesses incorporated here: Directing attention, energy, and behavior toward the dying patient, Resolution of personal relationship with the dying patient, and Helping the dying patient.

Directing Attention, Energy, and Behavior toward the Dying Patient

Remaining as involved as possible with the dying patient; avoiding withdrawal and promoting whatever continued communication, interaction, dignity, control, living, and meaning that remains available.

Directing increased attention to the patient and being hyperalert to cues pertinent to him or her.

Focusing energy (physical and emotional), behavior, thought, and resources (emotional, physical, time, financial, social) on caring for the patient.

Balancing the incompatible and conflicting demands of simultaneously holding onto, letting go of, and drawing closer to the dying patient.

Assigning the patient a considerable degree of priority in terms of giving consideration, fulfilling wants and needs, planning activities, and so forth.

Responding to the patient in ways that make allowances for deterioration, loss, and disability, without supporting inappropriate or prematurely regressive defenses.

Possibly doing painful things (for example, taking the patient for an uncomfortable medical procedure) or omitting pleasurable ones (for example, refusing to buy the patient's cigarettes) for the patient's own good that signal debilitation and/or the terminality of the illness.

Resolution of Personal Relationship with the Dying Patient

Finishing unfinished business with the dying patient. Although the term can refer to practical, financial, and business matters that remain to be settled, as used here unfinished business primarily focuses on the psychosocial issues that were never addressed or that lack successful closure in the relationship between the dying patient and the griever. It can incorporate such behaviors as expressing feelings, resolving past conflicts, saying goodbye, explaining past omissions or commissions, articulating important messages, tying up loose emotional ends, and manifesting or ceasing behaviors in accordance with the patient's preferences, values, needs, or desires.

Specifically informing or reinforcing what the patient means and has meant to the griever, providing other pieces of personal feedback, and stating promises and intentions for the future.

Recollecting the mutual relationship and shared memories from common experiences.

Planning the future with the patient so that such plans will not be felt as betrayals after the death.

At the appropriate time, saying goodbye to the patient and providing permission to die.

Helping the Dying Patient

Identifying, anticipating, and meeting the needs of the dying patient.

Tending to the last wishes of the patient.

Acting to facilitate an appropriate death for the patient (Weisman, 1972).

Assisting the patient with his or her own anticipatory grief, problem solving of specific fears and concerns, completion of terminal illness tasks (Kalish, 1970), and finishing of unfinished business with others in order to achieve the sense of closure that can provide the patient with a feeling of peace and the ability to let go when the time is appropriate.

Promoting an open awareness context (Glaser and Strauss, 1965) to the fullest extent possible.

Acting to minimize the psychological, social, and physical suffering and losses of the patient.

Providing the psychosocial support and acceptance necessary for the patient to cope with, express, and manage the feelings, thoughts, fears, concerns, and needs generated by the illness and impending death.

Assuming necessary body and ego functions for the patient without fostering shame, depreciation, or unnecessary loss (Pattison, 1969).

Joining the patient in a process of life review (Butler, 1963).

Working with the patient to determine how he or she wants to be remembered and attempting to bring this to fruition.

If desired by the patient, preplanning with him or her the type of funerary rituals preferred.

Familial and Social Processes

Finally, anticipatory grief stimulates a series of familial and social processes. These illustrate that the dying of the patient takes place in a social context, which in itself is affected by the loss.

The family starting to reorganize itself without the patient being available to fulfill the same number and types of roles or to fulfill them in the same manner or extent as previously.

Individual grievers beginning to assume and adapt to new roles and responsibilities because of the incapacitation and future absence of the dying patient.

Making plans with other survivors-to-be for what will happen later in the illness and after the death.

Negotiating extrafamilial relationships.

Networking with other people, institutions, and organizations to secure the best services and provide the patient the optimum treatment and quality of life possible.

Working with clergy and funeral service personnel to arrange for postdeath rituals to meet the dying person's preferences.

Conclusion

Anticipatory grief is a complex and multidimensional set of processes that may be called forth during the terminal illness of a loved one. It entails not only grief over future losses but over past and present losses as well. Contrary to popular misconception, the phenomenon does not have to eventuate in premature decathexis from the dying loved one and, in fact, has the potential for and capability of supporting and stimulating continued involvement with the dying patient.

References

Aldrich, C.K. 1974. Some Dynamics of Anticipatory Grief. In B. Schoenberg, A. Carr, A. Kutscher, D. Peretz, and I. Goldberg, eds., *Anticipatory Grief.* New York: Columbia University Press, pp. 3–13.

Ball, J.F 1976–1977. Widow's Grief: The Impact of Age and Mode of Death. *Omega* 7:307–333.

Benfield, D.G., S.A. Leib, and J. Reuter. 1976. Grief Response of Parents after Referral of the Critically Ill Newborn to a Regional Center. *New England Journal of Medicine* 294:975–978.

Binger, C.M., A.R. Ablin, R.C. Feuerstein, J.H. Kushner, S. Zoger, and C. Mikkelsen. 1969. Childhood Leukemia: Emotional Impact on Patient and Family. *New England Journal of Medicine* 280:414–418.

Bornstein, P., P. Clayton, J. Halikas, W. Maurice, and E. Robbins. 1973. The Depression of Widowhood at 13 Months. *British Journal of Psychiatry* 122:561–566.

Bowlby, J. 1980. *Attachment and Loss: Loss, Sadness and Depression.* Vol. 3. New York: Basic Books.

Burton, L. 1974. Tolerating the Intolerable—The Problems Facing Parents and Children Following Diagnosis. In L. Burton, ed., *Care of the Child Facing Death.* London: Routledge & Kegan Paul, pp. 16–38.

Butler, R.N. 1963. The Life Review: An Interpretation of Reminiscence in the Aged. *Psychiatry* 26:65–76.

Chodoff, P., S.B. Friedman, and D.A. Hamburg. 1964. Stress, Defenses and Coping Behavior: Observations in Parents of Children with Malignant Disease. *American Journal of Psychiatry* 120:743–749.

Clayton, P.J., L. Desmarais, and G. Winokur. 1968. A Study of Normal Bereavement. *American Journal of Psychiatry* 125:64–74.

Clayton, P.J., J.A. Halikas, W.H. Maurice, and E. Robbins. 1973. Anticipatory grief and widowhood. *British Journal of Psychiatry* 122:47–51.

Cohen, M.S., and E.K. Cohen. 1981. Behavioral Family Systems Intervention in Terminal Care. In H.J. Sobel, ed., *Behavior Therapy in Terminal Care: A Humanistic Approach.* Cambridge, Mass.: Ballinger, pp. 177–204.

Friedman, S.B. 1967. Care of the Family of the Child with Cancer. *Pediatrics* 40:498–504.

Friedman, S.B., P. Chodoff, J.W. Mason, and D.A. Hamburg. 1963. Behavioral Observations on Parents Anticipating the Death of a Child. *Pediatrics* 32:610–625.

Fulton, R., and J. Fulton. 1971. A Psychosocial Aspect of Terminal Care: Anticipatory Grief. *Omega* 2:91–99.

Fulton, R., and D.J. Gottesman. 1980. Anticipatory Grief: A Psychosocial Concept Reconsidered. *British Journal of Psychiatry* 137:45–54.

Futterman, E.H., and I. Hoffman. 1973. Crisis and Adaptation in the Families of Fatally Ill Children. In E.J. Anthony and C. Koupernik eds., *The Child in His Family: The Impact of Disease and Death.* Vol. 2. New York: John Wiley & Sons, pp. 127–143.

Futterman, E.H., I. Hoffman, and M. Sabshin. 1972. Parental Anticipatory Mourning. In B. Schoenberg, A.C. Carr, D. Peretz, and A.H. Kutscher, eds., *Psychosocial Aspects of Terminal Care.* New York: Columbia University Press, pp. 243–272.

Gerber, I. 1974. Anticipatory Bereavement. In B. Schoenberg, A. Carr, A. Kutscher, D. Peretz, and I. Goldberg, eds., *Anticipatory Grief.* New York: Columbia University Press, pp. 26–30.

Gerber, I., R. Rusalem, N. Hannon, D. Battin, and A. Arkin. 1975. Anticipatory Grief and Aged Widows and Widowers. *Journal of Gerontology* 30:225–229.

Glaser, B. and A. Strauss. 1965. *Awareness of Dying.* Chicago: Aldine.

Glick, I.O., R.S. Weiss, and C.M. Parkes. 1974. *The First Year of Bereavement.* New York: John Wiley & Sons.

Goldberg, S.G. 1973. Family Tasks and Reactions in the Crisis of Death. *Social Casework* 54:398–405.

Hamovitch, M.B. 1964. *The Parent and the Fatally Ill Child.* Los Angeles: Delmar.

Hofer, M.A., C.T. Wolff, S.B. Friedman, and J.W. Mason. 1972. A Psychoendocrine Study of Bereavement. *Psychosomatic Medicine.* 34:481–504.

Kennell, J.H., H. Slyter, and M.H. Klaus. 1970. The Mourning Response of Parents to the Death of a Newborn Infant. *New England Journal of Medicine* 283:344–349.

Kübler-Ross, E. 1969. *On Death and Dying.* New York: Macmillan.

Lebow, G. H. 1976. Facilitating Adaptation in Anticipatory Mourning. *Social Casework.* 57:458–465.

Levitz, I.N. 1977. Comments in section on "The Parents." In N. Linzer, ed., *Understanding Bereavement and Grief.* New York: Yeshiva University Press, pp. 179–186.

Lindemann, E. 1944. Symptomatology and Management of Acute Grief. *American Journal of Psychiatry* 101:141–148.

Maddison, D. 1968. The Relevance of Conjugal Bereavement for Preventive Psychiatry. *British Journal of Medical Psychology* 41:223–233.

Maddison, D., and A. Viola. 1968. The Health of Widows in the Year Following Bereavement. *Journal of Psychosomatic Research* 12:297–306.

Maddison, D., and W. Walker. 1967. Factors Affecting the Outcome of Conjugal Bereavement. *British Journal of Medical Psychology* 113:1057–1067.

McCollum, A.T., and A.H. Schwartz. 1972. Social Work and the Mourning Parent. *Social Work* 17:25–36.

Natterson, J.M., and A.G. Knudson. 1960. Observations Concerning Fear of Death in Fatally Ill Children and Their Mothers. *Psychosomatic Medicine* 22:456–465.

Parkes, C.M. 1970. The First Year of Bereavement. *Psychiatry* 33:444–467.

Parkes, C.M. 1972. *Bereavement: Studies of Grief in Adult Life.* New York: International Universities Press.

Parkes, C.M. 1975. Determinants of Outcome Following Bereavement. *Omega* 6:303–323.

Parkes, C.M., and R.S. Weiss. 1983. *Recovery from Bereavement.* New York: Basic Books.

Pattison, E.M. 1969. Help in the Dying Process. *Voices: The Art and Science of Psychotherapy* 5:6–14.

Pattison, E.M., ed. 1977. *The Experience of Dying.* Englewood Cliffs, N.J.: Prentice-Hall.

Pattison, E.M. 1978. The Living–Dying Process. In C.A. Garfield, ed., *Psychosocial Care of the Dying Patient.* New York: McGraw-Hill, pp. 133–168.

Peretz, D. 1970. Reaction to Loss. In B. Schoenberg, A.C. Carr, D. Peretz, and A.H. Kutscher, eds., *Loss and Grief: Psychological Management in Medical Practice.* New York: Columbia University Press, pp. 20–35.

Rando, T.A. 1983. An Investigation of Grief and Adaptation in Parents Whose Children Have Died from Cancer. *Journal of Pediatric Psychology* 8:3–20.

Rando, T.A. 1984. *Grief, Dying, and Death: Clinical Interventions for Caregivers.* Champaign, Ill.: Research Press.

Raphael, B. 1983. *The Anatomy of Bereavement.* New York: Basic Books.

Raphael, B., and D. Maddison. 1976. The Care of Bereaved Adults. In O.W. Hill, ed., *Modern Trends in Psychosomatic Medicine*. London: Butterworth.

Rees, W.D., and S.G. Lutkins. 1967. Mortality of Bereavement. *British Medical Journal* 4:13–16.

Richmond, J.B., and H.A. Waisman. 1955. Psychologic Aspects of Management of Children with Malignant Diseases. *American Journal of Diseases in Children* 89:42–47.

Rosenbaum, M. 1944. Emotional Aspects of Wartime Separation. *Family* 24:337–341.

Rosenblatt, P. 1983. *Bitter, Bitter Tears: Nineteenth-Century Diarists and Twentieth-Century Grief Theories*. Minneapolis: University of Minnesota Press.

Sanders, C.M. 1982–1983. Effects of Sudden vs. Chronic Illness Death on Bereavement Outcome. *Omega* 13:227–241.

Schleifer, S.J., S.E. Keller, M. Camerino, J.C. Thorton, and M. Stein. 1983. Suppression of Lymphocyte Stimulation Following Bereavement. *Journal of the American Medical Association* 250:374–377.

Schwab, J.J., J.M. Chalmers, S.J. Conroy, P.B. Farris, and R.E. Markush. 1975. Studies in Grief: A Preliminary Report. In B. Schoenberg, I. Gerber, A. Wiener, A. Kutscher, D. Peretz, and A. Carr, eds., *Bereavement: Its Psychosocial Aspects*. New York: Columbia University Press, pp. 78–87.

Siegel, K., and L. Weinstein. 1983. Anticipatory Grief Reconsidered. *Journal of Psychosocial Oncology* 1:61–73.

Silverman, P. 1974. Anticipatory Grief from the Perspective of Widowhood. In B. Schoenberg, A. Carr, A. Kutscher, D. Peretz, and I. Goldberg, eds., *Anticipatory Grief*. New York: Columbia University Press, pp. 320–330.

Sudnow, D. 1967. *Passing On: The Social Organization of Dying*. Englewood Cliffs, N.J.: Prentice-Hall.

Travis, G. 1976. *The Experience of Chronic Illness in Childhood*. Stanford, Calif.: Stanford University Press.

Vachon, M.L.S., A. Formo, K. Freedman, W.A. Lyall, J. Rogers, and S.J. Freeman. 1976. Stress Reactions to Bereavement. *Essence* 1:23–33.

Vachon, M.L.S., K. Freedman, A. Formo, J. Rogers, W.A. Lyall, and S.J. Freeman. 1977. The Final Illness in Cancer: The Widow's Perspective. *Canadian Medical Association Journal* 117:1151–1154.

Vachon, M.L.S., J. Rogers, W.A. Lyall, W.J. Lancee, A.R. Sheldon, and S.J. Freeman. 1982. Predictors and Correlates of High Distress in Adaptation to Conjugal Bereavement. *American Journal of Psychiatry* 139:998–1002.

Verwoerdt, A. 1966. *Communication with the Fatally Ill*. Springfield, Ill.: Charles C. Thomas.

Weisman, A.D. 1972. *On Dying and Denying: A Psychiatric Study of Terminality*. New York: Behavioral Publications.

Wiener, J.M. 1970. Reaction of the Family to the Fatal Illness of a Child. In B. Schoenberg, A.C. Carr, D. Peretz, and A.H. Kutscher, eds., *Loss and Grief: Psychological Management in Medical Practice*. New York: Columbia University Press, pp. 87–101.

Wolff, C.T., S.B. Friedman, M.A. Hofer, and J.W. Mason. 1964. Relationship between Psychological Defenses and Mean Urinary 17-hydroxycorticosteroid Excretion Rates: I. A Predictive Study of Parents of Fatally Ill Children. *Psychosomatic Medicine* 26:576–591.

2

An Agenda for Adaptive Anticipation of Bereavement

Vanderlyn R. Pine

The term "anticipatory grief" was used to close the 1944 classic article, "Symptomatology and Management of Acute Grief" by Erich Lindemann, the noted psychiatrist and researcher of the topics of death, grief, and bereavement. However, the term was not actively brought into the field of death studies until the early 1960s. The purpose of this paper is to clarify some of the issues that surround the definition of anticipatory grief, locate it in a general framework of grief, and deal with some practical applications and methods of helping people who are experiencing grief reactions.

What Is Anticipatory Grief?

Anticipatory grief suggests a temporal dimension in regard to grief. Before dealing with the anticipation aspect, however, it is important to clarify the issue of grief. The term "grief" refers to a psychological and physiological process that occurs in response to a specific loss. When one experiences grief, one feels a sense of loss in one's innermost self. The complex set of emotions and the behavior surrounding it are referred to as "grief manifestations" or "grief symptoms."

The term "bereavement" refers to an objective state or condition of loss. For example, if someone loses a physical object, that person would be bereaved of it. If one has a body part amputated, one would be bereaved of that. Bereavement of some body parts, for example, loss of a breast, arm, leg, and so forth, usually do elicit a grief response. There are other forms of body amputation that might not elicit a grief response, for instance, the trimming of one's hair or fingernails. Although the loss of a fingernail may be thought of as an amputation, for most people it would not cause a grief reaction. However, for

I am deeply indebted to Diane L. Carpenter, my editorial associate, for her help, suggestions, and comments throughout the revision process. I also want to express my thanks to Patricia P. Pine, Kathy D. Williams, and Therese A. Rando, all of whom provided comments on earlier versions. I had discussions with J. Eugene Knott, Robert Fulton, and Howard C. Raether regarding some of the ideas presented here and appreciate their suggestions.

a classical guitarist who depends on the nail for playing, its loss may be a bereavement that elicits grief.

Are We More Concerned with Grief Today?

Are we more concerned with grief today compared to the past? After all, people always have died, and the survivors always were likely to have felt a sense of loss when a death occurred. Death and grief always have been part of the human condition.

The answer is that we *are* and *are not* more concerned with grief today than in the past. Grief was a key subject in ancient myths, folklore, and literature into which many cultural values were woven in an attempt to explain grief and loss. For example, the ancient myths of Sumeria, which date to over ten thousand years ago, are replete with references to death and reactions to it. The myth of "Gilgamesh the Wrestler" recounts that, because he was stricken with grief, Gilgamesh set out on a trip to find immortal life. This is one of many examples of the pervasiveness and the powerful sentiments about death and loss that have existed throughout human history. Other notable examples include the Judeo–Christian Bibles and writings of other important world religions, all of which make numerous references to death and grief.

Clearly, interest in the human conditions of death and grief has always existed, but the manner and timing of death have changed drastically. Dying often takes longer than it did in the past. With the obvious exception of sudden, catastrophic death, almost all forms of dying have become protracted and extended over time. It is precisely this temporal change that has compounded the issues of dying and death in modern society. The prolongation of the dying process or the transition period from life to death is one of the major reasons for the increasing interest in and visibility of *anticipatory grief*. The dying process in its own right represents a kind of bereavement, for when a person begins to die, he or she begins to lose those attributes that we believe characterize life.

What Is Anticipation of Bereavement?

Since there is great confusion in this area of dying, let us conceptualize the term "anticipation of bereavement" rather than the term "anticipatory grief" because it is my contention that the anticipation of a particular bereavement elicits and triggers various grief reactions. An important caveat of which to be aware is that once death is viewed as imminent, the process of grief begins. Thus, the intial news about an impending death represents a type of loss. Moreover, it is unrealistic to say that once you know that someone is going to die you begin the process of *anticipatory grief* and that when that person dies, anticipatory grief ends and *normal grief* begins. Fixed starting and stopping points are not present in these processes. At issue here is the connotation that grief is segmented, whereas, in reality, this is not the case.

Let us return to the time dimension because, after all, the term focuses on "anticipation." It is important to recognize that grief may occur before bereavement, at the time of bereavement, and following bereavement. As is the case with so many other psychic processes, how and when it takes place depends on a number of factors, but it almost always is connected with a sense of loss.

The temporal dimension of grief calls for thinking of it as something that occurs along a continuum. It is not something that exists at a given moment and then stops; rather, it takes place over time. Along this continuum, we must consider the relationship of the bereaved person to this time dimension. Although a somewhat abstract step, it is necessary to understand the full meaning of the terms anticipatory grief and anticipation of bereavement. Once something occurs that triggers a sense of bereavement, there is active grief potential. The grief potential depends on factors such as the closeness of the relationship to the person who is expected to die or to the dead person. Furthermore, the nature of the cause of death is important in terms of whether the death is sudden or lingering. With a sudden, unexpected death there is no time to anticipate it, whereas a lingering death allows for more psychological preparation and anticipatory reaction.

Regardless of timing, there are at least three factors on which grief depends. First, one must be aware of an event that creates (or will create) a loss or bereavement. Second, there must be conscious perception of the bereavement as real. At this point it is important to be cognizant of the fact that it is possible to be *aware* that something has happened without consciously perceiving it. The third factor is the set of reactions that follows mere awareness versus the set of reactions that follows conscious perception.

A personal example will help illustrate this point. In my sophomore year at college my father died unexpectedly at the age of forty-eight. My grandfather, who was in his eighties, had been ill for a long time, and my family was somewhat prepared for his death. My college roommate gave me the news concerning the death. As he approached me, he had a look on his face that suggested something was wrong. Of greater importance is that he said to me, "Van, you had better come inside and call home, your father has just died." I reacted immediately by saying, "Oh, you mean my grandfather." Although I was aware that a death had occurred, I had not consciously perceived the particular death that had occurred. It was not too long until I allowed myself to admit that it might be my father rather than my grandfather who had died. The set of reactions I experienced varied. During the time that I was aware of a death but believed it to be my grandfather, I was calm and in control of myself and my emotions. However, as I began consciously to perceive my father's death, I became more anxious and increasingly nervous, and my grief reactions became more difficult to control. Furthermore, after the news of his death, my reactions vacillated from awareness to conscious perception, complicating both anticipatory and immediate acute grief.

How Does "Appropriateness" Affect Reactions to Dying and Death?

Another aspect that has an impact on and may complicate our reactions to dying and death is the sense of "appropriateness." This may be thought of as a culturally learned sense that is acted upon both individually and institutionally. David Sudnow (1967) discusses this topic and provides excellent illustrations of how dying and death are culturally constituted entities. As a result of his participant observation at two hospitals, he noted that dying in a medical institution is defined by the way professionals act toward a patient rather than the actual physical condition of that patient. Furthermore, these actions are influenced by the professionals' perceptions of the patient's social worth. Consequently, different people with the same disease will not necessarily be treated in the same manner. In one case, a terminally ill patient may be perceived as "having a chance" or "having some hope," whereas another patient with the same disease or condition may be perceived as "dying." For example, assume that a seventy-eight-year-old alcoholic with emphysema is hospitalized due to an acute lung infection. It is more likely that the medical staff, the social services staff, the religious staff, and virtually everyone involved in the care of that patient will react as though dying begins sooner than if the person were a forty-eight-year-old nonalcoholic with the same illness. This sort of institutional treatment revolves around the concept of "appropriateness," with death being "socially appropriate" regardless of or often in spite of medical conditions.

Weisman (1972) explains that "appropriate death for one person might be unsuitable for another. Finally, what might seem appropriate from the outside, might be utterly meaningless to the dying person. Conversely, deaths that seem unacceptable to an outsider, might be desirable from the inner viewpoint of the patient" (p. 37). Hence, as Sudnow implies and Weisman states, grief reactions to a particular death are conditioned and tempered by our sense of appropriateness.

It also should be recognized that many major bereavements (losses) are accompanied by minor bereavements that are just as real and that contribute to the process of anticipation for dying people as well as their families. This would include people who have suffered from a condition such as a near-fatal heart attack or have received radiation treatments or have undergone chemotherapy for cancer. All claim that so-called minor losses may be just as problematic as the major losses. For example, a man suffering from a congestive heart condition said that he missed the feeling that he could have sexual relations without experiencing the fear that he might die while doing so. The so-called minor loss (his diminished sexual capability) that accompanied the major loss (his impending death) was so powerful that he no longer felt free to engage in activities that he previously had considered commonplace. In dealing with dying, death, and bereavement, we must be cognizant of the fact that the matters of perception, appropriateness, and scope are important dimensions surrounding and affecting the issues.

What Changes Affect Our Consciousness of Death?

Because dying generally takes longer to occur and has become a more protracted process than in the past, a new set of psychological, social, and medical problems has come into focus. Therefore, grief today is quantitatively and qualitatively different from in the past. The change is quantitative in terms of the number of deaths that most people face in the course of their lives. Today, because death is less common among the young and tends to occur in institutions, most of us actually observe dying rather infrequently; therefore, the sheer quantity of "death experience" is lower today than in the past.

From the qualitative perspective, death today differs from in the past for a number of reasons. The individuals who grieve have changed. As a result of the increased number of people dying in hospitals, professional caregivers constitute an important group who have become increasingly involved in the grieving and bereavement process. Despite this involvement, their feelings toward those for whom they have cared largely have been ignored. Professional caregivers often find themselves in the predicament of caring (in the affective sense) more about the dying patient than the more traditional units of family and close friends.

This shift in affective concern has occurred because medical technology not only makes possible the prolongation of life but also is the basis for repeated and often extended separations of the chronically ill or dying person from his or her family. According to Fulton and Fulton (1971), such separations reduce familial and friendship contacts and also serve to weaken social and emotional commitments. In addition, there is growing evidence that medical personnel who have attended a deceased patient are highly critical of family members and friends whose behavior seems to be inappropriate, incongruous, or callous. Put simply, the professionals may respond negatively to family members who display seeming disregard for their dying or dead relatives.

Compounding these shifts are social changes that have affected our collective consciousness concerning death. The last thirty to fifty years have brought about significant social changes. The turmoil and the national sadness that was part of the economic depression of the 1930s brought about a social consciousness of mass deprivation or mass bereavement that was new to American society. Another change involves the acute grief syndromes that have accompanied the wars in which Americans have been involved. Since the early 1940s, there has been little respite from this type of grief. First, there was World War II, followed by the Korean War, followed by the Vietnam War, and followed by present terrorist and other warlike conditions. Therefore, our society has the legacy of the depression with one kind of deprivation or bereavement followed by actual deaths, loss of honor, and war-related bereavements.

The vast technological changes that have taken place in the last thirty years also are extremely important. In 1957 Sputnik was launched by the USSR, and western society was catapulted into the era of science nonfiction. Other technological changes suddenly came into the forefront around that time; changes in electronics, transistors, and telecommunications and the development and widespread use of computers represent technological advances that have changed our lives drastically. It is possible today to scan a human body with a computer and make judgments on its condition. Unlike physicians, the computer can make decisions unencumbered by social values. Although computer diagnosis is very costly, there are advantages to using computers that can make socially "value-free" evaluative assessments of physical conditions. It is not clear how this new power will be used, but it certainly alters the everyday concerns of medicine.

The considerable demographic shifts that have come about in the United States represent another change that affects our consciousness of death. In the United States, approximately 5,300 deaths occur every day, totaling about two million deaths annually. However, due to our population's rapid growth, the death rate (the number of deaths per one thousand live population) is *lower* than ever before. In the 1900s, there were approximately 17 deaths per one thousand live population, whereas today there are approximately 8.5 deaths per one thousand live population. Because the rate has decreased from 17 to 8.5 per one thousand, death is less common. It also means that although we have more deaths numerically we have proportionately less deaths occurring in our everyday experience.

Another important change that has occurred is that the average life expectancy has increased dramatically from about 47 years in the early 1900s to about 75 years in the 1980s. A more significant change, however, involves the ages of those who die. Specifically, in the 1980s nearly 75 percent of the deaths in the United States will occur to people age 65 and older. In 1900, 53 percent of the deaths that occurred were of people fourteen years old and under. This sizable shift has brought about many problems concerning the issues of dying and death, such as health care delivery to an increased number of elderly dying people, psychological difficulty in dealing with young people's deaths, and other similar age-linked matters.

Finally, "the right to die" movement and the growing concern for the care of the dying is an important change. The Hospice Movement, which originated in the 1950s in St. Joseph's Hospital in London, addressed both the above-mentioned concerns. In 1968, Cecily Saunders formed the famous St. Christopher's Hospice in London. Recently, the Hospice Movement has been credited with being the answer to our problems regarding death; however, although the original concept had strong grassroots appeal, a volunteer orientation, and did not accommodate itself to government regulations, it has become politicized and now is regulated by government rules, requirements, and funds. One of the problems with government involvement is the response to and accommodation of programs to dollars in the sense that "programs follow dollars." This could change the beneficial volunteer nature of a hospice to a more formal institutional atmosphere, an important issue since it was patient need that led Dr. Saunders out of the hospital and into the less restrictive hospice model. With these changing conditions the benefits of the original model may be lost.

What Complications and Paradoxes Affect
Death Consciousness?

Artificial life is a significant change that affects our consciousness of death. We create artificial life supports routinely. Moreover, we can change life and extend it. However, the creation, change, and extension have given rise to a host of perplexing and often unanswerable questions. Some of the consequences brought about by these changes contain some dying and death paradoxes. Consider some examples.

Karen Ann Quinlan elicited an enormous sense of empathy and hope that our society could somehow help this woman to have a dignified dying process. Nonetheless, we were not prepared to deal with the complicated issues raised by her situation, and her family was forced to take their concerns to the courtroom. The first court decision stated that this was *not* a matter to be decided on in the courtroom and received severe criticism from the press. However, the precedent for the decision was well documented. The presiding judge was aware that in Nazi Germany many deaths were decided in the courts. His reasoning was that he should not make a decision in the Quinlan case, but that the family, physician, and hospital should come to a decision without court intervention.

The family persevered in the courts, and the case finally was decided in a second hearing. The decision was not made on the grounds of Karen Ann Quilan's right to die, but rather on the grounds that she was being kept alive by machines, which constituted an invasion of her privacy. After the decision, the hospital staff disconnected her life support mechanisms. Although it was presumed that she would die, she remained physically alive. For ten years she confounded the medical community with her presence. She evoked the hostility of the tax-paying community due to the costs of her treatment, paid for by the county welfare system. However, during the time she was in a comatose state, she was dead by most people's definition of death, which is based on our sense that anyone who is socially dead is not alive.

An illustration of one of the many paradoxes of this situation is the fact that at the beginning of Karen Ann Quinlan's ordeal and that of her family there were strong sentiments about the religious and social reasons against pulling the plug on her life support system. After several years of costly life maintenance, however, there were protesters marching in the small community where she was institutionalized, carrying signs that read, "Put her in a bubble and charge admission so we don't have to pay for her."

The circumstances just cited contain an outrage at a social system that does not know how to confront the new issues and questions concerning dying and death that have been created by technology. Technology has altered significantly not only the manner in which people die but also our reactions to dying and death situations.

Another example of a paradox surrounding dying and death occurred in Texas in 1984, where J.D. Autry was to be executed in a "humane fashion." He was strapped to a guerney, wheeled into a room, and needles were inserted in his veins in a procedure designed to terminate life. In the middle of the process a stay of execution was granted and he was disconnected and sent back to his cell. The stay was not permanent and again he was scheduled to die. The second time the process of intravenous execution began, he stayed alert throughout the first ten minutes. Just before he died he said, "Tell them I kept my cool." Ironically, many of those present at the execution lost their composure due to the "bizarre" nature of the events. This is another illustration of how our reactions to such "not easily categorized" deaths are confusing.

The third and final paradox is that of Dr. Barney Clark. Dr. Clark's diseased and almost dead heart was removed, and he was given an artificial heart with which he lived an extra 112 days. For centuries, the absence of a person's heartbeat has been considered a legal sign of death. Thus, the question arises, was Barney Clark alive or dead when his heart was removed and a machine inserted? Did he actually live an extra 112 days or was he dead during those 112 days? Most of us believe he was alive because his mind was functioning. This illustrates western culture's belief that life resides in the brain, in contrast to some ancient societies' beliefs that life was breath or that death results from a nonfunctioning of the heart.

Interestingly, Barney Clark was given a key to turn off this artificial means of living if he could no longer deal with the situation. In regard to this, he said in an interview, "Well I haven't really thought much about it. I don't expect I'll use it." He did not use it, but he died of complications. If Dr. Clark had used the key, would he have been guilty of committing suicide? As a society, we do not know how to respond to that question because there are no clear-cut guidelines on which to base such a decision.

These paradoxes confound modern society and leave us ill-equipped to deal with death. We do not know what to do in regard to these dilemmas because we have no sociomoral standards to follow in our decision making. This lack of norms or standards is not unique to our society, it prevails whenever drastic and rapid changes occur and our laws as well as our way of thinking have not caught up with or addressed such changes.

What Do We Know about Grief?

The study of grief is a relatively new field whose origin can be traced to the writings of the noted psychoanalyst Sigmund Freud, who dealt with grief in the era of World War I. Freud's position (1957) was that mourning was normal but that melancholia, which he thought was similar to a lingering, maladaptive kind of mourning, was pathological.

In the 1930s, Eliot, (1933) a sociologist, posited that there was more to the grieving process than just the mind. Eliot also called for "a social psychology of bereavement." He explicitly specified that bereavement and grief constituted an important field for social research.

Lindemann's pioneering, classic article contributed excellent points regarding a wide range of grief concerns. The article, published in 1944, describes the specific manifestations of acute grief, provides clinical evidence, and makes sensible conclusions based on observations he made in his clinical efforts with survivors of the Cocoanut Grove Nightclub fire in Boston. Lindemann was the first to describe acute grief as an identifiable psychiatric condition. He explains that acute grief can happen prior to the death event, it can be exaggerated, it can be delayed, and it can be "apparently" absent. He further states that grief, which can be distorted and the cause for great concern, can be resolved if professionally treated.

From our perspective, one of Lindemann's most profound observations is reported in the closing paragraphs of the article. He found that patients experienced genuine grief reactions when a physical separation from a loved one occurred, as well as when "the threat of death" occurred. Lindemann's example of this situation is the grief reactions experienced by families during World War II when a member was absent due to military service. He labels these reactions "anticipatory grief."

Lindemann goes on to say that persons experiencing anticipatory grief focus on their adjustment after an anticipated potential death and thus go through "all the phases of grief—depression, heightened preoccupation with the departed, . . . and anticipation of the modes of adjustment which might be necessitated by it (the death)" (Lindemann, 1944, p. 147). Using the experiences of soldiers and their families during World War II, Lindemann points out that although anticipatory grief "may be a safeguard against the sudden impact of death, it can be problematic in its own right" (p. 148).

Worden (1982) writes about grief and grief counseling, specifying four main tasks of bereavement: (1) accepting the reality of the loss; (2) experiencing the pain of grief; (3) adjusting to an environment in which the deceased no longer is present; and (4) withdrawal of emotional energy and its reinvestment in another relationship.

The first task, accepting the reality of the loss, refers to the relationship between disbelief and eventual acceptance, and one of Worden's important points is that it may be problematic when a person gets *stuck* in grief and denies the loss. Such a reaction, for example, commonly occurs in the aftermath of an airplane crash in which all of the dead bodies are not recovered. In such cases, bereaved people have been heard to say things such as, "I think my daughter survived. Then she crawled off and is suffering from amnesia somewhere." Another way that accepting the loss may be subverted is by the bereaved denying the importance of the loss. For example, a child may say, "Well I never liked my father anyway, he didn't mean that much to me." In this way, the child attempts to deny the importance of the loved one's death and thereby avoids accepting the reality of the loss.

Experiencing the pain of grief is cited by Worden as a positive and necesssary task of bereavement. The "pain of grief" refers to both the physical and emotional pain suffered by the bereaved. Lindemann discussed people suffering from grief reactions at the time of the Cocoanut Grove fire who demonstrated no *psychological* manifestations of grief. However, a large number of them complained about having *somatic* problems such as tightness in the throat, choking, shortness of breath, and an empty sensation in the abdomen. Lindemann also detected a connection between ulcerative colitis and unresolved grief. Such physical symptoms may be a manifestation of emotional pain and should not be ignored.

In this regard, there are a number of ways that society may negate the physical and emotional reality of grief such as in effect saying, "Come on, get back to normal." In personal interviews with a number of young bereaved widows and widowers, one of their common complaints is their friends' desire to get them back into the mainstream too quickly. These well-meaning friends suggest activities such as attending singles clubs as early as six weeks after the death of a spouse, and this may be too soon for many bereaved people. This kind of social negation of the pain of grief is problematic and dangerous for all involved.

Still another aspect of avoiding the pain of grief is the use of drugs. One of the detrimental practices most obvious to funeral directors, clergy, and others who deal professionally with bereaved people is the prescription of heavy sedatives for the bereaved during the period immediately following the death, especially during the funeral. Several weeks later the bereaved person may turn to a family member, friend, counselor, clergy, or funeral director and say, "What happened?" According to most researchers, the pain of grief should be experienced as close to the event and as naturally as possible.

The third task that Worden stresses is the need to adjust to an environment in which the deceased is no longer present. The fact that people are multidimensional and simultaneously fulfill various roles adds to the difficulty of adjusting to an environment without that person when death occurs. For example, a deceased person may have filled the roles of mother, wife, sister, daughter, friend, and coworker.

Due to the large amount of time spent in the workplace, adjusting to this environment following the death of a colleague often creates a difficult situation. When a coworker dies those who have worked with the deceased may have no legitimate social avenues in which to direct their grief over the loss of a friend and confidante. The same sense of loss with no legitimate channels of grief expression also may affect health care professionals who become emotionally attached to a patient and who grieve about that person's dying and death. As a result, their adjustment following the death may be complex and problematic.

In regard to Worden's third task, there are at least three ways of dealing with a loss that can lead to future problems. The first involves the bereaved seeking replacements for specific roles previously filled by the deceased. The resultant new relationships are initiated on a weak and false foundation. The second involves the bereaved personally attempting to fill the role of the deceased. This, of course is a virtual impossibility and can lead to great frustration, anger, and maladaptive behavior. Third, the bereaved may pretend that no change has occurred as a result of the death. This can lead to masked grief symptoms such as physical ailments, delayed or distorted reactions, or avoidance of reality.

The fourth and final task of mourning that Worden identifies is the withdrawal of emotional energy and its reinvestment in another relationship. Perhaps the most difficult, this task must be accomplished in a manner that does not force the bereaved to forget or reject the memory of the dead person. Rather, it should enable the formation of new relationships *without* the dead person. This is what Freud (1957, p. 154) meant when he said "grief should free the bereaved from the dead" and what Lindemann (1944, p. 143) meant by "emancipation from the bondage to the deceased."

One problematic element may arise when this issue of freedom from the deceased is linked to anticipatory grief or to the anticipation of a bereavement. Due to the nature of anticipatory grief, a person close to someone who is dying can move too quickly through anticipation and be prepared for the person to die. However, in some cases the dying process may last longer than expected and the bereaved person may emotionally distance himself or herself from the dying person. Simply stated, problems can arise when a terminally ill person hangs onto life while significant others already have let go.

An example of this situation occurred to a young couple and their three children when they learned that the wife's unmarried sister, age thirty-five, had terminal cancer and was diagnosed as having three to six months to live. Since there were no other family members, the couple asked the sister to live with them for the remaining months of her life. The couple talked about the dying experience with their children and felt that the family could share it, even though it meant restructuring their home lives. After three months the sister was still alive. Another three months passed and she continued to live. After nine months the family sought therapy because one of the children asked, "Isn't she ever going to die?" The family had experienced the grief process too completely and too soon since the death had not occurred when anticipated.

Why Does Anticipation of Bereavement Call for Adaptation?

It is necessary to understand the many dimensions of bereavement because whether the grief is acute, anticipatory, delayed, or distorted, it ultimately is caused by a bereavement. In this sense, bereavement can be thought of as a tapestry of loss with psychological, social, and cultural dimensions woven together in a complex, little-understood pattern. Psychological dimensions involve one's self, social dimensions involve the interactive process with others, and cultural dimensions involve the larger society in which one lives and the commonly understood meanings that set the boundaries for one's socioemotional reactions to bereavement. The implication of this multidimensional perspective is that we can predict to some extent what a particular loss will mean to us. This sense of the future is the ultimate determinant of our anticipation of bereavement. Therefore, when we learn that someone will die or *may* be dead, we can quite accurately anticipate what that loss will mean to us personally. This provides the psychological–sociological–cultural skills or knowledge to set the grieving process in motion.

Bereavement per se is the *same* in every culture in the sense that the death of a person represents the same objective loss no matter where it occurs. However, grief reactions to a particular bereavement are culturally determined. For example, in some societies the death of a child's father has little impact on the child. However, if the child's mother's brother dies, the loss is significant because the kinship ties in some matrilinear societies are based on the mother's brother's property, rather than the father's property. The point is that when considering grief reactions, we must strive to consider the culture and accepted mores of those who are bereaved.

It is important to understand that a bereaved person does not get rid of grief after a specified amount of time has elapsed. It is more realistic to consider grief as a phenomenon that occurs along a continuum. In many cases, remnants of grief may be carried by a bereaved person forever. However, grief becomes a serious problem if it dominates the bereaved person's life and prevents him or her from adequately carrying out the normal activities of life.

Anticipatory grief or grief in anticipation of a bereavement is a *real* form of grief. Grief is experienced from the moment of awareness, through conscious perception, and throughout all the reactions that occur in response to dying and death; however, the ultimate purpose of the grief process is to achieve a level of resolution, and at this point we encounter a psychological–sociological–cultural bind. Namely, most of our everyday conventional wisdom and our social scientific literature only explicates the normal course of grief.

It is my present contention that we cannot *know* the normal course of grief for each individual. Moreover, it is the present belief that all one's grief reactions are linked together throughout one's existence. For example, someone's death may elicit feelings about the death of a grandparent who died many years ago. Similarly, the death of a friend may bring forth feelings about a death that previously occurred to another friend. These muted connections to previous deaths exist in everyone, and each new death provides the opportunity for these past feelings to be reexperienced, especially if grief over the previous deaths has not been resolved. Therefore, each individual's unique past experiences with death situations must be taken into account and incorporated in addressing the needs of the bereaved.

This perspective leads to the idea of adaptive anticipation, which takes into consideration common sense knowledge, professional judgment, reasonable prediction, and creative thinking. By combining the knowledge base discussed thus far and integrating it with the specter of a future loss, it seems possible to develop a rational approach to helping people cope with their grief reactions to an anticipated bereavement.

What is an Agenda for Adaptive Anticipation of Bereavement?

For a professional caregiver, the search for precise techniques by which to help bereaved people is not a useful endeavor. Rather, flexibility and adaptivity to fit the individual's needs, lifestyle, past losses, grief reactions, and so forth are the keys to coming to terms with loss. It is essential to be aware of the many factors that may affect the bereaved person's life. Following are four important ones to which special attention should be given.

First, know the changes that have occurred in an individual's life prior to, at the time of, and following the news of an impending death, as well as following a death.

Second, strive to understand each person's personal death history. The best way to accomplish this is to have the bereaved prepare an inventory of the losses they have experienced. This can assist in discussing the full scope of their particular reactions to a death or an anticipated death.

Third, treat each bereaved person as a unique individual as well as a member of a family unit or other group. This is important because the reactions within a particular family actually represent individual dilemmas and responses for each member of the family. The critical point is that although part of a unit, each individual reacts in accordance with his or her own personal relationship with the deceased.

Finally, recognize that a particular person's actual or anticipated death can have as many different effects as there are individuals experiencing the loss. In addition, each bereaved person will be touched on many different levels, and their lives will be altered in different ways.

In anticipation of bereavement when a death is expected to occur, a useful agenda of action that includes practical steps should prove beneficial to both professionals and their patients. It can assist the person seeking assistance to complete the tasks of mourning. It may be beneficial to have the bereaved ask the salient questions recommended by Weisman (1972):

If death is close, what matters most?

If death is inevitable, what would make it acceptable?

What can one do to prepare for a death?

What might lead one to want to die?

At what point do you want others to stop "keeping you alive?"

It is emphasized that answering these questions requires one to undergo stark self-examination. Furthermore, Weisman stresses that there are no correct answers to these questions. They are presented because society has been unwilling to ask realistic questions about impending death, and this avoidance makes the process of anticipation more difficult.

Rando (1984) suggests strategies for the professional and begins by emphasizing the griever's need for acceptance and nonjudgmental listening. This will help the client to express his or her emotions and facilitate a necessary review of the relationship with the lost loved one. Later, the bereaved person will need assistance with integrating the past with the present.

Among other strategies, Rando points out that social support is necessary, especially soon after the death, because the bereaved person may require caregivers in the midst of chaos. At the time of such intense emotional reactions, it is helpful and comforting to know there are others who lend security, order, and a sense of reality to the griever. Group therapy and particularly self-help groups can be helpful in this regard.

An atmosphere in which people have the freedom to choose their own style of grief will promote a feeling of ease in dealing with a death situation. Helping people deal with feelings of ambivalence in anticipation of bereavement is challenging but essential because ambivalence is pervasive to the person experiencing it. In fact, Freud (1957) refers to the conflict of ambivalence as one of the problems that needs to be resolved in the work of grief. It is even more problematic when unconscious feelings of ambivalence are unearthed as a result of the death and then are combined with conscious feelings of ambivalence.

Freud further states that ambivalence in the relationship with the person who died has the potential to develop into pathological grief, self-reproaches, and even may force the bereaved to blame themselves for the death of a loved one. Hence, any mixed feelings that the bereaved may have had toward the deceased should be explored and discussed. Again, this type of counseling should conform to the unique needs of the bereaved.

How Can We Synthesize This Information?

All facets of grief, including the physical, emotional, temporal, social, and familial, must be integrated and then modified to address the specific needs of the bereaved. Let us bring together the diverse perspectives presented by citing three noted studies of anticipatory grief that collectively help demonstrate the point of this chapter.

In 1944, Lindemann concluded his classic treatment of acute grief by describing what he called "anticipatory grief." He recognized the danger of not acknowledging the special reactions to anticipated bereavements and cautioned as follows:

> In such situations apparently the grief work had been done so effectively that the patient has [been] emancipated and the readjustment must now be directed towards new interaction [and not the object of the loss]. It is important to know this because many family disasters of this sort may be avoided through prophylactic measures. (p. 148)

Twenty-seven years later, Fulton and Fulton (1971) concluded their discussion of anticipatory grief by recognizing the potential dangers as follows:

> As a psychological phenomenon with social consequences, anticipatory grief . . . confronts us with a two-edged effect. It possesses the capacity to enhance our lives and secure our well-being, while possessing at the same time the power to undermine our fragile existence and rupture our tenuous bonds. (p. 99)

Forty years after Lindemann's original article appeared, Rando (1984) concluded her chapter on grief with the following admonition:

> It is important that anticipatory grief be recognized as a legitimate phenomenon for intervention. Interventions made at this point can prevent problems in mourning from developing; later interventions can only try to remedy difficulties that already have occurred. (p. 40)

This chapter has emphasized that in order to cope adequately with anticipation of bereavement, it is crucial to be adaptive. The way people react to loss depends on many factors, not the least of which involves the expectations and anticipations surrounding a particular bereavement. Awareness of the problems and a sensitive handling of those individuals experiencing them can help enhance the quality of the intervention during the period of anticipation as well as after the bereavement has taken place.

References

Eliot, T.D. 1933. A Step toward the Social Psychology of Bereavement. *Journal of Abnormal and Social Psychology* 27:380–390.

Freud, S. 1957. Mourning and Melancholia [1917]. In *Collected Papers*. New York: Basic Books, pp. 152–170.

Fulton, R., and J. Fulton. 1971. A Psychosocial Aspect of Terminal Care: Anticipatory Grief. *Omega* 2:91–100.

Lindemann, E. 1944. Symptomatology and Management of Acute Grief. *American Journal of Psychiatry* 101:141–148.

Rando, T.A. 1984. *Grief, Dying, and Death: Clinical Interventions for Caregivers.* Champaign, Ill.: Research Press.

Sudnow, D. 1967. *Passing On: The Social Organization of Dying.* Englewood Cliffs, N.J.: Prentice-Hall.

Weisman, A.D. 1972. *On Dying and Denying: A Psychiatric Study of Terminality.* New York: Behavioral Publications.

Worden, J.W. 1982. *Grief Counseling and Grief Therapy: A Handbook for the Mental Health Practitioner.* New York: Springer Publishing Company.

3
Anticipatory Grief and Reinvestment

J. Eugene Knott
Eugenia Wild

T he concept of *anticipatory grief* was so labeled first by Lindemann (1944) in his classic work on the symptoms and care of the acutely bereft. In it, he cited a syndrome in which a person evidences concern over adjustment to living following the death of a loved one such that anticipation of the modes of readjustment are engaged in prior to the actual death by the survivor-to-be. He further noted that this can (1) entail expression of many or all of the phases of grief; (2) involve precautionary psychic preparation sufficient to begin emotional decathexis or gradual disinvestment of emotional energy; and (3) prove problematic if such grief work is fully manifested far in advance of the actual death or if the presumed death loss subsequently proves erroneous.

Later examinations and formulations of this concept have pointed to the complexity of the phenomenon of anticipatory grief and its seeming contradictions. Fulton and Gottesman (1980) provided the most thorough address of this and have cautioned against too hasty and inconsiderate a view of what anticipatory grief may involve. For our purposes, the definition by Lebow (1976), and the accompanying array of tenets delineated, shall suffice. These tenets provide a backdrop against which the matter of reinvestment is discussed.

Lebow refers to anticipatory grief as the total set of cognitive, affective, cultural, and social reactions to expected death felt by the patient and family. Key to this view are the confluent psychological *and* social aspects, and the notion that the processes occur both for the patient and relatives dealing with protracted illness, although these may be quite different in their intensity, focus, duration, and timing. Lebow further lists the tasks faced by all those involved as they begin to adapt to the inevitability and finality of the death. The tasks include:

The authors of this chapter are both bereaved parents who personally have wrestled with the concepts of anticipatory grief and reinvestment. Coming to terms with the diagnosis of cancer in one's child, living through the experience with that child over many years, and surviving have helped to shape our perspective.

Editors note: Although many of the examples utilized in this chapter refer to dying children, the processes discussed are equally relevant for older dying individuals and their loved ones.

Continuing but shifting levels of involvement with one another

Altering role relationships

Doing the work of grieving and mourning (individual and relational behaviors)

Altering the context of decision making about the dying person's needs

Separating and saying goodbyes

The matter of reinvestment, by contrast, is less frequently written about, less appreciated, and perhaps fraught with too much anticipatory guilt making. Arising as it has from a primarily psychoanalytic tradition, reinvestment has been considered alternatively as necessary (Lindemann, 1944; Silverman, 1982), signal (Bowlby, 1980), appropriate (Parkes and Weiss, 1983), and adaptive (Pollock, 1961).

From our standpoint, reinvestment has all the above characteristics. It is also risky, probably less planful than would appear, and enables new meanings to be derived for the life, illness, dying, death, grief, and original investments in the loved one whom we mourn.

As Fulton and Fulton (1971) noted, anticipatory grief has the interlinking capacity for both a rehearsal of the death and preliminary attempts to adjust to the consequences of the loss. Rando (1984) further notes the qualities of preparing for reinvestment that are inherent in anticipatory grief's other allowances. They include, among others, "beginning to change assumptions about life and identity [and] making plans for the future [without the dying person] so that they will not be felt as betrayals of the deceased after death" (p. 37).

In all, reinvestment—call it reestablishment, recovery, recathexis, if you will—appears to be a normal, even critical phase of adaptation to one's bereavement and grief. As Parkes and Weiss (1983) noted, the recovery may entail accomplishment of three related tasks:

Recognition and cognitive explanation of the loss

Emotional acceptance of the loss

Assumption of the new identities and roles incumbent on the mourners in a community

This latter task particularly calls on the individual to begin the life's work of adjusting to being without the consistent presence of the loved one.

As some research has shown, when the loss is that of a child, the reinvestment may be somewhat more complicated, especially in this culture (Futterman, Hoffman, and Sabshin, 1972; Rando, 1983.) Futterman and his collaborators studied the anticipatory grief of parents and listed a set of five related, somewhat serial behaviors that functioned to aid parents anticipating the death of their child. These included:

Acknowledgment of the progression of the child's condition to inevitable death

Expression of grieving and all its possible associated experiences

Making sense of the child's life as worthwhile

Beginning to *withdraw emotional attachment*, particularly in future hopes for the child's life

Gathering a sense and mental picture that will *memorialize* the child in a personally meaningful way thereafter

Furthermore, the number and range of influencing factors of psychological, medical, social, physiological, and spiritual natures are critical variables in any consideration of bereavement outcome. Raphael (1983), Osterweis, Solomon, and Green (1984), and especially Rando (1984) have catalogued and summarized the differential effects of these dozens of factors, so we shall not repeat them here. For the rest of our discussion, suffice it to say these four things in summary of the research on our topics:

1. Anticipatory grief does appear to have a beneficial effect on bereavement outcome in many cases.

2. The varying temporal, social, psychic, and physical faces of the dying experience significantly determine those outcomes.

3. Grieving a lost child may present particularly challenging demands on the anticipatory mourning *and* reinvestment experiences of the bereaved.

4. Reinvestment is an important, even revitalizing component of adapting to death loss, but one that is not fully appreciated nor easily come by in our culture today.

Lindemann (1944) and others have described the difficulties of families in reintegrating absent members after World War II. These people had been missing long enough for their families to grieve them and move on to form new attachments. This phenomenon has been called "the Lazarus syndrome" after the biblical story of a man brought back from the dead. Easson (1970) discusses this with regard to children who have been diagnosed with a usually fatal disease and who unexpectedly recover or have long remissions. Families may find it difficult or impossible to reinvest emotionally in these children.

The experience of one author may serve to illustrate this point:

My daughter was diagnosed with cancer at age three. Several years after her diagnosis I was aware that while externally I was involved with her physical and medical care needs, I was not making an emotional connection with her. Lucky enough to hear a lecture in which the Lazarus syndrome was being discussed, I realized that I was afraid of the pain of investing in this probably dying child and that this was not my own lack but a commonly observed phenomenon. This knowledge allowed me to make a choiceful decision between the natural process of decathecting or reinvestment. I chose the latter.

Often, discussions of reinvestment focus exclusively on the survivor's ability to make new love bonds, reintegrate into the community, and move on after the loss. Long-term living–dying processes engendered by the advances of modern medicine have created a need to look from another perspective: reinvestment in the face of dying. Disease remissions inevitably create hope for cure, long-term survival, or more time. They allow one to reinvest. Relapses kill such hopes and hard work must be done to stay in contact with the ill person. Consciousness of the process, of decathecting and recathecting, if you will, is imperative if we are to avoid premature withdrawal.

One of the authors expressed these sentiments:

Since my son's diagnosis, one of the ways I think about myself, my life, and my family living is that blue skies are not universally there anymore. There's a cloud and I, in some metaphorical way, expect life will never be the same again. I thought my son might die immediately when told he had leukemia. Then I dealt with the concept that two-year survival was a good sign and he relapsed at twenty-two months. I had to focus again on whether or not to reinvest. But I think family members, and perhaps caregivers, don't have the luxury of making that decision. There are some choices about how, but not about whether.

Being with a loved one through the dying process brings a succession of little deaths as debilitation narrows horizons. It has been thought that the more dysfunctional an individual became over time during a protracted illness, the more each of these incremental losses became an opportunity for the survivor to let go of a piece of that relationship. These losses and the increasingly diminished capacity for normal living are thought to make it easier to let go and even see death as acceptable. Both authors view this as a contrivance, a way to try to justify the expected loss. Our experience was that we continued to reinvest even as our children's losses, such as legal blindness and sterility, mounted.

In essence, it must be remembered that the person who is anticipating the death of a loved one is in a process that requires two different things. One is to separate, to withdraw from that painful situation and reinvest elsewhere or risk losing the context for one's own life. At precisely the same time, one ought also to continue to be involved with the dying person or risk losing connection with that life before it is over. The need for both separation and involvement should be simultaneously reinforced for the person who is anticipating loss.

We learn early to pull away from pain; it seems natural, we don't need to touch a hot stove often. Reinvesting in a painful situation, such as a loved one's dying, requires overcoming that learning. This takes energy. If the dying continues over a long period of time, the amount of psychic and physical energy required is enormous.

Recathecting, rather than decathecting, may increase the time needed for recovery after the death, mitigating against the salutary effects of anticipatory grief that have been suggested by some. One of us, whose child had lived thirteen years after the initial diagnosis, found it took several years to feel at normal energy level and fully back to work. A colleague shared her impatience with that slow return, reflecting probably both a belief that having all the time to prepare should have enabled her readjustment to be completed sooner and a loving wish that suffering should finally end.

Finally, the ability to reinvest is the acknowledgment of our survival. It's one of the few ways we have of literally saying to ourselves, "I'm not dying, _____ is." Anticipatory grief involves losing another and being able simply to know you are the survivor-to-be. Saying it to yourself and grappling with your imminent losses in that life may be the whole essence of reinvestment.

References

Bowlby, J. 1980. *Attachment and Loss: Loss, Sadness and Depression.* Vol. 3. New York: Basic Books.

Easson, W.M. 1970. *The Dying Child: The Management of the Child or Adolescent Who Is Dying.* Springfield, Ill.: Charles C. Thomas.

Fulton, R., and J. Fulton. 1971. A Psychosocial Aspect of Terminal Care: Anticipatory Grief. *Omega* 2:91–99.

Fulton, R., and D.J. Gottesman. 1980. Anticipatory Grief. A Psychosocial Concept Reconsidered. *British Journal of Psychiatry* 137:45–54.

Futterman, E.H., I. Hoffman, and M. Sabshin. 1972. Parental Anticipatory Mourning. In B. Schoenberg et al., eds., *Psychosocial Aspects of Terminal Care.* New York: Columbia University Press, pp. 243–272.

Lebow, G.H. 1976. Facilitating Adaptation in Anticipatory Mourning. *Social Casework* 57:458–465.

Lindemann, E. 1944. Symptomatology and Management of Acute Grief. *American Journal of Psychiatry* 101:141–148.

Osterweis, M., F. Solomon, and M. Green, eds. 1984. *Bereavement: Reactions, Consequences, and Care.* Washington, D.C.: National Academy Press.

Parkes, C.M., and R.S. Weiss. 1983. *Recovery from Bereavement.* New York: Basic Books.

Pollock, G.H. 1961. Mourning and Adaptation. *International Journal of Psychoanalysis* 42:341–361.

Rando, T.A. 1983. An Investigation of Grief and Adaptation in Parents Whose Children Have Died from Cancer. *Journal of Pediatric Psychology* 8:3–20.

Rando, T.A. 1984. *Grief, Dying, and Death: Clinical Interventions for Caregivers.* Champaign, Ill.: Research Press.

Raphael, B. 1983. *The Anatomy of Bereavement.* New York: Basic Books.

Silverman, P.R. 1982. Transitions and Models of Intervention. *Annals of the Academy of Political and Social Science* 464:174–187.

Part II
Anticipatory Grief and the Principals Involved

4

Effects of Anticipatory Grief for the Patient, Family Member, and Caregiver

Marion A. Humphrey

Anticipatory grief differs from postdeath grief in both duration and form. It affects the patient, family member, and caregiver in similar, yet dissimilar ways. This chapter explores the similarities and differences of anticipatory grief for each of these individuals, along with the adaptational tasks with which each is confronted. It will conclude with specific intervention strategies for facilitating healthy anticipatory grief in each of the parties. Throughout, the constant interplay among these three principals will be noted, with an analysis of how their different experiences of anticipatory grief impact upon the interpersonal relationships of this triad.

The Experience of Anticipatory Grief

Anticipatory grief is a multidimensional experience. Fulton and Gottsman (1980) describe it as occurring on three levels:

The Psychological Level. On this level there is a complex interplay of factors affecting other levels, which include individual coping abilities and feelings of guilt, responsibility, anger, and despondency.

The Interpersonal Level. Like a pebble dropped in a pond, grief has a ripple effect on the individual's total life situation. In other words, one individual's grief will affect, in varying degrees of intensity, all those in his or her family system. This includes the extended family, of which caregivers are a part. Because impending death is an anxiety-provoking crisis, the dying person and those close to him or her will naturally experience varying degrees of anxiety and stress. They may feel the need to conceal this from each other, thus isolating themselves from their natural support systems. Research has pointed out that the manner in which families and dying persons deal with or deny their impending loss will have an effect on their anticipatory grief, as well as possibly influencing their long-term adjustment. The reactions of the caregivers involved in the patient's care, from prediagnosis to death and bereavement, can have a facilitative or detrimental effect on the emotional state of the dying person and the family. Caregivers and friends who cope by using avoidance of this painful emotional situation, deny the patient and family an important means of support in dealing with the impending loss. Opportunities for expression of feelings, teaching, and meaningful interpersonal interactions go by the board and the patient and family are left to deal with an overwhelming situation with whatever resources they have on hand.

The Sociocultural Level. Funerary and mourning rites today are in a state of flux. Memorial services, in which the body is not viewed (except by immediate family members and sometimes not even by them), are more prevalent than ever before. Closed caskets and less or no calling hours seem to indicate a trend toward downplaying traditional mourning rites. Although this is not necessarily wrong, it does leave us with fewer role models for bereavement and fewer norms for appropriate mourning behavior. Davidson (1975) described the "waiting vulture syndrome," in which survivors-to-be are left in an extremely awkward position. They are compelled to cope with their loss without having learned appropriate coping strategies from societal or family role models. In some cases, because of the need to protect children and young people from the experience of death, this segment of the population may have little previous experience to help them cope with their own impending loss. Thus, anticipatory grief can have a positive or negative effect, depending on how it is experienced and the response one may have to that experience.

The dying person experiences anticipatory grief in the present sense. He is grieving for what he has already lost in the past, and also what he is in the process of losing in the present. From the moment of a fatal diagnosis, he is faced with a multiplicity of losses both symbolic and physical. For example:

Loss of being a healthy person functioning in society.

Loss of the ability to live at home without interruption by hospitalization, painful treatment, or doctor's appointments.

Loss of the ability to plan for the future.

Eventual or sudden loss of job role.

Loss of the ability to care for the home and family.

Loss of the ability to perform sexually.

Loss of the ability to care for one's own bodily needs and functions.

The family member experiences anticipatory grief in a similar, yet unique way. Although experiencing all the above mentioned losses with their loved one, the family member still has a future. The most devastating aspect for the family member is the disequilibrium experienced with family shift and role reassignment. This is compounded by the need to begin to perceive a future in which the loved one no longer exists.

The professional caregiver (and this includes clergy, social worker, psychologist, therapist, nurse, physician, or any other member of the interdisciplinary team who has interaction with the dying patient and the family) also experiences some of the losses described above with the person in their care. However, the caregiver, although not as intensely as patients or family members, can face death situations as often as two or three times a day, with different dying persons and their families. The professional caregiver, in being exposed to a multitude of potentially tragic situations, is hard pressed to keep a healthy balance between his or her professional and personal life demands and the need to maintain the inner person intact. In other words, caregivers are uniquely vulnerable to suffering from an accumulation of grief.

These three viewpoints, briefly outlined here, are the fulcrums from which the behaviors of the individuals involved are simultaneously being played out in the cruciblelike setting of the hospital, the nursing home, the hospice, the physician's office, or the home. The potential for a volatile situation is readily apparent.

Fulton (1978), Rando (1983), and Lebow (1976) are some of the researchers who have studied anticipatory grief. All agree that certain amounts of anticipatory grieving are clearly associated with fewer atypical grief responses following death. However, Rando's work in 1983 on the anticipatory grief of parents whose children had died from cancer, illustrated what appears to be an optimal amount of anticipatory grief. Parents with too few anticipatory grief behaviors, or those with too many, appeared to be compromised in terms of their participation in the hospitalized child's illness and their own adjustment after the death. This research has implications for the anticipatory grief of others whose loved one is dying as well. It clearly suggests the therapeutic necessity of avoiding too little or too much anticipatory grief. For example, Rando noted that too much anticipatory grief appeared to have interfered with the parents' ability to continue interacting with their child. This may provide some empirical support for concerns about premature detachment. She also noted that in contrast to those who engaged in a medium amount of anticipatory grief behaviors, those in low and high anticipatory grief behavior groups evidenced more anger and hostility following the loss and reported higher loss of emotional control after death. Rando concluded that individuals who had engaged in an optimum medium amount of anticipatory grief behaviors (1) appeared to be better able to participate with the child during the illness; (2) sustained more therapeutic levels of anger and hostility and emotional control after the loss; and (3) reported higher ratings of subsequent adjustment after the death.

In other writing analyzing both the costs and benefits of anticipatory grief, Rando (1984) observes that the clinical and empirical evidence suggests that in its role as a preparation for death, anticipatory grief is critical because it ensures that the loss is not unexpected. However, it can well interfere with the individual's experience with the dying person during the illness, and high amounts have been associated with less satisfactory bereavement experiences.

Adaptational Tasks in Anticipatory Grief

Each of the principals involved—the patient, the family member, and the caregiver—is confronted with a series of adaptational tasks in the process of anticipatory grief. The relative importance of each task for a given individual will vary widely, depending on such factors as the personality of the individual involved, the nature of the illness, the environmental circumstances, and so forth.

Adaptational Tasks of the Dying Person

The following adaptational tasks of the dying person have been delineated by Kalish (1970).

Getting Affairs in Order. The effects of the illness may make it difficult for the patient to participate in this due to physical or mental impairments, or seriously depleted energy levels. Denial by the patient and/or family members may mean this issue will not be addressed at all. For example, Joe was a fifty-four-year-old married man with two college-age sons. He owned his own jewelry business. Despite the fact that physicians and nurses were very realistic with the patient and family about his impending death from cancer, the patient and family style of coping with adversity in the past was to deny it. This resulted in the patient making inappropriate business changes just prior to his death that had serious consequences for his family's financial survival.

Coping with the Loss of Both Loved Ones and Self. The realization of the totality of the loss for the dying person can be overwhelming. Not only must he consider the loss of relationships but also of the very world around him, his inner identity, his body, everything. The dying person must contemplate life going on for his survivors without him. Who will care for them, share in their joys and sorrows? This is an especially poignant issue for the dying person.

Considering Future Medical Care Needs. Options for care of the dying are becoming more difficult to provide as resources for third-party payment become increasingly limited, and hospitals and nursing homes have to cope with guidelines such as Diagnostic Related Groups (DRGs). The Hospice Movement provides some interesting and important options for home care of the dying but even this model of care is experiencing financial difficulties during the present state of health care payment flux. Careful planning of the terminal care of the patient can be one of the most critical issues that needs to be addressed. How, where, by whom, and how much it costs will have an effect on the quality of the last days of the patient's life. It will also have a far longer effect on the memories of the survivors.

Planning the Future. With the patient and family aware of a limited length of time left, how that patient and family chooses to use their time, energy, and financial resources becomes of paramount importance. For example, May, a sixty-seven-year-old widow, lived alone. When she entered the final stages of her illness, it became important for her sense of identity, worthwhileness, and control to visit several nursing homes and to make plans for where her final days were to be spent while she was still physically capable of accomplishing this.

Anticipating Possible Future Pain and Facing Possible Losses of Sensory, Motor or Cognitive Abilities, Changes in Appearance, Loss of Performance and Function—All Suggesting a Loss of Identity. The issue of pain needs to be realistically addressed. The specific meanings of pain for this particular individual must be explored. The anticipated loss of identity that naturally accompanies a terminal illness is extremely threatening, difficult to cope with, and yet unavoidable. For example, Janice was a forty-three-year-old unmarried woman with leukemia. She had been a successful businesswoman and her physical appearance was important to her. She took pains to wear an attractive wig, makeup, and so forth. However, she related to her therapist one day, "I can pretend I'm okay, except when I step out of my morning shower and I see the reality of my death reflected in my bathroom mirror." Future (as well as present) losses must be grieved and the patient assisted in coping with them in a fashion that will minimize the shame and guilt that can be experienced.

Considering Being a Nonperson. This existential issue is almost impossible to comprehend, and yet must be confronted when one is facing imminent death. Just as one cannot look at the sun without looking away, we cannot look at our nonbeing without looking away. This anticipatory issue can best be dealt with in small doses over a reasonable period of time. Life review can be helpful here, as a sense of fulfillment and satisfaction with life aids the dying person in letting go. The fear of the rite of passage can also be helped by religious or philosophical discussion.

Deciding to Speed Up or Slow Down the Dying Process. In losing one's life, one loses ultimate control. In anticipating one's death, it is helpful to know that we do have some control over the actual death trajectory. It is not at all unusual for people to hold on until some special event has taken place or some special person has arrived. It appears that the individual makes a type of decision to let go and death usually follows very closely.

Adaptational Tasks of the Family Member

At the same time as the dying person, the family member is presented with a series of tasks in anticipatory grief. These have been articulated by Lebow (1976) and include:

Remaining Involved. This means participating in the reality of the other, responding to what the dying person is going through, as well as sharing with him some of the family members' experiences. For example, it is easy to feel isolated, especially if in the hospital or nursing home. A dying person needs to have a part in the decisions about family, finances, and home. For the dying person, this emphasizes that he still has some control, his opinions still matter, indeed, he is still living. The family member can still share some of the burden of family life with their loved one, allowing him to finish unfinished business and to temporarily lower the feelings of abandonment.

Remaining Separate. This is the task of individuation. The family member needs to develop an appreciation of his or her own sense of self, separate from the patient. He or she must come to grips with the fact that the loved one will die and must start to contemplate a future in which the loved one does not exist. The family member must begin to differentiate his or her own needs from those of the sick family member.

Adapting to Role Change. This refers to the reassignment of roles within the family and adapting to new demands in reasonable ways. This role shift is one of the most difficult tasks the family member will undertake. This can include, for example, husband/father assuming the mothering role; an adult child assuming the parent role with a dying parent; a widow assuming financial and property maintenance responsibilities; or a child assisting in taking over a deceased sibling's chores. In the terminal illness of a family member, family system functioning is highly threatened. There may be power struggles, especially when the dying person has been the strong one in the family, as well as reluctance to assume responsibilities that appear to be overwhelming. The struggle for the family to achieve a new homeostasis is a stressful, albeit necessary one.

Bearing the Affects of Grief. This necessitates managing the feelings aroused by the event of terminal illness. In addition to the more usual feelings, such as sadness and guilt, memories, and affects of past losses are commonly revived in grief. For example, Janet was a thirty-two-year-old wife whose thirty-four-year-old husband of two years was dying of cancer. The anticipation of this loss reawakened old, unresolved issues surrounding the sudden, accidental death of a sibling when Janet was eleven years old. It also raised issues about her divorce from her first husband five years previously. These issues had to be dealt with in therapy, along with her anticipatory grief over the impending death of her husband.

Facing Reality. The family member needs to face the reality of the anticipated loss. This needs to be done as a process, allowing time for comprehension and internalization of this painful information. Brief, imaginary glimpses into the future in which the loved one no longer exists need to be normalized for the family member as part of the process of anticipatory grief. Discussion of medical requirements, plans for care, funeral arrangements, and financial concerns may need to be addressed over and over again.

Saying Goodbye. This acknowledges the reality of the impending loss and may be communicated verbally and nonverbally. This is a critical area that requires much support and role modeling from caregivers. The family member may have difficulty recognizing when the end is near. Goodbyes left unsaid, or not completed in a way that is satisfactory to the survivor, can be devastating to the grief experience. For example, Louise was highly stressed by the hospital death-bed scene with her husband in which both nurses and doctors withdrew during the death trajectory. Having no previous experience with death, Louise could not recognize the signs of imminent death. The actual death surprised her and left her feeling that she had failed her husband by not saying or doing some of the things she had imagined saying and doing when she had previously anticipated the death scene.

Adaptational Tasks of the Caregiver

Simultaneously, with both patient and family member, the caregiver must face a series of interrelated tasks if the anticipatory grief experience is to be as successfully negotiated as possible.

Accepting the Loss of Power and Ability to Control Death. Caregivers working in university or research-oriented facilities, where the underlying philosophy is cure-oriented, will find this an especially difficult task. This is true of the physician in particular. Gerber (1977) points out that medical training unwittingly influences the manner in which physicians care for the dying:

> Medical education tends to encourage physicians to define a patient as "a case," that has a diseased part which can be healed with the use of appropriate medical technology. The medical skill is present, the illness is located and defined, and

technical care is offered. But where is the patient? The learned orientation of treating the part rather than the whole is directly related to the medical care of the dying patient. If a physician has limited interest in the social and emotional aspects of patient care, this learned orientation will be very evident when the physician is confronted with a terminally ill patient. The proper medical care of the dying patient necessitates that the physician functions beyond his learned technical skills. The question is, how can the physician be a comforter, as well as a healer, when his training discourages social and emotional skills. (Gerber, 1977, p. 74)

To a lesser degree, this phenomenon is also true for nurses. Nursing education underscores the three most highly esteemed attributes of a nurse interacting in the presence of a patient as being composure, control, and competence. Nurses are taught to manage or prevent emotional displays with drugs or by referring difficult cases to special agents, such as the clergy, social workers, and psychiatric services.

Ultimately, nursing's goals are care- rather than cure-oriented. This often puts a nurse in conflict when performing as a member of the team that is basically cure-oriented. This conflict filters down to other caregivers such as social workers or clergy, whose educational and philosophical orientation is to have a more holistic approach to patient care but who have less power in participating in decision making and planning that care.

Finding Satisfaction in Achievement of Patient–Family Comfort Rather Than in Cure of the Disease. There must be a dramatic shift in focus of care here. The heaviest burden for decision making falls on the physician. He or she must bear the brunt of accepting that cure goals are no longer relevant. Then, he or she must inform the dying person, family members, his or her peers, and the health care team of the change in focus from cure to palliation. Once this has taken place, nurses, for the most part, are usually comfortable and extremely expert at providing care that is comfort-oriented. Other team members can also make this transition once the ultimate decision has been made. A problem arises when the physician is unable to make this transition, thus blocking everyone, including the patient and family, from making it as well.

Recognizing and Adjusting to Emotional Reactions That May Be Precipitated by the Impending Death. Because of the highly charged emotional impact of our concerns with death, it becomes difficult to prevent our feelings and needs from interfering with those of the dying person and his family. Caregivers are likely to assess the dying person's needs in relation to their own needs, unless that caregiver has at least partially worked through his or her own feelings about dying and death. When the caregiver is aware of these personal feelings and beliefs, he or she is then capable of seeing beyond them and keeping them from interfering with the ability to provide support to the patient and family. Being in the presence of impending death often evokes memories of previous experiences, both professional and personal. The experiences, especially if they occurred when the person was vulnerable, color all further reactions to situations involving dying and grief. It cannot be stressed enough: most of us experience unpleasant reactions of fear and anxiety or even revulsion when we begin to think about death. It is important to continually remember how normal these feelings are.

Maintaining a Balance between Involvement and Objectivity. Because we are human and mortal before we are professional caregivers, it is sometimes difficult to maintain a therapeutic distance between those persons in our care and our own personal lives. Therapeutic distance is the ability to be empathetic, to emote, and yet maintain a sense of individuality. It requires the ability to recognize when transference and countertransference take place. It implies an ability to know when to step back or when to let go. The struggle for balance can go on not only with the dying person and the family, but also between the caregiver and the other members of the health care team. It is necessary to continually ask oneself, "Whose needs am I meeting?"

Recognizing and Adjusting to the Need to Change the Focus of Care from the Dying Patient to the Family Members. In traditional medical settings, the focus of care has always been the patient. As death approaches, caregivers need to recognize and be comfortable with beginning to transfer the focus of care to the family members. In hospitals and nursing homes, this can be most difficult as family members and relationships tend to be viewed as existing in the periphery. However, when family members are viewed as an extension of the dying patient and are encouraged to be present and participate in the care, a great deal can be done for the dying patient's peace of mind as well as that of the ones who will survive the death. Family member needs are legitimate concerns for the caregiver.

Recognizing and Adjusting to the Multiplicity of Demands Inherent in Providing Care for the Dying. Health caregivers, in general, deal with a multiplicity of simultaneous demands. At times, these demands can be in conflict as one struggles to meet (1) one's own expectations of professional performance; (2) patient and family expectations; (3) expectations of physicians; (4) expectations of other interdisciplinary team members; and (5) expectations of the institution. Nowhere is this more acute than when dealing with the dying patient and his family. Overriding the situation is the knowledge of a lack of time. Given this knowledge, we know we cannot undo, redo, or postpone events. This heightens anxiety and tension and places a special burden on the caregivers.

Recognizing Caregiver Potential for Accumulated Grief and Seeking Appropriate Ways to Care for the Caregiver. These issues have been explicated by Fulton

(1978), who states that frequently professional caregivers experience grief at the loss of a patient and in many ways react as bereaved survivors themselves. Nurses, in particular, are prone to this reaction because of the intimate role they play in caring for the patient and family. The uniqueness of the constancy of this role fosters ties with the patient and family from which other caregivers may be excluded. For example, the primary care nurse, assigned to the 11:00 p.m. to 7:00 a.m. shift in a hospital, may have the opportunity to interact with the dying patient during one of the most emotionally unbearable periods of the day. These kinds of intimate interactions tap emotional responses in the caregiver that can be intense, crossing the boundaries of professionalism, and touching on our humanness, vulnerability, and finiteness. This kind of involvement brings with it new responsibilities and new emotional risks.

Patient care populations, formerly comprised of many acutely ill and relatively younger individuals, now are comprised of a high number of elderly, chronically ill people. For this population, death is a long-anticipated fact. This can result in caregivers becoming caught up in patient and family lives, causing them to find themselves grieved persons when the patient dies. Caregivers also grieve the loss of family members no longer available to them. This phenomenon of anticipatory grief helps turn caregivers into what Fulton (1978) calls "surrogate grievers."

The Hospice Movement has paid considerable attention to this caregiver need, making clear standard statements about the need for staff support. This is usually accomplished through death education for their workers and volunteers, as well as with frequent, planned support meetings. Hospitals, nursing homes, and home care agencies need to follow this example.

Clinical Interventions

When we consider each of these diverse perspectives being maintained concurrently within the crucible of the hospital, hospice, nursing home, physician's office or home, we have an amalgamation of discordant experiences, needs, and demands. What can we do in the face of these conflicting scenarios? There are specific interventions to help us deal with these dilemmas.

Interventions for the Dying Person

Intervention to assist the dying person must derive from realistic perceptions about and appropriate postures with the dying individual. They must necessarily include an admixture of various types of informational, familial, and social support.

Perceive the Dying Person Holistically. How easy it is to forget that health care personnel always see patients and their families in a stressful and artificial situation! We tend to ignore the fact that the dying person and his family had a lifetime of experiences, both positive and negative, before he became a patient. They had hopes and dreams, plans and responsibilities that shaped and molded them into who and what they are now. We need to look beyond the disease experience to the whole, wonderfully complex person and family that this illness has infringed upon. Only when we begin to know and understand this person, will we be able to comprehend and appreciate what this dying experience is like for him.

Provide the Information Dying Persons Need in Terms They Can Understand. Be prepared to repeat information several times, as only through repetition can some of the difficult and threatening information be absorbed and accepted. Listen carefully to what is being asked and avoid giving more information than is being requested. Caregivers sometimes err in their own need to have bad news off their chests prematurely. Be sure other members of the team are apprised of what information the dying person has been given. Strive to give pertinent information to the dying person and family together, particularly when the information being given is bad news. Such bad news, when given with compassion and followed by a supportive surrounding, is more comprehensible.

Facilitate Meaningful Discussions by Assisting the Patient in Reviewing What Meant the Most During His Healthy Life. Ask about people, possessions, and pursuits. Encourage the dying person to talk about how the illness has changed him. Preservation of communication also preserves self-esteem. The ability to maintain the patient's self image is even more important than the fact of the illness itself.

Be Aware of The Patient's Values and Your Own. Caregivers should take time to explore their own values and beliefs. What, if any, are their religious and philosophical beliefs? How do they feel about themselves, their sexuality, their role in life? Working with the dying patient and his family can open doors for personal growth never before imagined. Caregivers should not be afraid to cross that threshold and find out who they actually are. Most importantly, when a value conflict arises, they should remember that it is the patient and his family's values that must be the deciding factor. Caregivers may embrace their own values, but they must remember that they are their own and must keep them from interfering with the provision of support.

Do Not Take Over for the Dying Person or the Family. Do not exclude the dying person from discussions and information about the illness or about family concerns. Encourage family members to make decisions with the dying person. Encourage the patient to maintain control as long as he wants to or for as long as he can. Avoid getting caught in the good deed whirlpool. For example, the hospice volunteer experiences a certain amount of gratification upon therapeutically meeting some of his or her assigned patient and/or family needs. This can result in a desire to do more to experience more gratification. This whirlpool of good deeds can create a situation where the volunteer begins to assume responsibility that belongs to patient or family members, thus crossing the therapeutic line.

Assist the Dying Person in Developing Support Networks and in Maintaining Important Relationships. Be sure that the dying person has adequate resources for terminating his business of living. This will include professional as well as family support. Facilitate adequate access to this support. The physical presence of family members is especially imperative at this time. The concept of the family as an extension of the patient makes it natural and important for significant family members to be present, if at all possible, during the death trajectory. This will promote peace of mind for the dying person as well as aid the grieving process for the survivors.

Spend Adequate Time with the Dying Person. Time is an extremely precious commodity for the dying person. Quality is much more important than quantity here. Short intervals of time on a regularly scheduled basis foster a sense of control that is comforting to both the patient and family. In this regard, the caregiver should not make promises that may be difficult to keep, for example, saying "I'll be with you," if this may be impossible.

Monitor Your Own Feelings. Caregivers must be aware of their own feelings and how they have an impact on them and their work. They are not immune to denial, dissimulation, antipathy and fears of personal annihilation and must not be ashamed to admit that caring for the dying is itself exposure to endangerment. (Weisman, 1977) Because of this, caregivers must not hesitate to enlist the assistance of other persons and sources of support to help them provide care for themselves so that they can care for others.

Surround with Empathetic Support. Empathy is the ability to perceive and experience a situation from the point of view of the other person. The optimal attitude toward the dying person and the family is one of compassionate objectivity. It is helpful to realistically assess the changes caused by the impact of the illness and impending death. This intervention will return some sense of control to the patient and family, while preparing them for situations that for most will be a first-time experience. Reducing fear of the unknown facilitates the ability to process anticipatory grief. For example, one hospice program encourages primary care nurses to review a handout text, describing the physical changes to be expected in the last hours or days of life. Such things as skin color changes, breathing pattern changes, and so forth are described in detail. At the appropriate time, the nurse reviews and discusses this handout with family members caring for the dying person. This normalizes, as much as possible, a potentially frightening situation. Family members whose anxiety is reduced can communicate a sense of competence and peace to their loved one.

When one considers that these will be the dying person's last human experiences, the importance of addressing these issues is underscored.

Interventions for the Family Members

As a unit of care in terminal illness, family members require their own specific interventions to help them cope with and in the experience of their loved one's terminal illness and death. These have been extrapolated from Lebow's tasks of anticipatory grief and are listed below.

Maintain the Relationships between Dying Person and Family by Encouraging Open Communication to the Extent Family Style Allows. It is essential to understand the family system and its style of communication. Interventions should be individualized with this realistic information in mind. Caregivers should not let their own values or needs interfere here. For example, conflicts in values between caregivers and patient and/or family can readily surface when dealing with communication. When conflicts arise, the question "Whose need is it?" can be most helpful. It is also important to recognize that now is not the time to try to remake the family's communication into something it has never been before. Many families will not be able to be as open and communicative as one would like. Try to help them to be open, but be realistic in attempts and expectations.

Support the Family Members' Unique Identities and Their Own Capabilities in Differentiating Their Own Legitimate Needs from Those of the Dying Person. A family member may need permission to spend time alone, to go out, to attend to some personal needs, to seek some solitude or privacy. Recognition of these needs can arouse feelings of shame and guilt for that family member. Help the family understand the normalcy of these needs and the problems that will develop if they fail to adequately attend to them. As death grows closer, at the appropriate times and in gentle ways encourage them to begin to think about their future lives after the death.

Assist and Support Family Members to Cooperatively Assume New Roles. There will be immediate additional duties and roles that will become apparent as the illness progresses. Guide the family in anticipating more permanent role changes and direct them in restructuring their roles in mutually adaptive ways. The use of frequent family conferences is an invaluable tool in assisting family members to adjust to these role changes.

Encourage the Family Members' Expressions of the Various Affects and Support Them in Bearing Their Emotions. It is exceptionally important to assist family members in expressing their emotions of grief and to normalize those for them. This is especially true with regard to negative feelings about the dying person, the illness, caregivers, God, and so forth. An assessment and knowledge of family members' previous experiences with loss will be useful in assisting caregivers in supporting the normal recapitulation of old griefs that typically will be precipitated by their present situation.

Continue Reality Testing and Planning to Assist the Family Members to Understand and Absorb Pertinent Medical Communication about the Course of the Illness and Treatment. Assist the family members in making practical plans for such things as patient care, caregiver communication, finances, wills, a burial place, and so forth. Encourage the repetitious recollection of events leading to the illness and dying as a means of assisting the family member to master, in small doses, the reality of the situation. Again, family conferences are helpful here.

Assist Family Members to Recognize That the End Is Near. Caregivers should encourage goodbyes through role modeling, that is, by communicating their own farewells to the patient. The final deathbed scene is one that family members always will carry with them. The opportunity to say goodbye in a mutually satisfactory fashion will have both short- and long-term effects on the grief of the surviving family members. Caregivers, by taking the opportunity to say goodbye, demonstrate the desirability and need to do this. There may be situations where family members are not present at the moment of death, but arrive shortly thereafter. Caregivers should encourage these family members to talk to their loved one, expressing their goodbyes as a viable and appropriate means of communication, citing the fact that hearing is one of the last senses to leave us.

Interventions for the Caregivers

Caregivers must care for themselves or they will be unable to effectively care for others. Following are interventions to assist the caregiver in caring for himself or herself.

Take Responsibility for Making the Decision to Work in Situations That Deal with Intense Life and Death Dilemmas. Caregivers who work in situations where there is high exposure to death *do so by choice.* It is essential to take personal responsibility for choosing this type of work. Professional caregivers and the agencies that employ them must take responsibility for preparing themselves and their staffs both intellectually and emotionally to face death. Classes on personal death awareness and grief and bereavement are essential tools in caring for the caregiver.

Develop a Philosophy of Involvement. How much does the caregiver want to be involved? Personalized care, responding to individual patient needs, cannot be provided without the caregiver having some involvement with the persons for whom he or she is caring. Before deciding on a philosophy of involvement, the caregiver must know the side effects of that involvement. With deep involvement, his or her feelings may become more apparent to the dying person, family members, other staff, and himself or herself. More importantly, when the caregiver allows him- or herself to "feel" with the patient and/or family, he or she will be open and vulnerable to more pain.

How much of a professional barrier or distance should be maintained when relating to the dying person and the family? Should the caregiver attempt to know the dying patient as a person, removing many of the barriers? Professional distance protects the caregiver from threatening feelings in himself and herself in response to a dying person's situation or behavior. Yet, care that is technically competent, but performed at an emotional distance, dehumanizes and encourages social isolation and powerlessness. Caregivers must learn to know their limitations. They must be more careful about taking care of themselves and more careful about meeting their own needs in their personal life.

Develop a Network of Support. No matter how idealistic the intent, a person can continue to expose himself or herself without support for only a limited period of time before beginning to raise defenses to insulate himself or herself. As a consequence, it is important to develop networks of support both in and out of the work situation. If support groups for caregivers do not exist, seek out those persons who may be able to assist in starting one. Chaplains, social workers, psychologists, and psychiatric liaison nurses are good resources to begin with. Do not forget peers, an often overlooked resource. A professional mentor can be of enormous help in providing caregivers with insight and support.

Share the Responsibility. Do not assume more responsibility than is necessary. Sharing the burdens, as well as the joys, with team members is appropriate behavior. When the caregiver begins to perceive himself or herself as the only one who can really help the patient, the question again must be asked, "Whose needs am I meeting?"

Take Care of Yourself. Caregivers should keep in good health physically. They should not let work upset the delicate balance of life, taking time to eat, sleep, love, and play. The urgency associated with caring for the dying may influence the individual's ability to prioritize personal needs. "I will have tomorrow, my patient will not." Caregivers need to constantly remind themselves that they also can only live "in the moment." Nothing is guaranteed to them merely because they are not terminally ill. Relationships with family and friends and activities and interests outside of work are the essential nutrients that keep caregivers healthy, both physically and emotionally.

Recognize the Beauty of Being Imperfect. Learn to say "No, I can't," "I don't know," "I need help," or "I need time for myself." Caregivers, by their very nature, are rescuers. This trait tends to foster feelings of "I must fulfill all needs." There is a tremendous liberation in recognizing our human imperfections and limitations.

Get in Touch with Feelings. This may be the single most crucial process necessary for the caregiver and the most difficult. Caregivers need to explore their feelings about death, suffering, and the meaning of pain. What does quality of life mean? They need to consider their own finiteness. To effectively deal with feelings about death, one must also explore feelings about strong emotions such as anger and sorrow. Grief requires an active expression of both angry and sad feelings. Typically, in today's society these feelings are kept under control, with minimal outward expression. The caregiver who reacts negatively to the expressions of strong feelings will find it extremely difficult to assist people facing death. Caregivers who work with the dying and their families must pay careful attention to the need for ongoing processing of their feelings in order to avoid the problems of accumulated grief and burnout.

Recognize the Need to Get Out. Caregivers need to ask "Am I happy with myself and my work?" "Do I feel fulfilled at the end of the day, or exhausted and frustrated?" Caregivers are in the right place, doing the right thing when they feel *synergized*! When they recognize they are in the wrong place, they need to seek support, explore their options, consider their alternatives and *move on*!

Conclusion

The period of anticipatory grief confronts patient, family member, and caregiver with a series of individual yet interrelated experiences and tasks that can be assisted by a number of specific interventions. These have been addressed here in the hopes of promoting healthy anticipatory grief in all parties involved.

As Fulton (1978) has noted, the effects of anticipatory grief may be felt on a personal or collective level. The increase in human longevity brings with it an increase in chronic diseases. The advances in technical medicine have opened up possibilities of prolonging life far beyond previous expectations and capabilities. Death has become an event that is often prolonged and anticipated by patient, family members, and caregivers over an extended period of time. These factors have introduced new dimensions of stress for all concerned. For the dying person, it is an intensely felt experience that ends with death. For the family member, dealing with separation and loss of a loved one, it can often be muted and possibly sublimated. Professional caregivers, whose exposure to patient and family suffering is extended, experience anticipatory grief in a more profound and intense manner, thus increasing the stress they must endure.

It is crucial that we recognize our individual roles and the effects anticipatory grief will have on us, for we will play at least two of these roles in our lifetime.

References

Davidson, G. 1975. The "Waiting Vulture Syndrome." In B. Schoenberg, I. Gerber, A. Wiener, A. Kutscher, D. Peretz, and A. Carr, eds., *Bereavement: Its Psychosocial Aspects.* New York: Columbia University Press, pp. 357–361.

Fulton, R.L. 1978. Anticipatory Grief, Stress, and the Surrogate Griever. In R. Fulton, E. Markusen, G. Owen, and J. Scheiber, eds., *Death and Dying: Challenge and Change.* San Francisco: Boyd & Fraser, pp. 241–245.

Fulton, R., and D.J. Gottesman. 1980. Anticipatory Grief: A Psychosocial Concept Reconsidered. *British Journal of Psychiatry* 137:45–54.

Gerber, I. 1977. The Making of a Physician: The Socialization Process and Medical Care of the Dying Patient. In D. Peretz, N. Lefkowitz, A. Kutscher, D. Hammond, N. Huber, and M. Kutscher, eds., *Death and Grief: Selected Readings for the Medical Student.* New York: Health Sciences Publishing Corporation, pp. 71–77.

Kalish, R. 1970. The Onset of the Dying Process. *Omega* 1:57–69.

Lebow, G.H. 1976. Facilitating Adaptation in Anticipatory Mourning. *Social Casework* 57:458–465.

Rando, T.A. 1983. An Investigation of Grief and Adaptation in Parents Whose Children Have Died from Cancer. *Journal of Pediatric Psychology* 8:3–20.

Rando, T.A. 1984. *Grief, Dying and Death: Clinical Interventions for Caregivers.* Champaign, Ill: Research Press.

Weisman, A.D. 1977. Psychosocial Considerations in Terminal Care. In D. Peretz, N. Lefkowitz, A. Kutscher, D. Hammond, N. Huber, and M. Kutscher eds., *Death and Grief: Selected Readings for the Medical Student.* New York: Health Sciences Publishing Corporation, pp. 189–199.

5
Anticipatory Grief from the Clergy Perspective: Presuppositions, Experience, and a Suggested Agenda for Care

David M. LaGreca

"Pastor, my sister just called from Ohio, her husband is dying."

"Rabbi, my father has been told that he has six months to live."

"Father, my child is ill. It's terminal. Can you come over?"

W
e define such invitations to minister, invitations common to all
clergy, as the "stuff" of anticipatory grief. The expectation of loss
calls many to thrash about for help in facing the "why" and the
"what does it mean" questions. Although anticipating loss is not limited to
life-threatening illnesses and does, in fact, include geographical relocation,
divorce, changes in job status and much more, the examples and reflection
here are limited to the anticipatory grief that precedes loss of a loved one
through death.

In this general setting, I try to situate the unique response that can be called the clergy role. I first look to some presuppositions and definitions. I then
try to describe the type of experience a clergy person might have within a situation of anticipatory grief. As part of that experience, I survey the clergy role
and the factors that can prevent clergy from functioning as facilitators or com-
panions in anticipatory grief situations. Finally, I suggest a few steps that might
help define a new agenda for the care that clergy offer to their people in such
times of need.

Presuppositions

The first presupposition quite simply is that we believe anticipatory grief exists. Anticipatory grief can be defined loosely as the feeling of anticipating a loss, whether it be loss of life, loss of a role in life, loss of another person, or even an object. I use Speigel's divisions of grief (1977) to define the stages in anticipatory grief. The initial response is one of *shock*. Soon that shock is replaced by attempts at *control*. There sets in a busyness with its own series of do's and don'ts. This stage gives way to a *regressive* one. At this stage of anticipatory grief can be found the most problematic behavior. In fact, this stage is simply the continued attempt by each personality involved to deal with the crisis at hand. Finally, we reach the *adaptive* stage. At this point in grief work, the person is ready to face some reintegration with self and others.

The second assumption sounds as simple as the first. Anticipatory grief is different for the patient, the patient–family unit, and the patient's caregivers (defined in the widest possible sense). The crux of the difference for each group is the time perspective that each holds. Anticipatory grief ends for the patient with death. The family unit and the caregiving team must face another grief process after the death, which consists of factors and experiences too numerous to mention here. With all three groups experiencing some amount of anticipatory grief, the clergy person is often called on to function in a somewhat confused and confusing setting.

Catalyst people can help in such a diverse and delicate situation. This is the third presupposition. Such a role is often the one assumed by the clergy person. He or she is usually one of the people called on to help. It should be remembered that although this catalyst role is often assumed by the clergy person, it need not be and, in fact, can be the role of any number of other influential people within the patient caregiving team.

Finally, the fourth and last assumption defines the clergy role as that assumed by any member of the caring world around the patient–family unit who takes a transcendent view toward life. What is popularly defined as a "religious view" is the domain of the clergy person in an anticipatory grief situation.

Experience of Anticipatory Grief from a Clergy Perspective

Working out of the assumptions presented above, and with confidence that the clergy person has something to offer those in an anticipatory grief situation, let us look more closely at the phenomenon described as anticipatory grief and also at the content, roles, and problems that clergy face when addressing such situations.

The range of responses that present themselves in the setting of anticipatory grief is extensively varied. Returning to Spiegel's division of grief work (1977) above, let us look at some of the responses that might be encountered at each stage.

Shock is the most common point at which a clergy person enters the lives of those who have begun the anticipatory grief process. A young friend, Scott, whose wife was dying at the age of twenty-five, spent most of the week she was in a coma unable to do more than stumble around hospital waiting rooms. The morning of her death, he sat at the edge of their bed in their home, unable and unwilling to come to the hospital.

For some patients, the beginning of the anticipatory grief process is one in which they desire to assert *control*. Another patient, Jack, spent a good deal of his time immediately after the diagnosis playing with diets, exercises, fad medicines, and what seemed to be purely quack advice. Only much later was he able to begin the work of grieving.

The *regressive* stage of grief work presents the most problems to those involved with the care of patient families. At this point, the patient and/or family members seem to regress to a stage of their lives when either all things were fine, or they handled their problems in a specific concrete way. One image comes to mind. When all else failed, a woman, who was attempting to cope with her husband's impending death, resorted to a tried-and-true method of their common life experience. For years, he had sold vitamins and vitamin supplements, so she proceeded to treat the disease with massive amounts of those vitamins they had used their entire lives to treat any illness whatsoever!

Finally, a stage of anticipatory grief can be experienced that, at its height, is *adaptive* and creative. It manifests itself in an honest, get-down-to-work attitude: Ruth wanting to leave something of herself behind and therefore cooperating with an audiovisual project; Steve wanting to help plan every last detail about his funeral down to the serving of wine at the funeral home; and Stacey wanting desperately to talk through the plans for leaving her five-year-old daughter behind and the pain of those plans as well.

The wide range of responses outlined above have generated some specific points of view that can be held in anticipatory grief. From a clergy perspective, the following viewpoints, their complete opposites, as well as anything in between, may and have been observed.

One may encounter a healthy look at death by some people. Death may be viewed as an ordinary part of life and may even be an object of serious and honest study on the part of the patient and the patient's family. The opposite is also true. Death can be seen as unnatural; something to be denied and avoided whenever possible.

Death may be the occasion for a seeking after closure, a finishing of business, within the work world or within personal relationships. Death may be the occasion for saying important things to important people. It may be a time of giving life, even as life itself is slipping through one's fingers. Or indeed, it can be the opposite of all this.

The impending loss may be the occasion for looking for help just to handle the myriad problems and possibilities present. Anticipatory grief begins in earnest whenever and wherever there is some sort of acceptance of the terminality of the patient on the part of the patient, the family, or the care team. The uniqueness of the phenomenon of loss is that it is interpreted through the relationship one has to the person being lost. As such, grief (anticipatory or otherwise) is never the same for any two people even if they grieve the same person.

The "stuff" of anticipatory grief work in the relationship between clergy person and patient, family, and/or caregivers can also be described in broad terms. The following list of items reflects some of the content discussed in a clergy setting but does not preclude the addressing of other issues as well.

God, prayer, and religiosity are the first matters that seem to be raised, whether out of recognition of the clergy person's field or out of the belief that this should be the place to begin with a clergy person. The entire gambit of guilt issues is also the raw material of many clergy–patient–family relationships. Guilt, both as the human phenomenon of interpersonal relationships and as a response to an often distorted image of God presents itself at this time.

Alienation, isolation, companionship, and premature detachment make up a great deal of the subject matter that can be and often is discussed with a clergy person in an anticipatory grief situation. Feelings of alienation from normal life, isolation from the decision-making process, premature detachment on the part of the patient or a significant other, as well as the question of who walks the road of life and death with a particular person, can fill the hours the patient spends alone and the time he or she sits and discusses matters with the clergy person. Finally, anger and its manifestations in depression and tension within a family unit can be raised as an issue with a clergy person who comes into the situation as an objective outsider.

Into this maze of God, guilt, and anger comes the clergy person. What roles are either expected or helpful in such a situation? Such expectation can be either on the part of the patient–family unit or on the part of the clergy person himself or herself.

The first role, seemingly too simple, is that which could be called the "transcendent stance." The clergy person's role is to bring the religious questions to the foreground. A significant part of this stance proclaims in word and deed that life is more than death, that a life well lived is a moral victory.

Another clergy role is that of bridging gaps. In most situations of anticipatory grief, the circumstances, personalities, and even the environment can change quickly and dramatically. In this situation, the clergy person can stand as someone bridging gaps for the patient–family unit.

The clergy person also can function in the role of listening board. Throughout a series of situations, often demanding important and sometimes critical decisions from the patient and the family, the clergy person just listens. A great deal of healthy anticipatory grief just needs to be expressed to someone who is willing to listen.

The patient and the family often find themselves in a position where they simply are responding to demands made on them by others. The clergy person can free up such a situation by being one of the people who gives the patient–family unit permission to be as they are, or want to be, at any given moment. Often the world in which a terminal patient lives is compartmentalized beyond our wildest imagination. The clergy person approaches each person as a whole, helping grief work to continue.

The time perspective of a patient–family unit is thrown out of kilter by an impending death. In this situation, where memories and medical histories seem to rule supreme, the clergy person can allow people to look forward. This allows the patient to participate in some planning that might be critical to him or her. It also gives the family permission to plan for next year's weddings and graduations and other transitions.

Finally, into the world of science comes a person who calls all involved to remember their shared humanity. The clergy person loves, questions, laughs, mourns, and cries. At times, this role can be the greatest challenge and the more rewarding one as well.

Before looking at the tasks that clergy persons might undertake to facilitate the work of anticipatory grief, we need to look seriously at those things that stop clergy from facilitating the roles outlined above. What problems are unique to clergy as they approach the demands made on them in the anticipatory grief situation? And what problems face patients and families in dealing with clergy in those same situations?

Perhaps it need not be said, but in the interest of completeness we will say that clergy are as different in dealing with the issues of anticipatory grief as any other group of people. In fact, they bring to such situations some strong disadvantages in addressing those situations.

The first and probably most common problem is that of the formal role that is demanded of most clergy in grief situations. The ceremonies and rituals of dying and death are standard in most faiths. In fact, some of the answers sound as standard as the rituals! It is difficult, therefore, for some clergy to deal with some modern situations; the two most common being patients who choose to die at home and patients who are conversant about their own dying process and their feelings as well.

Many clergy, as do doctors and nurses, view their ministry in terms of healing. For those with a strong focus on healing, impending death and death itself is as much an insult as it is to someone who has spent years in medical training.

For a clergy person, the unfinished business involved with a death can be a greater insult. Many cannot tolerate endings that are not neatly and succinctly packaged.

Finally, although age and experiential differences are to be expected among clergy, many people cannot understand or tolerate the personal hangups and/or problems that any particular clergy person brings to this part of his or her ministry. Clergy are often afraid of death; they walk to the grave so often and then walk away that many of them see death as unreal. Clergy people are not exempt from bringing their own unresolved grief experiences to an anticipatory grief situation. They often are afraid of hospitals and the settings in which they find their sick people. Also an unspoken mutual intimidation can exist between medical caregivers of all kinds and clergy persons. Just like anyone else, clergy bring to an anticipatory grief situation an often acute inability to deal with a caring team made up of diverse persons and personalities.

In defense of clergy, there are also barriers erected by patient, family, and care team that impede the work of the clergy person. A clergy person is often looked on as associated with death. Clergy arrive often when medical people fail. There is a standard social response to clergy that is gentle and proper in its religiousity, that is, a type of good conduct. Finally, for many people, the clergy are supposed to remain uninvolved, which translates in the eyes of many people as unemotional. Help is requested but not personal involvement.

Suggested Agenda for Caring

> No one ever told me that grief felt so like fear. I am not afraid, but the sensation is like being afraid. The same fluttering in the stomach, the same restlessness, the yawning. I keep on swallowing.
>
> At other times, it feels like being mildly drunk or concussed. There is a sort of invisible blanket between the world and me. I find it hard to take in what anyone says. Or perhaps, hard to want to take it in. It is so uninteresting. Yet I want others to be about me.
>
> When I lay these thoughts and questions before God, I get no answer. But a rather special sort of "no answer". It is not the locked door. It is more like a silent, certainly not uncompassionate, gaze. As though God shook his head, not in refusal but waiving the question. Like, peace, child; you don't understand. (*A Grief Observed* by C.S. Lewis, 1961, pp. 1, 80–81)

Is there a way that our stance as clergy within a situation of anticipatory grief can help to penetrate that invisible blanket, that mildly concussed feeling of which Lewis speaks? I shall look at three necessary requirements in the approach to that question and then at some possible directions that a new agenda could take.

The first requirement in regard to clergy participation in an anticipatory grief situation is for a team approach. This would allow the clergy person the ability of helping with part of the work being done, while at the same time offering him or her the personal support that is necessary.

A requirement in favor of the psychological as well as physical health of the clergy person is a second important factor. It is critical that the caring clergy person exhibit, first and foremost, a care for himself or herself. Some arguments can be made for total and full involvement, but there are already enough stressed people present in an anticipatory grief situation. The clergy person is often the only person who can, by example, give permission to others to take the time and space necessary to care for themselves.

The last requirement is a recognition that as in any chemical reaction, the catalyst is changed. Within a situation of anticipatory grief, as a group of people struggle to maintain health in a physical, social, and spiritual sense, a caring and honest clergy person will be changed. We must accept such a change, being honest and caring enough to share it with patient and family alike.

With these requirements met, a new agenda for caring should include some, if not all, of the following:

An ability to reflect with patient and family on the ordinariness of the death experience in a world that sees each new scientific–medical discovery as extraordinary. Death is not something stuck on the end of life, it is part of living!

An ability to reflect on the moral victory that claims that life is more important than death!

The need to balance the seriousness of life with the levity that is our gift from God; the ability to appropriately maintain the stance of the clown.

The need to show, by example, that caring professionals care for themselves and allow others to do the same.

An approach to problems that is at once creative and practical and full of risks gladly taken.

The need to help survivors in their transition from anticipatory grief to the grief work of survivors.

Conclusion

After having traced this long and, at times, winding path, I end with some conclusions and a call to ministry.

As clergy people, we may be the only outsiders who enter an anticipatory grief situation who are known in some way from before. Either through personal contact or reputation, the people that we minister to often know who we are. We may be the only people in the lives of a patient and/or family who have participated in another event in their lives other than this grief and dying process. We must learn that this is a privileged position that allows us to intervene and help in creative ways.

We also may be the only people who are present to all members of the anticipatory grief situation. Although this brings a certain amount of confusion and chaos to our work, we do bridge various personalities and that linking is worth the risk it entails.

Within the situation of anticipatory grief, we may be the only people who can articulate, or at least begin to articulate, how we have been changed in the process. Because of that, and if we truly allow ourselves to do that, we can help others by giving them both the permission and the example to begin the articulation of change in their own lives.

Finally, we stand to gain and share a heightened sense of awareness concerning our own life, its intensity, and goals. In helping another to face their dying, and truly living that process in anticipation of the moment of death, we learn a great deal about our own deaths and our lives. This happens when we are free enough to allow our patients and their families to teach us!

Clergy have a role in anticipatory grief. Many of us have experienced that role and have experienced the good results of taking the risk and plunging ahead. I suggest we get on with it! When we walk with others, we learn, we are changed, we help, and we are helped.

References

Spiegel, Y. 1977. *The Grief Process: Analysis and Counseling*. Nashville, Tenn.: Abington Press.
Lewis, C.S. 1961. *A Grief Observed*. New York: Seabury Press.

6

A Physician's Acquaintance with Grief

Stanley M. Aronson

We remember those times in life when we become intimate with deep grief, whether it be grief in response to a pressing, immediate reality or grief in anticipation of future tragedy. At such dark times, as in the lamentations of Jeremiah, the hurt seems incurable, the wound grievous, and there is no healing.

Immediate grief is one of the solitary passions, experienced as a mourning for that which is lost and a despair that life can provide nothing to replace it. Anticipatory grief, on the other hand, intrudes at a time when the sky is undarkened and the feared storm, if it indeed be a storm, is at the far margins of visibility. Although immediate grief does weep alone, we often attempt to share our episodes of sorrow, seeking out those who have risen from previous grief or who are strong enough not to run from it. Commonly we find such individuals among our enduring friends, members of our family, members of the clergy and, at times, physicians.

Most people agree that providing necessary solace is part of the unwritten covenant between the patient and his physician, and, tacitly, society delegates this particular responsibility to the medical profession, although it is clearly not an exclusive assignment. Customarily, during times of personal sorrow, support is provided by professional persons from the caring elements of society. In actuality, it is a task to be assumed by whomever can willingly accept it. For, the sharing of grief not one's own is a rare capability that requires neither formal accreditation nor reward for its fulfillment.

The caring physician, in abiding with a grieving person, inevitably feels the margin of that person's sorrow but will not typically share the unrelieved sense of despair that immediate grief so often generates. In these encounters, the physician's personal sadness rises from his greater familiarity with the many faces of tragedy. It is tempered not only by his sure knowledge that life is most times stronger than grief but also by his awareness that true grief is not a commodity to be transferred.

Yet there is a form of grief—anticipatory grief—that is peculiar to the physician. He accepts this burden, perhaps unknowingly, when he learns that his knowledge of the pathophysiology of disease has afforded him a small window of access to the future.

A century ago medicine was capable of curing very few illnesses. Yet, the profession was more than the art of placating the patient while nature provided an occasional cure. Physicians were skilled, for example, in handling selected technical problems such as the repair of bone fracture; in reducing the levels of pain through the use of drugs; in advocating hygienic measures for the control of communicable disease; and, through their special awareness of the kinetics and trajectory of diseases, in providing reasonably accurate forecasts of each patient's future.

To a large degree, Western medicine is distinguishable from other schools of the healing arts in its reliance on the notion of the individuality of diseases and that once a particular disease is identified, its evolution and likely outcome is predictable. Non-Western medicine has been more concerned with the pragmatic relief of symptoms and, accordingly, has paid little attention to the mechanics and nomenclature of the underlying illnesses. To non-Western practitioners, sickness is an inchoate state, something to be suppressed rather than understood. The dissection of the dead body for anatomic or pathologic inquiry, and the companion disciplines of the laboratory sciences, are uniquely Western contrivances. Indeed, so much emphasis has been placed on the rational analysis of disease that the Western physician has been accused of ignoring the disabled while confining his attention to the disability.

The securlarization of Western medicine, in the last three centuries, saw great emphasis placed on the nosology and etiology of each disease. The separateness of each illness was repeatedly verified by objective criteria, named, and classified. To this day, much of formal medical education is invested in the precise identification (diagnosis) and natural history (prognosis) of human disease. Beyond its expanding ability to provide comfort and occasionally cure, contemporary Western medicine has refined, albeit imperfectly, the art of predicting the future. In many ways, this has been the profession's greatest accomplishment: to confront the aggregate of organic suffering and to perceive within this population of distressed persons separate maladies each with their unique risks, etiologies, and histories. Thus, two ill persons may seek help each because of severe headache. In one, the physician may recognize the characteristics of migraine and may then offer the patient the assurance that the pain will inevitably resolve within twelve hours; and in the other person, the physician may detect the subtle hints of a brain tumor as the cause of the headache and foresee in a seemingly healthy person the remorseless inevitability of seizures, blindness, coma, and death in the measurable future. The trained physician perceives more than that which is apparent to the intelligent but untrained eye. His skills in diagnosis allow him to review the inadequate fragments of available information and to arrive at some explanation, a tentative diagnosis that will account for the various clinical signs and symptoms that have been

noted, together with their sequence and velocity. Account is also taken, ordinarily, of the patient's genetic heritage and socioeconomic station. At times,
the diagnosis is unambiguously apparent; at other times, multiple diagnoses
are under active scrutiny, each with some assigned level of probability. In the
days that follow, the physician will reassess each conditional diagnosis in light
of new test results, the emergence of new clinical signs, as well as new diagnostic
perceptions derived through professional consultation. The principle of
establishing a diagnosis before beginning therapy is usually observed, particularly in teaching hospitals. Indeed, antibiotics are customarily withheld in instances of suspected infection until the inciting organism is identified in the
laboratory. Only then can the appropriate antibiotic agent be given and in a
dosage largely dictated by the laboratory-determined sensitivity of the infec-
ting microbe.

Physicians, and particularly internists, therefore invest much of their energies
into the establishment of a confident diagnosis. The path toward achieving this
diagnosis is typically strewn with discarded alternatives. Each lump looms as
a cancerous node and every chest pain as the harbinger of coronary artery
disease until ruled out by some further clinical or laboratory information. In
each excursion into the dark realm of diagnostic possibilities, the physician
is compelled to anticipate the consequences to the patient should the more
serious possibility turn into reality. The forty-seven-year-old married accountant, the father of three children and the sole support of his aging parents, visits
the office because of some intermittent rectal bleeding. The likeliest cause is
benign hemorrhoids, but the possibility of an underlying colorectal cancer must
be considered and diligently explored. Between the time of conjecture and the
time of verification, perhaps an interval of a few days, the physician is the private
bearer of a terrible weight: the knowledge that this currently functioning family
may soon face serious problems, some of which may be insoluble. During this
interval of anxiety before a diagnosis may materialize, the prudent physician
keeps the many possibilities, especially the more remote ones, behind a bland
facade. Nature is generally kinder than a human's diagnostic exercises and most
lumps are eventually shown to be benign and most chest pains turn out to be
of noncardiac origin. The interval of diagnostic doubt cannot be avoided and
it becomes a matter of tender charity to withhold from the patient all the various
clinical possibilities. If indeed the worst scenario is verified, there is sufficient
time to share the truth; and if no cure or specific treatment is available then
the future path must be jointly appraised by patient, family, and physician.

The skilled and sensitive physician accepts anticipatory grief as a near-
constant companion when he embraces much of the conjectured future as a
necessary part of his professional duties. Ninety-nine negative tests do not provide the emotional compensation to balance but one positive screening procedure that predicts some human tragedy in the near future. In such instances,
the physician's grief is increased by the inevitable conflict that arises between

the desire to provide the patient with peace of mind on the one hand, and the obligation to provide him with the truth on the other. Sometimes the truth must be unfolded slowly, otherwise much harm may be done. Emily Dickinson once said that the truth must dazzle gradually, or else every man be blinded. The heartache borne by the concerned physician in such a situation cannot be discarded without also discarding his humane commitments. He knows that giving the patient truth without mercy is a sanctimonious cruelty, whereas providing mercy without truth is a maudlin sentimentality. There are times when the diagnosis remains elusive, and the patient continues to deteriorate, when neither truth nor mercy can be served, leaving the physician to endure his own personal, immediate, and anticipatory grief alone. Indeed, this grief, which is inherent to medicine, may be a major factor contributing to the hazards of the profession with its little-publicized but high rate of emotional impairment and chemical dependencies.

There are other grievous burdens that the dim knowledge of the future places on the concerned physician. Should he attempt to orchestrate the grief within the patient and his family, making its intensity appropriate to prognostic reality? Not too little, as when generated by futile denial of the facts, and yet not too much, potentially leading to a rejection of the patient by the family. Despair may cause a premature entombment of the dying patient who still has weeks or months of conscious existence before him.

Anticipatory grief also accompanies the surgeon who must envision what his patient will experience as a result of the surgical removal of an important body part. Knowing that the procedure, an amputation for example, may be immediately lifesaving will not lessen the grief that pervades both the making and the imparting of this critical decision. The woman facing mastectomy for breast cancer must confront the threat to her life as well as the parallel assault on her sexual identity. Death, then, is clearly not the only outcome that may provoke anticipatory grief in the physician. The anticipation of limb amputation, the likelihood of surgically induced blindness, paralysis, or impotence in a currently functioning human being will inevitably bring great sadness and grief to the physician who must ultimately share this sobering information with the patient and his family.

Certainly the physician's license to see beyond today deprives him of some peace of mind, whereas his intimacy with aging permits him but a meager collection of comforting illusions. Aging is sometimes a graceful event, a work of art, with much wisdom and insight replacing the inevitable loss of certain faculties. More often, it is a poignant, demeaning, and graceless thing, filled with memories that are both bitter and failing. As a larger fraction of our population survives beyond the age of seventy-five years, an erstwhile rare disease is becoming increasingly frequent, achieving what has been described as the next great epidemic. This illness is Alzheimer's disease and by its nature the source of great anticipatory grief. It is a lengthy and progressive illness that finally deprives its victims of memory, orientation, identity, clarity of thinking, and even the capacity to tend to basic everyday needs. Ultimately there is a loss of spirit, memory, and even personal identity with the individual reduced to a mean vegetative existence, incapable of recognizing even his closest relatives although yet surviving for years under nursing home shelter. At this moment, there are no therapeutic interventions that might prevent, cure, or even retard the desolate journey of the disease. It destroys the mind of the victim, while permitting him a sham existence at a fearsome emotional and financial cost to the immediate family. Imagine then the grief in the physician who detects the earliest hint of memory lapse or cognitive misjudgment in an otherwise vigorous, characteristically healthy person. It requires little imagination to envisage the stretch of years ahead with its destructive effects on spouse and children.

Until fundamental research illuminates the causes of Alzheimer's disease, the physician can offer little more than his diagnostic conclusions. Although he may be a compassionate source of support to the family, his professional words are now of no particular value and at times, therefore, abiding silence may be the only honest response.

It has been said that every cradle asks us "Whence?" and every coffin, "Whither?" The poor barbarian, weeping above his dead, can answer these questions as intelligently as the robed priest of the most authentic creed.

Part III
Clinical Interventions In Anticipatory Grief

7

Understanding and Facilitating Anticipatory Grief in the Loved Ones of the Dying

Therese A. Rando

I n many families, when a loved one is dying, so too are the other family members. While their "dying" is not of a permanent, irreversible, physical sense, it does constitute the permanent and irreversible death of psychosocial aspects of themselves, their lives, their family, and their world. This chapter explores the experience of the loved ones of the dying and identifies treatment interventions designed to facilitate their anticipatory grief.

Concepts Pertinent to the Family in Anticipatory Grief

It is important that the reader maintain a family systems perspective as this chapter progresses, keeping in mind the following four facts: (1) The family is a constellation that is more than the sum of its parts. (2) Anything that affects the system as a whole affects the individual members, whereas anything that affects the individual members necessarily affects the family as a whole. (3) The family is a system and as such struggles constantly to maintain its homeostatic balance and equilibrium. The terminal illness of a family member imposes great strain on the family system that has to reorganize itself to adapt to this strain and reestablish its stability. (4) Each family has its own distinct characteristics, such as specific roles, rules, communication patterns, expectations, and patterns of behavior that reflect their beliefs, experiences, coping strategies, system alliances and coalitions. These work to keep the system consistent and stable. Clinically, they are some of the most important variables influencing how the family copes with the terminal illness of one of its members.

This chapter is dedicated with great respect and affection to Father Frederick W. Kelly, S.J.

Some portions of this chapter are adapted from material in *Grief, Dying, and Death: Clinical Interventions for Caregivers* by T.A. Rando. Published by Research Press, Champaign, Illinois. 1984. Used with permission.

Finally, it is important that the reader appreciates that there are numerous psychosocial realities that have contributed to making the American family uniquely vulnerable to bereavement (Volkart, 1957). A series of recent sociological changes—industrialization, urbanization, greater social mobility, increasingly rapid social changes, and the proliferation of technology—have altered the family as an institution. Today, family integration and primary group interaction has declined and the family increasingly has become limited in its ability to meet the needs of all its members. Consequently, familial tasks increasingly have been delegated to society. This makes the family dependent on society for many more supportive functions than before; leaving it much more vulnerable to stress and less able to provide for its members.

The death of a family member in American culture causes greater psychological impact than in other cultures (Volkart, 1957). This stems from the fact that the limited range of interaction possible in the American family fosters unusually intense emotional involvement. In societies where psychological involvement is spread over more individuals, and the extended family is more prevalent and allows more than just the biological parents to be actively involved with child rearing, emotional involvement is more dispersed. Death of a family member in these societies does not generate such overwhelming responses nor have the same impact as it does in America where the relationships are more exclusive. Also, in this society there is a greater potential for ambivalence and hostility to arise as a consequence of death. This occurs since in the American family self-identification and personal dependency are rooted within the limited scope of family members and because there is a social tendency for families to breed overidentification and overdependence. Although family members are major sources of love and gratification, they are at the same time also sources of punishment, frustration, and anger. This necessarily leaves American individuals with more negative and ambivalent feelings to contend with after a death. The fact that emotional attachments to particular people, as opposed to their roles, is the norm in the American family further increases the risk for complicated bereavement responses. All of these factors contribute to the American individual's high vulnerability to the death of a family member and, by implication, to the terminal illness experience leading to that death.

Experience of Family Members When a Loved One Is Terminally Ill

Family members involved with a terminally ill individual are in a singularly unenviable position. In most cases, they are forced to witness the progressive debilitation of their loved one without the power to stem the inevitable course of loss and death. They suffer as they watch the dying patient in physical and psychological pain, frequently suffering additionally either because they cannot bear the pain for the loved one or because they recognize that they are relieved that they are not called on to do so. Often through an uncertain up-and-down course, they are expected to adapt to a patient who may feel fine one day and feel quite ill the next. Already present confusion is magnified by situations in the terminal illness that breed inconsistency, resentment, and ambivalence. The lack of norms and clearly specified expectations and responsibilities, along with the depletion that results from the stress of demands for major readaptations and investments of self, time, and finances, all contribute to the psychological conflicts, emotional exhaustion, physical debilitation, social isolation, and family discord so routinely reported by those whose loved one is dying.

The family has to develop strategies for meeting the needs of the dying person. Depending on the nature of the illness, the family may be required to adapt to a loved one who, though slowly dying, will go on living for an extended period of time. Many times this results in a living–dying interval (Pattison, 1977) in which the patient sometimes appears completely normal, allowing family life to be resumed as before, and at other times becomes severely ill, creating demands for major readaptation in the family system. This up-and-down nature of the illness does not preclude the fact that the patient, although perhaps somewhat changed due to the confrontation with mortality, pain, or disease, is in most cases still much the same person as before. In all probability, until the point relatively close to death, the patient still expects to be treated as he or she always has been, having the same preferences, hopes, and desires as previously, and still requiring intimacy, enjoyment, productive work, and social and intellectual stimulation. The diagnosis of a terminal illness does not take away the human needs of the dying patient; if anything, it heightens them. Consequently, the family requires assistance to resist the tendency to socially bury the dying person prematurely. Fear and anxiety often cause families to decathect too much, creating precipitous separations much too early in the dying process. Families have to struggle not to allow their awareness of the patient's dying to be psychologically destructive to their relationship with him or her. They must balance relating to their loved one as a living person with recognizing and adjusting to the fact that he or she is dying. Family members are expected to continue to relate to the patient in ways that evidence their concern about the oncoming death, yet continue the ongoing relationship as it was previously sustained. They have to be honest with the patient and not be afraid to disagree simply because the patient is dying, avoiding condescension or placation, which would be demoralizing and infantilizing, only serving to increase the patient's isolation and decrease his or her trust.

Family members are the commonly overlooked secondary victims of the terminal illness. Although they continue to live, parts of them die with the patient. These are the parts of the self that have been constituted by the interactive relationship with the dying person; for example, the special and unique part of the self and identity that has been the daughter to the mother now dying. Additionally, although the family continues on after death of a loved one, it too is forever changed by the irretrievable loss of the presence and role-fulfilling behaviors and functions of the dying patient and the various subsystems within the family system that had been formed by the relationships of individual family members with the dying patient. Consequently, the mourning of family members is not solely for the terminally ill loved one but also for themselves and their families. This leaves them in the position of coping with multiple grief experiences occurring simultaneously: a situation that in other instances would be clearly viewed as comprising "bereavement overload" (Kastenbaum, 1969) but that in this case is construed as merely part and parcel of the anticipatory grief experience.

Complicating Issues in Anticipatory Grief

There are three courses of action toward which family members ideally direct themselves when another family member is dying.

> The main tasks of the dying patient's family can be synthesized into three aspects. First, the family must begin a joint process of anticipatory grief and finishing unfinished business with the dying member to prepare for the decathexis that must ultimately occur. Second, the family must accomplish the first task while supporting the dying patient and struggling to find ways to continue to live with her as fully as possible until the moment of death. The dying patient must be given as much control as possible, despite the ongoing process of relinquishing family roles and responsibilities. Third, the family must start to reorganize itself to maintain its stability following the imbalance fostered by the illness of the dying patient. It must ensure the continued survival of the other family members and commence the change process that must be completed following the death of the patient. This also entails grieving for the death of the family unit as it has been known to all of the family members (Rando, 1984, p. 340).

Family members must strike a delicate balance: they must cope with the terminal illness of the loved one, while continuing to take care of the family unit. Competing demands in these two areas often leave individuals feeling guilty because there is never sufficient time or energy to attend as completely as possible to both sets of needs. When visiting at the hospital, they may be concerned about the children at home; when at home, they may constantly wonder what is happening at the hospital in their absence. Atlhough this problem may be slightly attenuated when the loved one is dying at home, this situation is replete with other conflicts for family members that stimulate the tug-of-war between attending to the needs of the dying and those of the survivors-to-be. In situations where the family member is tending to the patient at home, there are often fewer chances for respite and more guilt when respite is taken. For example, it is not uncommon for discomfort or guilt to develop when family members know that the dying loved one has observed them in situations of levity or hears them talk about an enjoyable night out, almost as if there is a sense of betrayal with the momentary putting aside of pain and grief.

While providing care for the dying person and being immersed in the context of death, the family must continue to meet its members' needs, function as a social unit in society, and provide a structure for the growth and development of its members (Barton, 1977). It must struggle to continue to perform those functions it is charged with providing to its members—nurturant functions (caring for both physical and psychological needs); relational functions (developing interpersonal abilities for relating to others); communicative functions (educating family members in verbal and nonverbal skills); emancipative functions (equipping family members to attain physical, emotional, and economic independence, along with the desire and ability to begin their own family); and recuperative functions (providing family members with a setting allowing them rest, relaxation, and reconstitution of energies for continued participation in society) (Fleck, 1975).

Caregivers must be mindful of these opposing tasks with which family members must simultaneously contend. This confrontation with, at times, opposing needs is not unique to this specific area. Indeed, family members must regularly manage clashing responsibilities, discordant roles, and antagonistic tasks repeatedly if they are involved to any serious extent with the terminally ill individual. Some of these include:

Holding on to the patient vs. letting go

Increasing attachment to the patient during the illness vs. starting to decathect from the patient in terms of his or her existence in the future

Remaining involved with the patient vs. separating from the patient

Planning for life after the death of the patient vs. not wanting to betray the patient by considering life in his or her absence

Communicating feelings to the patient vs. not wanting to make the patient feel guilty for dying or bound to this world when the patient needs to let go

Balancing support for the patient's increased dependency vs. supporting the patient's continued need for autonomy

Focusing on the past and recollecting with the patient vs. focusing on the future

Redistributing family roles and responsibilities vs. not wanting to do anything that would call attention to or cause more losses for the patient

Taking care of the patient's needs vs. taking care of one's own needs

Being immersed in participating in the patient's care vs. living one's own life

Experiencing the full intensity of the feelings involved in anticipatory grief vs. trying not to become overwhelmed

Focusing on the patient as a living person vs. remembering that the patient is dying

Continuing reinvestment in the patient who has multiple remissions and relapses and who is going to die anyway vs. not reinvesting as much any more

Treating the patient as one always has in the past vs. taking into account the patient's situation and treating him or her differently

Rushing to create memorable experiences in the patient's last days and pushing for as much meaning as possible in the time remaining vs. allowing nature to take its course, reminiscing, and just passively being present with the patient

Identifying a loss so it can be grieved by the patient vs. focusing more positively on the remaining potentials

These are only some of the dilemmas inherent in caring for a dying family member. The stress of trying to decide how to proceed in any one, or combination, of them only exacerbates the quandary. It heightens the normal emotional responses that accompany the experience of losing a loved one.

Emotional Reactions and Therapeutic Interventions

Caregivers must recognize, normalize, and legitimize the characteristic difficulties of the family member's experience with the dying loved one: the confusion, the up-and-down nature of the illness, the competing demands, and the present and future losses of the loved patient and of parts of the self and the family. Along with these, they must work to help the family member cope with the intense emotions stimulated by the illness and impending death. Major feelings with which family members must contend are guilt, sorrow and depression, anger and hostility, and anxiety. These are each analyzed below and then a discussion of treatment interventions follows.

Guilt

Experience of Guilt. During the illness, family members almost always can be expected to experience some amount of guilt for many of the feelings, thoughts, and behaviors that are a natural outgrowth of living with a dying person. There are numerous precipitants of this very painful and anxiety-provoking emotion. Guilt may accompany the recognition of anger and other hostile feelings toward the terminally ill patient. It frequently develops from the interpersonal conflicts that often arise during a terminal illness, when frustration, anxiety, and irritation are so much a part of the experience. Guilt is not an uncommon emotion when family members feel responsible for the illness in any way, either through heredity, omissions, or commissions; because they failed to protect the loved one from the illness; or since they will survive the loved one. It also can be stimulated by the repugnance family members feel when they confront the ravages of the illness; for example, the scars, the smells, the medication side effects. Guilt is also experienced when family members wish that the end would come. The normal reactions to the arduous task of contending with the illness usually are major factors prompting guilt; for example, the normal ambivalence about being in the situation; the family members' feelings about the demands of the patient and the illness; the resentment of resources spent on the patient; the discomfort when family members violate unrealistic expectations and/or standards suggesting that he or she devote all time, energy, and focus solely to the dying person without regard for personal needs; the stress of making choices about incompatible responsibilities, roles, and tasks; the relief felt by family members because they themselves are not dying, and so forth.

Intervention in Guilt. It is critically important that the caregiver be aware of opportunities to sensitively intervene in the family members' struggles with guilt. The caregiver must observe the family members' reactions and encourage their expression of negative feelings whenever appropriate. The caregiver can assure the person of the normalcy of some negative thoughts toward sick persons and note that these are human reactions to stressful situations, which are acceptable providing they do not prompt hostile or destructive actions. The caregiver may want to educate family members that angry feelings can coexist with loving ones and that one does not preclude the other. It may be important to point out the positive feelings that have been observed in the relationship with the dying patient. Additional education about the normalcy of ambivalence, especially in this situation, can be most therapeutic. It may also be important to convey to family members that in times of stress people sometimes dwell on the negative aspects of a relationship, foregetting the positive ones. All of this is geared to help family members better tolerate negative or ambivalent thoughts, allowing such thoughts to coincide with positive and constructive ones without fear. Unrealistic and irrational expectations of self and situation must be identified and more appropriate ones offered. Family members will then be able to care for the loved one with more realistic self-expectations and, as a result, will sustain less guilt and self-reproach for failure to meet unrealistically high standards. Further relief or prevention of guilt can be provided by enlisting family members' appropriate participation in the dying person's overall treatment program. This gives them the opportunity to make restitution for any acts of omission or commission in the past, and provides them with experiences that illustrate to themselves and others their concern for the patient. However, this must be monitored to assure that the participation allows for enough time to attend to critical personal needs or else it will become destructive to both the patient and family members.

Family members may respond to their guilt by putting all their time, energy, and resources into the care of the dying patient. This overextension can stimulate further resentment and consequently more guilt for feeling this way. When such behaviors are recognized, caregivers should speak to the family member about the need for rest and replenishment of energy. They can explain that continuous neglect of one's own needs ultimately leads to resentment. Caregivers are in an excellent position to time interventions sensitively, promoting a break or time out between family and patient when both parties could benefit from it. For example, it is at times helpful to encourage family members to go home and rest, shower, change clothes and then return more refreshed to spend time with the patient. For those caring for the patient at home, they can be encouraged to arrange for respite care to allow themselves the freedom to leave the house, tend to their own personal needs, and get a different perspective for awhile. The patient can benefit from this as well, if the timing is correct and the separation not made to feel as abandonment.

Although family members recognize that they require such respites, they may be reluctant to initiate them themselves. Giving them permission implicitly or explicitly can be most therapuetic, especially near the end of an illness when they may be keeping a vigil with the patient. Obviously, this does not diminish the importance for family members to be present for the dying person, but even in the best of circumstances people need time away from each other and from the contemplation of threatening situations if they are going to continue to cope in healthy ways. Therefore, for the caregiver who wants to facilitate appropriate anticipatory grief, it is important to attend to the family members' needs for rest and replenishment in order to provide fertile soil for that healthy anticipatory grief. Grief before or after a death requires energy. The emotionally and/or physically exhausted, depleted person is simply unable to attend to the requisite tasks of this important work.

Sorrow and Depression

Experience of Sorrow. Sorrow is the sadness, pain, and anguish that family members feel in their grief over losing a loved one. Many individuals fear that they will be overwhelmed by this mental suffering. Because of this, they may distance themselves emotionally or physically from the dying patient, only contributing further to the patient's own sorrow. Many may overcompensate for this fear with aggressive or demanding actions to hide their true vulnerability, whereas others may use an attitude of indifference to camouflage their feelings. Caregivers need to recognize that sorrow, and its frequently accompanying depression, are difficult emotions to cope with, especially when the individual involved is concerned about remaining in emotional control.

Intervention in Sorrow. Caregivers should keep a number of points in mind when intervening in the sorrow of family members (Rando, 1984). They must identify, legitimize, and normalize these feelings of sorrow to reduce family members' fear of such feelings and to help them develop appropriate responses to them that do not interfere with the remaining time with the dying patient. They must redefine terms such as "lose control" or "break down," acknowledging the intensity of the feelings but reframing them more positively, using such terms as "emotional release" or "intense feelings." They should inform family members that these are normal reactions often requiring strong expression that, in this case, follow different norms than usual. This does not denote loss of control. Caregivers will do well to assist family members in understanding that it is those emotions that go unexpressed that prompt "loss of control" responses and that there is great value in expressing a little emotion at a time in order to avoid an accumulation that will explode later on. It helps family members to understand that they hurt so much precisely because they love the dying person so much. Placing the sorrow in a context of meaning, personal or religious–philosophical, will help them to avoid being overwhelmed by it. Family members can be given a sense of control of their feelings if they are helped to understand that the processing of emotions must take place but that they can choose how and when, with the caregiver encouraging expression of feelings in those places that are comfortable and without much threat. Hospital corridors and waiting rooms do not offer the appropriate privacy family members may require. Caregivers must legitimize the pain while still holding out the expectation that, although the situation is difficult and the emotions hurtful, the family member will be able to bear them and that at some future point there will be less pain. Caregivers need to be mindful of the limits and capabilities of the individual family members. They must recognize when one or all of them may need assistance, such as to be given information in smaller bits and pieces or at a slower pace, or may require gentle closure in a situation in order not to be overwhelmed. This does not mean patronizing the family nor helping them to avoid reality. Rather, it means modifying the experience to maximize their ability to cope with it and not be so inundated with it that they give up. Most importantly, caregivers must focus on enabling family members to experience the joys and pleasures that are still available, so as not to prematurely detach from the dying patient and relinquish remaining satisfactions that are still possible in the relationship with him or her.

Experience of Depression. Feelings of depression normally are expected to arise in those who are losing a loved one through a terminal illness. This emotion is both a natural aspect of the grief over the past, present, and future losses that comprise anticipatory grief and an expected consequence of the multileveled depletion that occurs during the course of caring for a dying individual. It is concomitantly an indication of and tool for preparation for the loss of the patient.

Bowlby (1961) has written that depression is adaptive in the mourning process. His theory can be extended to the anticipatory grieving that occurs during terminal illness. Bowlby views depression as the subjective aspect of the state of disorganization ensuing when one's behavior is no longer organized and self-sustaining. Such a state typically arises when the functioning interaction ceases between oneself and important aspects of one's world. In anticipatory grief, this refers to the loss of the relationship with the loved one as it existed prior to the illness, when all of the hopes, dreams, and expectations attendant to that relationship were still intact. It also refers to the other past, present, and future losses inherent in the loved one's dying. In anticipatory mourning, the patterns of behavior that have developed in interaction with the loved one are ceasing to be appropriate, as loss follows loss and the patient relinquishes roles, capacities, and abilities. This presents the mourner with losses that signal the ending of the relationship as it used to be. Consequently, these feelings lead to a disorganization of the mourner's usual behavior patterns, which in turn results in his or her feelings of depression. Although painful, disorganization and depression are both necessary and adaptive in that they facilitate the requisite breaking down of old patterns of behavior (based on the old relationship) and make way for new ones in the future. Failure to relinquish patterns of behavior that have grown up in interaction with the dying patient and that are no longer appropriate would result in maladaptive behavior if they persisted. Only if such patterns are broken down will it be possible for new ones, adapted to new objects (or, in the case of the dying patient, to the new realities of his or her current situation), to be built up. Numerous symptoms are either pathognomonic of this depression or are in some way related to it. These include:

Vegetative Symptoms of Depression

weight loss or gain

sleep difficulties

social withdrawal

anhedonia

apathy

decreased energy,
    initiative, and
    motivation

decreased sexual desire

psychomotor retardation
    or agitation

anorexia

Cognitive Disruption

confusion

feeling out of control

depersonalization

disorganization

lack of concentration

decreased effectiveness or
    productivity

feeling overwhelmed

problems with decision making

Combination of Anger and Depression

irritability

anxiety

tension

frustration

heightened psychological arousal

restlessness

feeling as if something is about
    to happen

Subjective Feelings of Depression

despair

deprivation

separation anxiety

anguish

yearning and longing for a
    different reality

loneliness

sadness

feelings of hopelessness or
    abandonment

feelings of meaninglessness

tearfulness and/or crying

guilt

self-reproach

lack of concern for the self

ambivalence

shame

feelings of inadequacy

sense of worthlessness

regression

dependency

feelings of helplessness

Intervention in Depression. Therapeutic intervention in the depression that accompanies anticipatory grief should focus on the encouragement of the expression of feelings associated with the impending death of the loved one, while continuing to facilitate whatever ongoing involvement and relationship remains possible. Past, present, and future losses can be identified and mourned. (See Rando [1984] for a complete discussion of intervention in the grief process.) These entail not only the tangible or well-recognized losses that are experienced, but also the symbolic or psychosocial ones, such as losses of status, roles, relationships, meaning, beliefs, dreams, hopes, and expectations. It will be helpful to assist family members in identifying and labeling the specific emotions and thoughts they are experiencing. Not doing this allows such emotions and thoughts to accumulate and act as an undifferentiated mass of painful stimuli. In such instances, family members lose the ability to clearly understand the experience, cannot problem solve or deal with its specific components, and tend to feel overwhelmed by its sheer mass since they feel there is too much to be managed or controlled. Family members can be assisted in identifying any unfinished business that remains with the dying person and in discovering appropriate ways to facilitate closure without premature detachment. Physical activities and social support can be of great assistance in providing family members with outlets that facilitate expression of emotion and reduce the intensity of affect.

Anger and Hostility

Experience of Anger and Hostility. Whenever a person is being deprived of someone or something valued, anger is always a natural response. Indeed, it reflects an innate biological predisposition to attempt to find and recover what has been (and is being) lost and to ensure that no future separations occur (Bowlby, 1961). Obviously, both these goals can be expected of family members whose loved one is dying. Anger, hostility, and frustration may be expressed in myriad ways, for example, negative verbalizations, aggressive behavior, sarcasm, negativity, irritability, tension, anxiety, obstinacy, passive aggressiveness, withholding, withdrawal, jealousy of others, and stinginess. Unfortunately, anger is dealt with very poorly in our society and, as a consequence, problems with this very understandable emotion consistently and adversely affect the experience of anticipatory grief for all involved.

Anger can be directed at the dying patient, the self, or third parties. Frequently, it is vented without family members' conscious knowledge or intent. Although anger at the dying person for abandoning the family is quite common, it is most difficult to admit to and is not deemed socially appropriate. Often, it is evidenced in the frustration, impatience, resentment, and withdrawal of family members vis-à-vis the dying loved one. In lieu of dealing directly with this anger at the patient, family members retroflect it inward and may become depressed, experiencing such feelings as worthlessness, self-reproach, and guilt. These feelings may also emanate from the guilt, loss of control, or frustration that normally accompany terminal illness. Not infrequently, the anger is displaced onto other persons who may or may not be directly involved in the terminal illness. Frontline caregivers are frequently the most easily identified targets for such aggression. Theirs is a most delicate position. They are cognizant of the fact that there are inordinant and excessive amounts of aggression and hostility that must be channeled to others beside the dying patient, and yet they are also aware that they must set appropriate limits in terms of what they should tolerate from the family.

Anger may also result from loss of faith in God or philosophy. The illness may precipitate a quest for meaning to make sense out of it, the impending death, and their impacts on and consequences for the survivors-to-be. "Why my loved one?" and "Why me?" are common questions that usually fail to elicit acceptable answers. Many mourners have a profound sense of injustice and disillusionment, feeling that they have played life by the rules but have lost the game. Values and beliefs that formerly were comforting may now be useless. Some will alienate others with their bitterness when their value systems fail them in their attempts to undertand and control what is happening to their dying loved one and themselves.

The experience of the illness itself, and what it does to all involved, also stimulates anger. There are few things that would generate such feelings more than watching unstoppable misery continue and seeing a loved one suffer in pain. The vicissitudes of the disease, its ravages, the continuing process of loss it involves, the sense of impotency it generates, the pain, the confusion, the unfairness, the frustration, the ultimate separation of the impending death all give rise to feelings of anger. In addition, family members must struggle with their anger over the consequent emotional, physical, economic, and social drains along with their impacts on lifestyle and standard of living. This becomes increasingly problematic as the resource drains escalate and, despite the sacrifices, the patient declines anyway.

Other sources of anger are the failure of the loved one to fulfill the dependency needs of family members due to decreased ability to function and the shifting of roles and responsibilities to other family members in order to cope with this reduced functioning. Disappointment over unfulfilled ambitions, unfinished business, and expectations that will never be realized also serves as a catalyst to the anger and frustration of family members; the latter an emotion that fuels the flames of anger throughout the entire illness experience.

The patient may also contribute to the aggression felt by family members through personality changes due to the illness, previous personality traits, or if the illness is perceived as having been self-inflicted or caused by neglect. When the anger of family members, or of any others involved with the dying patient, is acted out by withdrawal or avoidance of the patient, serious problems can ensue. Such behavior is always recognized by the patient who may escalate his or her own aggressive behavior and/or experience increased feelings of loss of control, anxiety, grief, and anger at being in the situation. For this reason, it is important that family members receive assistance in coping with these feelings and channeling them in the most appropriate and therapeutic fashion available in this very difficult situation.

Intervention in Anger and Hostility. A number of therapeutic interventions assist family members in coping with the anger and hostility generated in the anticipatory grief experience. First and foremost, there consistently must be a recognition of the normalcy of these emotional responses under the conditions of terminal illness. This must be communicated by caregivers implicitly, and sometimes explicitly, to all concerned. Likewise, permission is given implicitly or explicitly to ventilate these feelings, as long as this is accomplished in appropriate ways. For example, although verbalization of anger under most conditions must be understood and tolerated, the physical attacking of another cannot be tolerated and appropriate limits have to be established. It is imperative that caregivers offer physical, as well as psychosocial, outlets for discharging aggression. Similar to other instances of human aggression and anxiety, physical release of emotion during terminal illness is most therapeutic. Too often the physical effects of emotions are overlooked by caregivers who fail to capitalize on this important dimension of intervention. Offering physical outlets, such as pounding a pillow, playing a sport, smashing old dishes or glasses in a safe area, punching a punching bag, kicking an empty and open paper bag, and so forth, will provide avenues for the siphoning off of emotions that, lacking other means of release, may prompt emotional and physical acting out in inappropriately aggressive ways. Similar intervention is also suggested for other emotions of anticipatory grief such as guilt, sorrow and depression, anxiety, and frustration as it can offer a means of therapeutic catharsis for all types of emotions. Implicit in this is the caregiver's having given permission for family members to both experience these feelings and to take a break from the dying patient in order to deal with them. This is necessary to ensure that these emotions do not build up to unhealthy levels.

Obviously, it is important for the caregiver to understand the many emotions that may be hidden under the facade of anger. Feelings of grief, fear, anxiety, frustration, impotence, sadness and depression are not infrequently present underneath the aggressive feelings and behaviors. Effective and therapeutic intervention will seek to address these feelings as well and will not become exclusively focused on the anger. Also, caregivers do well not to take a patronizing attitude toward the aggressive feelings, nor to push family members to experience them as they (the caregivers) feel that they should.

As with all other emotions, feelings of anger and hostility will be manifested by the family members according to a variety of idiosyncratic psychological, social, and physical determinants. Family members must be allowed to express their feelings in ways that are consistent with these individual influences and should not be forced into predetermined types of feeling manifestations. Related to this is the importance of analyzing each person's specific reactions and looking for the emotions, thoughts, fears, and concerns that give rise to them. Similar to what caregivers must do when attempting to help delineate the component fears of death that contribute to a dying patient's anxiety, the causes of aggressive feelings and behaviors must be investigated and then specified in order that family members cope with them more effectively than if they tried to confront them en masse. Only when the underlying, real concerns are known will family members be able to respond to them effectively. The caregiver must help family members identify these specific, idiosyncratic concerns and refrain from assuming that their actions necessarily are based on what the caregiver has previously learned from personal or professional experience. For example, "I know that he is really angry that I am healthy while he is dying, and that is why he is saying that I don't understand him" may be more a statement about the speaker's guilt than about the patient's true feelings. In fact, the speaker may not sufficiently understand the patient. This can only be determined if and when the caregiver assesses the situation without overuse of or overreliance on preconceived notions that have been generated either personally or through theoretical models in the field; for example, stages of dying patients.

A lack of information about what is happening to their loved one and what they can do to help often prompts feelings of resentment and infantalization in family members, as well as feelings of being out of control, unprepared, and frustrated. Caregivers must recognize that information seeking is frequently an adaptive coping response to stress used by healthy individuals. Consequently, it is important to provide family members with appropriate information in order not only to allow them to prepare for what is going to occur and to maximally participate in the care of their loved one but also to avoid the negative feelings that result when they are prohibited from receiving requisite information. Although in some cases caregivers may feel that family members want to know too much, the importance of their need to be included and not feel that the care of their loved one is exclusively taken from them by strangers cannot be overstated. This must be recognized by caregivers and each request for information should be evaluated with these normal psychological needs of the family members kept in mind. For those caregivers who routinely hold family conferences and treat the patient and family as a unit, this will not be a new notion.

It may be helpful for caregivers to remember that family members may have difficulty admitting to being angry at their dying loved one. In these cases, it may be more prudent to use less emotionally charged words that convey sentiments to which family members may more readily admit. For example, instead of using the word "angry," it may be more acceptable for some people to admit to being "irritated" or "annoyed" (Lazare, 1979).

The proximity of family members, usually confined with one another under one roof, raises quite high the potential for volatility and explosion. Each family member, struggling to cope with the aggression that is part of the experience, will have the normal tendency to displace it onto those closest. When everyone in a household is feeling this same way, or intensely feeling different emotions, they can tend to potentiate one another's anger. This is another reason why it is imperative for caregivers to be aware of aggressive feelings as well as of those emotions, thoughts, and behaviors that prompt them. Only then can adequate and appropriate intervention be provided to reduce the level of aggression that can build up in a family and initiate a chain reaction among its members. While this can happen with other emotions as well, it tends to occur more frequently with anger and its variations.

Anxiety

Experience of Anxiety. Anxiety on the part of family members is probably the emotion that is least appreciated by caregivers and others dealing with the family of a dying patient. Whereas there may be allowances made for these individuals to experience the other more expected emotions such as sorrow, depression, anger, and even guilt, there tends to be insufficient sensitivity accorded to the manifestations of anxiety and the need for interventions to address it.

Anxiety has been defined as "the apprehension cued off by a threat to some value that the individual holds essential to his existence as a personality" (May, 1977, p. 205). The threat may be to physical life, as in the threat of death, or it may be a threat to psychological existence, such as meaninglessness or the loss of one's sense of identity.

In the situation of anticipatory grief there are many sources of the anxiety that family members experience. Anxiety is predictable in the circumstances of losing a loved one through a terminal illness, since it arises in all situations that confront the individual with the unknown and the unfamiliar. This, plus concerns about life without the loved one, fright arising from the sense of vulnerability caused by the process of loss, distress associated with memories of earlier losses and separations that are resurrected by this loss, and heightened emotional and physical arousal, are all parts of the sense of panic and anxiety that may occur to family members either intermittently or chronically during the anticipatory grief period.

Anxiety is also a normal accompaniment to the uncertain, sometimes mutually exclusive demands of the terminal illness. This anxiety can be exacerbated as continual changes and losses occur either unpredictably or as part of an unstoppable process that the family sees bearing down on them but that they are powerless to deter. Other reasons for the anxiety include the frightening sense of helplessness aroused when a loved one is endangered and the outcome cannot be altered; the flood of acute emotion experienced during the illness process and the reactions to it; the defenses used to cope with the terminal illness and gradual loss of the dying loved one; the intense separation anxiety experienced because of anticipation of parting from the loved one; and the contemplation of one's own death that is stimulated by the entire experience of watching another die (McCollum and Schwartz, 1972).

Unexpressed emotions and thoughts are additional sources of anxiety in the terminal illness period. This is frequently seen in instances such as when a family member struggles to hide her sadness from the dying patient or when a friend wants to talk with the patient about the illness but has been forbidden by the family to do so. Psychological conflicts in one's feelings, thoughts, or impulses concerning the dying patient can also stimulate feelings of anxiety. This is exemplified in the family member who becomes anxious at his recognition of wishing for some relief through the death of the patient.

One of the greatest stimulators of anxiety is the disorganization that occurs both intrapsychically and intrafamilially. It occurs intrapsychically as the mourner is attempting to replace old patterns of behavior with new and more adaptive ones that reflect the current reality (Bowlby, 1961). Correspondingly, it occurs within the family system as family members must cope with illness-generated altered lifestyles and reassignment of roles and responsibilities. Along with these are the anxiety-provoking issues of uncertainty of the patient's deterioration; concern about depletion of emotional, physical, financial, and time resources; and the stress of decision making and balancing mutually incompatible demands.

Intervention in Anxiety. Treatment of the anxiety of family members is much the same as for that of the dying patient. Since anxiety is apprehension in the absence of a specific danger and differs from fear in that it is nondirected, the major way to assist an individual is to help him or her break down the anxiety into its component parts. In this fashion, specific fears and concerns are delineated and each one can be addressed and problem-solved individually. It is always easier to cope with well-defined, explicit fears than to attempt to grapple with more global, undifferentiated, and thus more terrifying anxiety.

Each individual has his or her own unique combination of specific fears about death. What is of the utmost concern is to one person may be negligible to another. The individual's response is influenced by a host of idiosyncratic psychological, social, and physical variables that in turn interact with the distinct factors associated with the particular illness and its characteristics (see chapter 1 for more on this). It is the caregiver's goal to work with the family member to ascertain which specific fears and issues are of concern to him or her, and then to assist the person in confronting them, isolating each one, and addressing them individually to reduce the overall level of anxiety. Among many examples of such concerns might be fears of: the unknown, loneliness, loss of identity, not knowing how to accept the sympathy of others, being overwhelmed by sorrow, missing the loved one at happy occasions in the future, economic problems, disintegration of the family after the death, guilt for previous omissions or commissions, unceasing sadness and grief, loss of social status, inability to cope with practical matters in the absence of guidance from the loved one, and so forth. To the extent that the individual's anticipatory grief contains some contemplation of his or her own death, a certain amount of normal annihilation or existential anxiety would be expected to be present.

As with anger and hostility, it is clear that a remedy for many of the aforementioned sources of anxiety revolves around the provision of information. Offering education and information minimizes the uncertainty and the unknown with which family members must contend. It promotes the legitimization and normalization of feelings, thoughts, and impulses that heretofore may have been unacceptable to family members and therefore conducive to anxiety and the assorted defense mechanisms mobilized to handle it. In other words, the caregiver offers information that allows the family members' experiences to be less of a threat to them. Where threat is diminished, anxiety is lowered.

As an adaptive coping behavior, information seeking is helpful on several accounts, and in appropriate amounts should be facilitated by the caregiver. It gives family members the ability to actively take some control, which is a critical issue since they have so little power to challenge the ultimate threat of the terminal illness taking their loved one. This has the added benefit of generating treatment options, which also renders more control, and it works against the passivity of victimization. It is a vehicle for the family members' participation in the care of the dying patient; with such participation, when it is in appropriate amounts, noted to be an important positive factor in postdeath grief and adjustment.

Other forms of anxiety intervention can be equally as therapeutic in attempting to intervene in anticipatory grief. Education about relaxation techniques has been shown to be quite positive for all who must cope with chronic stress. This, coupled with encouraging and providing permission for respites away from the dying patient to provide much needed replenishment and suggesting physical activities to afford outlets for tension, can go far in assisting family members to cope with the anxiety inherent in anticipatory grief. In a recent study investigating group treatment of cancer patients and their spouses, it was found that education and information about the illness, its treatment, its stress, and methods of coping with its changes, especially relaxation techniques, were reported to be the most helpful aspects of intervention (Heinrich and Schag, 1985). Of course, some anxiety will not be assuaged since it is a normal response to current and potential separation; nevertheless, such intervention can ameliorate much of the anxiety stemming from other sources.

Treatment Interventions in the Component Processes of Anticipatory Grief

At this time, the goals of treatment with the family of a dying patient entail being supportive of their adaptive functioning. The three areas of focus for intervention are (1) communication and awareness contexts; (2) the anticipatory grief and unfinished business of the family; and (3) clinical therapy intervention and clinical education and advocacy (Rando, 1984). In this chapter, devoted as it is to the facilitation of appropriate anticipatory grief, the focus will be mainly on the second goal. However, issues involving the communication and awareness contexts are subsumed as well under the experience of anticipatory grief. There are related clinical therapy interventions and clinical education and advocacy strategies that will also be helpful to anticipatory grief. Therefore, a few comments about goals one and three are in order.

Communication and Awareness Contexts

The key to family support and intervention is the communication process. The hallmark of healthy families is flexible, open communication. In contrast, family disturbance is marked by distorted, unclear, and disqualifying messages. Variables such as family rules and decision-making processes, as well as the relative openness or closure of the family system, both affect and are revealed through the communication processes. When a terminal illness afflicts a family member, patterns of communication may be strained by both the emotional content and the coping mechanisms that are employed by the family to deal with the impending loss. Consequently, the communication patterns in the family may be an indicator of how well the family is handling the loss.

In addition to verbal communication, nonverbal communication occurs. Distancing from the dying patient and changing the patterns of relating to him or her are obvious ways of communicating discomfort with the situation. Research indicates that one of the most frequently reported problems for cancer patients is the absence of open communication within the family. It is mentioned as often as physical discomfort and more frequently than difficulties with medications or overall treatment (Gordon et al., 1977.) Frequently, even in families with open communication patterns, the desire to protect the dying patient or other family members from the pain of the situation eventually restricts communication. The withholding of information results in closed awareness contexts (Glaser and Strauss, 1965), and the concealment of emotions often disrupts relationships and causes emotions to explode later on. Ideally, an open awareness context, one in which there is shared knowledge, information, and communication about the patient's dying, is the goal to strive for since the other contexts (closed awareness, suspicion awareness, or mutual pretense) rob the dying individual of the intimacy of genuine communication (Glaser and Strauss, 1965).

Although caregivers might wish to foster an open awareness context for all families in which the members could share feelings, give and receive clear and congruent messages, and have flexible interactions with each other, the truth is that many families have never had open and fluid relational patterns. As a result, to expect them to communicate in an open and honest way about their feelings, fears, and thoughts during such an anxiety-provoking and stressful time is totally inappropriate. In such cases, caregivers must strive to promote whatever amount of open communication the family system can tolerate.

Clinical Therapy Intervention and Clinical Education and Advocacy

In terms of *clinical therapy intervention,* it is assumed that the caregiver possesses the requisite knowledge of not only anticipatory grief but the experience of the dying patient, family systems theory, children's reactions to death, and the problems accompanying illness in general and the patient's illness in particular. Such interventions must be based on a recognition of the properties of the family as a system. This recognition stimulates meeting with the entire family whenever possible, while still striving to establish a personal relationship with each family member when and if feasible. Children are always included if possible. The entire family is involved in as much care and treatment of the dying patient as reasonable in order to facilitate the therapeutic benefits of such participation—reduction of anxiety; provision of a sense of control, contribution, involvement, and support; atonement vehicle for past guilt; expression of sentiment; and the opportunity to finish unfinished business and appropriately grieve in anticipation of the death. The caregiver must recognize the individual strengths and weaknesses of family members, and of the family system as a whole. Strengths must be capitalized on and areas of weaknesses offered support. He or she must appreciate the differences among families and be realistic about what can be expected given each family's psychosocial history.

The family needs to be assisted in understanding the dying patient's responses and feelings. At some point(s), the caregiver will most probably have to interpret the dying patient's responses for the family and educate them about the patient's feelings. Family members need help to understand the dying experience from the patient's perspective, the intense anticipatory grief the patient feels because he or she is losing everything he or she has ever known, the patient's specific fears, the patient's emotional reactions and coping mechanisms stimulated by thinking about the oncoming death, his or her struggles with dependency and independence. The family should be helped to appreciate the patient's fears of dying in pain and dying alone, along with any other idiosyncratic fears the patient may have and what they can do to assuage them. Caregivers can explain the concept of social death and work with the family to avoid its occurrence. The family can be shown how to support the dying patient's self-esteem and sense of control and will benefit from recurring guidance from the caregiver on how to help the patient achieve an appropriate death (Weisman, 1972).

Within their limits, families need to be helped to appropriately express their anticipatory grief, develop or maintain open communication, identify and finish unfinished business, and avoid distancing themselves from the patient. Families must be encouraged to participate in a normal relationship for as long as achievable with the dying patient. However, they also require permission and encouragement to take time out to replenish themselves and meet other ongoing needs of family members. They need help in maintaining realistic hope and will benefit from having their reactions normalized (if appropriate), especially those generated when the patient relapses or the vicissitudes of the illness impinge too greatly on the family.

Clinical education and advocacy interventions provide practical information to help the family members cope. They support strength and offer alternatives for deficient skills and weaknesses. Usually they involve teaching family members about the illness and the medical treatment, as well as providing them with information pertinent to the institutions with which they must deal and helping them identify current and potential resources. For example, families require specific guidance in identifying, locating, and utilizing material, financial, and social assistance. They need concrete information to help them deal with other practical realities of the illness and death, such as how to meet future medical care needs, plan needed respites, and arrange postdeath rituals. Families benefit from the caregiver's discussion with them in coming to a decision on how to explain the illness and its implications to others. Family members should be instructed as to what can be expected at the time of death and afterward. Most importantly, they are greatly helped by explanations about what dying patients undergo, the experience of anticipatory grief for families, the functioning of the family system and how it needs to reorganize itself. This information should not be offered in a didactic or self-fulfilling prophecy format but shared during the course of the illness as normative information that can provide both a context against which family members can understand their own responses and a preparation for what they will confront.

General Therapeutic Interventions with Grievers

There are seven broad areas of interventions with grievers. These are applicable to both anticipatory and postdeath grievers. They provide a matrix from which other interventions in the specific area of anticipatory grief can be extrapolated. These have been articulated by Rando (1984) and each one is briefly discussed below.

Make Contact and Assess. In this phase, caregivers must reach out to grieving individuals. They must be present physically as well as emotionally to offer security and support, working to keep the griever from becoming isolated. Maintaining a family systems perspective in dealing with the griever is helpful. An important intervention is to give the person implicit and explicit permission to grieve. Early in treatment, it is imperative to conduct a thorough assessment of the mourner's grief and to have an understanding of the person in order to have a context in which to put this particular loss. Indiscriminately promoting grief without an understanding of the particular griever and the variables that influence his or her grief can be countertherapeutic at times.

Maintain a Therapeutic and Realistic Perspective. If caregivers are to be helpful, they must view both their own role and the griever in proper perspective. Expectations must be appropriate. For example, the caregiver must remember that the pain cannot be taken away from the griever and that the critical therapeutic tool he or she has is his or her own personal presence with the griever. The caregiver must not let his or her own sense of helplessness prevent him or her from reaching out to the griever, and he or she should be able to demonstrate genuine concern and caring without letting personal needs determine the experience for the griever. It is expected that a caregiver may have to tolerate volatile reactions from the bereaved. However, the caregiver should never tell the griever to feel better because there are other loved ones who are not dying or try to explain the loss in religious or philosophical terms too early. The caregiver must not forget to plant the seeds of hope, and must indicate that the pain will subside at some point in time, yet must balance this with not minimizing the situation or causing the griever to fear that the loved one will be forgotten. The caregiver must hold out the expectation to the griever that the tasks of mourning eventually will be completed successfully. All of this is greatly assisted if the caregiver does not encourage responses antithetical to appropriate grief.

Encourage Verbalization of Feelings and Reminiscences of and with the Dying Patient. Grievers must be helped to recognize, actualize, and accept the losses they are sustaining. This is facilitated if the caregiver listens nonjudgmentally, with permissiveness and acceptance. Grievers require help in identifying, accepting, and expressing all the various feelings and thoughts of anticipatory grief. The caregiver can help the griever find ways of expressing these feelings and thoughts in ways which are most congruent with the griever's idiosyncratic personality. It would be inappropriate to overlook the importance of finding individualized modes of expression and to try to force everyone to express their anticipatory grief in the same way. Grievers need to be allowed to cry, talk, and review about the dying patient and their mutual relationship without the imposition of the caregiver's structure. If the griever appears to be resisting the grief process, it is helpful to explore the defenses to discover the reasons behind them.

Help the Griever Identify and Resolve Secondary Losses and Unfinished Business. The caregiver's focus here is on assisting the griever to specify current and potential secondary losses and to work on grieving these without prematurely detaching from the dying patient. It is critical for the caregiver to work with the griever to identify any unfinished business with the dying patient and to look for appropriate ways to facilitate closure.

Support the Griever in Coping with the Grief Process. One of the most important things that the caregiver does is help the griever see that he or she will experience many uncomfortable stresses, demands, and reactions to both. Again, if appropriate, grievers need to be assured that this is normal, as long as this is accomplished in a fashion that does not minimize their particular experience. Grievers can benefit from normative information about expectations in anticipatory grief, as long as these are not put forth as self-fulfilling prophecies. They must be helped to maintain a perspective on the anticipatory grief experience. Also, they must understand that grief reactions are unique and that, despite the natural wish to avoid it, the painful process must be yielded to if they are going to emerge therapeutically from it. The caregiver can help the griever find ego-syntonic ways of expressing the pain and all the emotions and thoughts attendent to the loss(es). The griever must be encouraged to be patient and not expect too much of him or herself. The importance of respites from the anticipatory grief experience and from caring for the dying patient should be underscored, with the caregiver working with the griever to find a variety of ways to replenish him or herself.

Help the Griever to Accommodate to the Loss. This area stresses giving assistance to the griever in incorporating changes into his or her identity, roles, experiences, beliefs, assumptions, and expectations that reflect the reality of the dying patient's deterioration and of the world that will exist as that deterioration progresses and after the patient dies. For example, a spouse who will lose a husband has to start to change from thinking of the world in terms of "we" to thinking of the world in terms of "I." Or, in the absence of the wife's ability to care for the children, a father needs support in learning to "mother" the children as well as be a father, and so forth. The caregiver can assess with the griever which new roles and skills must be assumed in light of the patient's illness and can work to help him or her accomplish this. After the death, there should be attempts at helping the griever recognize that a major loss always changes individuals to some extent and that these changes need to be identified and integrated. The griever needs to be made aware that he or she must come to a healthy new intrapsychic relationship with the deceased loved one, without equating the length and amount of suffering with some kind of testimony of love for the deceased. At that time (although for some this will occur during the illness), it may be helpful in working with the griever to reestablish a system of belief or meaning that can support or explain the loved one's illness and death. Also, after the death, it will be helpful to work with the griever to decide in what appropriate ways the deceased's memory may be fostered and how he or she can continue to relate to the deceased loved one through rituals, memorials, and so forth.

Work with the Griever to Reinvest in a New Life. Most of these interventions are appropriate after some time has passed and grief work is undertaken following the death of a loved one. They seek to encourage the griever to find rewarding new things to do and people to invest in and to identify the gain that has derived from the loss. For some individuals whose loved one dies from an overly extended illness and/or whose loved one has a medical condition that precludes awareness of the griever's presence and interactions, it may be helpful to encourage the griever to find some meaningful people or activities to invest in as diversions. However, this must *not* be seen as a suggestion to prematurely detach from the dying loved one. It is offered here only as a statement of recognition that in some illnesses, such as when a patient is in a coma for many years, life must go on for the family.

Specific Therapeutic Interventions for the Component Processes of Anticipatory Grief

The discussion above briefly touched on some of the general interventions suggested for grief. This section examines specific interventions that promote the processes of anticipatory grief. The components of these processes are listed below. (See chapter 1 for a specific delineation of these processes.) It is to be remembered that (1) these must be integrated with the aforementioned general treatment strategies in order to be most therapeutic for anticipatory grievers, with the interventions listed in this section not being exhaustive by any means and (2) some of these interventions will be more appropriate for end-stage anticipatory grief situations than for these earlier in the illness. The caregiver must always evaluate a proposed intervention based on the needs of the particular patient and family at a given point in the illness. See chapter 1 for further discussion.

Components of the Three Interrelated Processes of Anticipatory Grief

I.   **Individual Intrapsychic Processes**
     Awareness and gradual accommodation to the threat
     Affective processes
     Cognitive processes
     Planning for the future

II. **Interactional Processes with the Dying Patient**
     Directing attention, energy, and behavior toward the dying patient
     Resolution of personal relationship with the dying patient
     Helping the dying patient

III. **Familial and Social Processes**

Individual Intrapsychic Processes. In these processes, the griever becomes increasingly aware of the threat of the patient's impending death and copes with the reactions generated by this awareness. This involves affective processes dealing with the emotional responses that are stimulated, as well as cognitive processes pertaining to changing one's sense of self, attempting to crystalize memories for the future, bargaining for a reprieve, and contemplating one's own death. These processes also interface with those involved in planning for a future that is an uncomfortable but natural outgrowth of the increasing recognition that future losses will occur and that the griever must be prepared for dealing with them.

For family members to come to an *awareness and gradual accommodation to the threat* of the loved one's death, they must have been given appropriate warnings that are clearly understandable to them. Frequently, diagnoses delivered in medical jargon are proffered, with insufficient time allowed for processing of implications. It is not unusual for many family members to have a knowledge of the name of a disease, but no understanding of what the implications are. If the impending loss is not made real for the family members, they are not able to prepare for it. Ths does *not* mean that one takes away all the hope family members need or that a self-fulfilling prophecy is established. It simply means that unless the reality is clearly presented to them, they are unable to prepare appropriately for it. Like the griever who cannot start to mourn the death of a loved one if the status of that loved one is unknown, such as in the cases of individuals who are Missing In Action or where bodies are not found, so a family member will have difficulty commencing his or her anticipatory grief if it is not clear what the reality of the impending loss is. This reality can be presented very gently and does not have to be given in a crude or insensitive way that would not respect the needs for the family to hear the news in a compassionate fashion. For example, the crass statement, "The cancer will kill your husband in a straight, down-hill course real quickly" may be changed to "Your husband has a cancer that will soon make it increasingly difficult for him to function. It is not clear exactly how long your husband's body will be able to tolerate the illness. However, you should know that in the near future he will start to experience a series of debilitations and that this, in most cases, eventuates in death very rapidly once the process has begun."

Caregivers must be supportive, yet at the same time as specific as possible, in informing family members about what to expect in order that they can be adequately prepared. They should ask the family what they have understood about what has been told them in order to check their comprehension. Caregivers should be prepared to deliver impactful information more than once, since the emotional defenses of family members may have precluded their taking it all in at once. Recognizing the confusion family members often feel, caregivers should ask for questions from the family and then give adequate time for response. Family members should be informed that it is acceptable to ask questions in the future as they occur to them.

There are times when the caregiver may have to be blunt. This occurs when the illness is progressing, and it is very clear that the family is denying the illness and/or its implications. At this point in time, the caregiver may have to be very specific and to the point, such as "Mrs. Smith, it is important that you understand that your husband is not going to recover from this illness. As far as medical knowledge can predict, he will not be able to make it to the holidays to see your children. I suggest you contact them and have them see their father now." In the same manner, some family members may have to be confronted in cases where time is limited and unfinished business will complicate their grief after the death. For example, in some instances caregivers actually may have to prompt family members to talk with the dying patient by saying such things as "You only have a limited amount of time left. Make sure that you say or do the things you need to in order that you will not feel guilty later on." At these times, it is permissible to be more direct than normal with family members. Although their desires ultimately must be respected, the deleterious consequences of leaving unfinished business must be pointed out to them.

The goal of the caregiver always must be to assist in reality testing and appropriate planning. At times, this entails helping the family understand the implications of medical information; at other times it means assisting them to make practical plans for pre- and postdeath activities. The caregiver must also encourage repetitious recollection of events leading up to the illness and the patient's current condition to assist the family in gradually adapting to the shock of the losses they are encountering. Normally, the experiences of the illness itself prompt family members gradually to realize that the loved one is dying. As the patient deteriorates, as hopes must be relinquished, and as medical interventions are of little use, family members are confronted with the reality to which they must accommodate.

The terminal illness of a loved one engenders a host of *affective processes*. The major ones are discussed above as they impact on the grieving over past, present, and future losses that are attendant to the terminal illness and death of this patient, or that are associated with unrelated losses that have been revived in the current situation (see "Emotional Reactions and Therapeutic Interventions" above). It is imperative that caregivers keep in mind the delicate situation in which the family members exist. The knowledge of the threat of death and potential loss will intensify the levels of emotion that are present. The remissions and relapses of the illness may bring about shifts in the type and intensity of emotions that the family members experience. With the presence of a dying individual, there may be attempts at modulation or suppression of negative feelings in order to eliminate potential stress. These can later erupt in less appropriate ways and can increase the resentment that exists, eventually undermining family cooperation. It is helpful for caregivers to anticipate with the family the emotional reactions that they may experience, to normalize them when they are encountered, and to suggest ways for the family to appropriately express and cope with these feelings, while providing the family with support during the process. Caregivers have to identify family members' idiosyncratic fears, concerns, and needs in the specific situation, as well as those that are ongoing, if they are going to have a more complete understanding of the family's emotional reactions and the ways in which each member chooses to cope with them.

Cognitive processes also are stimulated by the loved one's terminal illness. As with any stressful event, the threatened loss of a loved one causes an individual to be hyperalert and to scan the environment for potential cues related to the stress. The threatened loss strikes at family members' security, sense of self, perception of the world, and so forth. Obviously, family members increasingly will be preoccupied with the loss. In addition to this, over time, as losses and changes accumulate, family members will start to recognize that the world is now different and that they must start to change to adapt to that new reality. This means changes in identity as they start to accommodate to the gradual transformation of going from a "we" to an "I" in terms of their interactive relationship with the dying loved one.

Because it is very important for family members to construct a composite image of the patient that can endure after the death, it is quite helpful for caregivers to encourage reviewing the past in order to crystalize memories to keep after the death. The "life review" (Butler, 1963) is beneficial to the patient as well as to family members in that such a review puts the patient's life in perspective and may help him or her to integrate it. For family members, this can assist in developing a view of the loved one that perhaps is more balanced than previously and has a more longitudinal dimension. Many times it affords insight into the loved one that heretofore has been lacking.

This also meshes with other cognitive processes, such as thinking about one's own death and bargaining for a reprieve. In the former, thoughts of one's own demise are stimulated by watching the dying of another. This gives rise to its own death anxiety. In these cases, caregivers can allow ventilation and encourage planning for how one would like one's own death. In terms of family members attempting to bargain for the life of their loved one, it is best if caregivers do not interfere, unless it is a process that is either distinctly unhealthy for the family member or interferes with the patient's receiving appropriate treatment or tending to medical needs. Taking away the hope that one's bargaining will work is not in the purview of the caregiver, although this does not mean that he or she should support unrealistic hopes.

At this time, many family members implicitly and without conscious knowledge develop a philosophy of how to cope with the patient's remaining time. Some will try to do as much as possible to create memories of the dying patient from which they can later receive sustenance. Others prefer not to feel so pressured and take a more passive, laissez-faire approach, not letting themselves get caught up in that whirlwind. The caregiver can help by asking the dying patient and family members how they are most comfortable in spending the time left. Problems can arise when the dying patient's attitude differs from that of the family members', in which case the caregiver has to mediate to help them come to a mutually agreeable arrangement or, at the very least, to understand one another on this issue. However, the dying patient should be given as much consideration as possible since it is his or her remaining life that is being debated.

Related to this is the need many family members have to be able to put their loved one's suffering and death into some philosophical or religious context that will lend it some meaning or afford it some explanation. For many, this occurs after the death; but for others it occurs during the illness. The best posture for the caregiver to assume is a nonjudgmental and empathic one, supporting the family members' quest for meaning if it is not detrimental to the person or patient.

Old issues (previous losses, griefs, vulnerabilities, and experiences) that may have been revived by the current loss are also contemplated by family members. In this regard, the principles of promoting the ventilation that is felt necessary by the family member would best guide the caregiver's interventions.

When the awareness of the threat has been recognized and the feelings and thoughts associated with it are being processed, *planning for the future* becomes a natural outgrowth. Of course, by definition, this implies having some understanding of what the future will bring in terms of how it will entail losses and changes to come. Caregivers should support family members' attempts to incorporate the dying patient in planning discussions (although it also must be recognized that some of the planning will be for the family members themselves and they may want to consider privately how they will respond to certain future issues). Caregivers can facilitate appropriate planning for the future by asking what specific plans have been made for certain events. For example, the soon-to-be widow can be asked how she will manage child care once she returns to work. This must be done in a way that will help stimulate planning; the griever should not be bombarded, overwhelmed, or frightened. It is often uncomfortable for family members to recognize that they are considering a future without their loved one, so it is imperative that caregivers normalize this and inform them that this is a natural part of accommodating to the undesired, but inevitable, loss. When the dying patient can be a part of that process, in addition to rendering him or her some control, such involvement also decreases family members' guilt over contemplation of the future without the loved one and can increase their opportunities to benefit from the patient's input, guidance, and preferences. A caveat: it is important that such planning and discussion occur at the appropriate time in the illness. When broached prematurely it can isolate the patient and/or create premature detachment.

Interactional Processes with the Dying Patient. In these processes, the griever actively continues to be involved with the dying loved one. Such involvement is necessary not only to continue to support the dying patient and to ensure there is no premature detachment but also to provide the time and opportunity for the griever to care for the loved one and to resolve their mutual relationships—actions that can be therapeutic for postdeath grief adjustment.

In a loved one's terminal illness, it is normal for family members to find themselves *directing attention, energy, and behavior toward the dying patient.* The main issue here is to promote whatever communication, interaction, control, living, and meaning remains available to the dying patient. Family members must be assisted in adopting a commitment to this as well as in remaining as involved as possible with the dying patient. Withdrawal from the patient will not only accentuate the patient's losses but will deprive family members of the therapeutic benefits of appropriate participation in the patient's care and the opportunities to minister to the patient's needs. Caregivers can explain to family members that they will have to struggle with mutually conflicting demands. In terms of their orientation vis-à-vis the patient, anticipatory grief necessitates their simultaneously moving toward the patient (directing attention, energy, and behavior toward the patient), staying the same with the patient (remaining involved with him or her), and moving away from the patient (decathecting from the image of that patient in the future). (See chapter 1 for further discussion of this subject.) The caregiver will have to help the family member balance these conflicting demands and cope with the stress their incongruence creates. The family member will need guidance in identifying how to simultaneously yet differentially respond to these demands. For example, one can move toward the patient behaviorally (in terms of increasing the time spent talking about feelings), while moving away (through starting to decathect from the image of the patient in the future) by and dealing with it on another plane (i.e., cognitively, not behaviorally), such as through starting to consider how to become more self-reliant. Thus, the competing demands may be met in different realms of the personality since one can move closer behaviorally or socially, while starting to move away intrapsychically. The ability of such differential responding means that the patient does not have to be prematurely abandoned despite the decathexis process. It will be critical for the caregiver to assist the griever with this complex realization and the discerning intellectual and emotional analysis it requires. The caregiver must continually emphasize the importance of ongoing involvement, modeling this for family members by the actions that are undertaken with the dying patient and the incorporation of the dying patient in all family activities.

Family members often require the assistance of the caregiver in learning how to balance the myriad other competing demands they will be subject to during their loved one's illness. (See "Complicating Issues in Anticipatory Grief" above.) In this regard, caregivers must also work with family members to educate and assist them in taking respites, in order that when they are with the patient they are able to focus themselves toward caring for the patient. When such things as normal resentment, ambivalence, and frustration arise and are explained as part of the process of living with a dying individual, this will help liberate family members from guilt and other negative responses that could interfere with their relating to the patient.

Family members must be assisted in doing those things necessary for the patient's treatment that are painful for them to do. It often takes a great deal out of family members to have to participate in those activities that are painful for their loved one (for example, taking them for painful medical procedures) or that prevent their loved one from having access to things that are enjoyable (for example, refusing to buy cigarettes). Caregivers can assist family members by encouraging them to discuss such matters and, in situations where the omissions or commissions do not seem to make sense to the family members, helping them decide whether or not they want to continue with them. In situations where palliative care is practiced and the "cure mentality" is minimized or absent, family members will not have to be put in such situations as frequently.

One of the most important aspects of anticipatory grief is that it allows time for *resolution of the personal relationship with the dying patient.* The most critical aspect of this is finishing unfinished business with the dying loved one. Addressing psychosocial issues that have never been addressed or that have lacked successful closure in the relationship with the dying patient can involve many behaviors. Such behaviors include not only expressing feelings and resolving past conflicts but encompass actions such as saying goodbye, explaining past omissions or commissions, articulating messages that are important, informing the patient of the meaningfulness of the relationship, or providing other pieces of feedback that may be important. Again, the ability of the family to withstand open and honest communication must be taken into consideration when caregivers consider prompting family members to be open and disclosive to the dying patient. As noted previously, it may be necessary to urge family members to do or say those things that need to be done or said so they do not feel guilty later on. Often it is helpful for caregivers to ask family members to identify what they think they will feel uncomfortable, incomplete, or guilty about six months down the road and then, if these are issues that can be addressed presently, to suggest they pay attention to them now in order to finish the unfinished business and to come to closure with the patient.

It is critically important, although frequently quite painful, for family members to say goodbye to the patient and to give him or her the permission to die. Saying goodbye to the patient can be done both verbally and nonverbally. Caregivers frequently need to model saying goodbye to the dying patient at the appropriate time. This can be done through such things as letting the patient know how he or she will be remembered; for example, "I will miss you when you are gone. Whenever I watch *Casablanca* I'll remember you and how much you loved that movie." It involves acknowledging that leave taking is occurring and can be demonstrated through concrete or symbolic actions as well as through verbal communication. The caregiver should be aware that different words or actions will be meaningful for different people in saying goodbye.

Permission to die is essentially what family members convey to the dying patient, making it acceptable for him or her to go. They thus refrain from attempting to keep the patient alive through guilt, responsibility, or unfinished business. It does not mean that the family is unmoved that the patient is dying. Rather, it signifies that, despite their wishes to the contrary, they love the patient enough to recognize that death is natural and inevitable, therefore they do not act in ways that will meet their needs at the expense of the dying patient's needs to let go. They can allow the peaceful transition. Sometimes just making a verbal or nonverbal statement that recognizes that the patient is dying gives the patient the message that the family members understand and reluctantly accept what is happening.

Throughout the period of anticipatory grief, family members ideally work on *helping the dying patient* to cope with his or her own anticipatory grief, to deal with the specific fears and concerns that confront him or her, and to achieve a sense of closure that can provide him or her with the feeling of peace and the ability to let go at the appropriate time. This entails facilitating an appropriate death, tending to the last wishes of the patient, determining and meeting the needs of the dying patient, and assuming necessary body and ego functions. Most importantly, it involves providing the psychosocial support and acceptance necessary for the patient to communicate about and cope with all aspects of the illness and impending death and with the consequent feelings, thoughts, fears, concerns, and needs that are generated by it. (The reader is referred to Rando [1984] for a complete discussion of how to be therapeutic with a dying patient.) Again, this will help not only the dying loved one, but the family members' adjustment after death will be better facilitated if there has been appropriate involvement in the illness of the patient.

In order to meet the needs of dying patients, family members must be aware of what they are. Therefore, a major responsibility of the family is to create an atmosphere in which the dying person feels free to make needs and wants known without fear of incurring resentment or disapproval. Caregivers can help facilitate an open awareness context in this regard. Family members can be directed not to assume what the patient's needs may be, but instead to ask the patient directly. Caregivers must advise the family to balance support for the patient's increased dependency with the continued need for autonomy. Too much of either can be countertherapeutic. Family members require help in coping with those processes that mark the decline toward death, without abandoning the loved one in order to avoid seeing it happen. It is particularly painful for family members to watch the loved one deteriorate and be forced to relinquish the roles and responsibilities that were once sustained. Their feelings of helplessness and lack of control are frequently defended against through a variety of coping mechanisms. Those mechanisms that are (1) expected and appropriate at the time; (2) safeguard the individual against incapacitating anxiety or depression; (3) enable the individual to maintain need-fulfilling relationships; and (4) do not interfere with the medical care of the patient may be appraised as functional for the individual in a given situation (McCollum and Schwartz, 1972.) A therapeutic task of the caregiver is to support those mechanisms that are healthy, functional, or adaptive, and work to gently supplant those that are not.

Along with helping the dying patient in the aforementioned ways, family members can help the patient to have continued control and self-determination by asking how the dying patient wishes to be remembered and then attempting to bring this to fruition. For example, the caregiver can suggest that the family member ask the patient how he or she would like to have his or her memory kept alive. Suggestions include writing letters or making video tapes for young children who will be left behind, establishing an endowment in the patient's name, bequeathing precious possessions to certain loved ones, choosing a headstone, and so forth. If desired by the patient, the family member can help him preplan the type of funerary rituals preferred. Ongoing communication can be facilitated by the caregiver between family member and patient, with the caregiver serving as a reality tester, a source of comfort, and a resource for helping to discharge negative feelings that could impinge on the relationship between the dying patient and family member.

Familial and Social Processes. Like all other systems, the family system will have to struggle to achieve homeostatic balance after there has been a change. This will necessitate the reassignment of roles and responsibilities to other family members. Caregivers can be helpful by explaining this process and by advocating the most appropriate assignment of roles for given family members. The family will be called upon to maintain a functional equilibrium in the sense of preserving normalcy and routine, while also making role shifts necessitated by the illness as well as balancing the special needs of the dying member with those of other members. Caregivers can assist the family to reassign current responsibilities cooperatively, and to anticipate future permanent changes, directing them toward restructuring their roles in mutually adaptive ways. However, they must always resist the impulse to take over for the family, either with the dying patient or among the members themselves.

Family members also will be called on to negotiate extrafamilial relationships. Some of these will involve establishing a relationship with caregivers. In this, it will be helpful for caregivers to teach family members to be assertive and how to express constructive anger and discontent in ways that will not jeopardize either their future relationship with caregivers or the care of the patient. Other social relationships are often put under stress when a family member is dying. This results from the family disruption that occurs during the illness, as well as from the lack of energy that many family members experience because of the illness and the interference this causes in their ability to maintain and nurture outside relationships. Caregivers can be helpful in explaining the social avoidance that often arises as friends become distant due to the anxiety-provoking nature of the terminal illness or the lack of knowledge of what to do to be supportive. Family members may have to be guided in taking the lead in dealing with friends who many times are interested in helping but do not know what to do.

Caregivers may also have to normalize the resentment that family members experience over the good fortune of friends or over their feelings that others cannot understand their plight. Support groups for family members of terminally ill patients can be exceptionally helpful and caregivers should be aware of these resources.

Finally, not only must family members learn how to communicate with the dying patient and with extrafamilial friends and health caregivers, they must also learn to work with one another. This will be especially important when the family is in flux due to the reassignment of roles or when they need to make plans for the future. Caregivers can work to facilitate and reinforce intrafamilial communication and should demonstrate the importance of this by including all family members in relevant meetings as often as possible and practical, demonstrating respect for the feelings and opinions of all and modeling healthy communication skills.

Conclusion

The anticipatory grief of the loved ones of a dying patient is a complex phenomenon encompassing a number of emotional responses and a host of psychosocial processes. These occur during a time of intense confusion, chaos, and competing demands. This chapter has endeavored to investigate this phenomenon during this unique experience and has offered treatment interventions designed to facilitate the most appropriate anticipatory grief, with the hope that it will be therapeutic for both patient and family.

References

Barton, D. 1977. The Family of the Dying Person. In D. Barton, ed., *Dying and Death: A Clinical Guide for Caregivers.* Baltimore: Williams & Wilkins, pp. 59–71.

Bowlby, J. 1961. Processes of Mourning. *International Journal of Psycho-Analysis* 42:317–340.

Butler, R.N. 1963. The Life Review: An Interpretation of Reminiscence in the Aged. *Psychiatry.* 26:65–76.

Fleck, S. 1975. The Family and Psychiatry. In A.M. Freedman, H.I. Kaplan, and B.J. Sadock, eds., *The Comprehensive Textbook of Psychiatry* (Vol. 1, 2nd ed.). Baltimore: Williams & Wilkins, pp. 382–397.

Glaser, B.G., and A.L. Strauss. 1965. *Awareness of Dying.* Chicago: Aldine.

Gordon, W., I. Feidenberg, L. Diller, L. Rothman, C. Wolf, M. Ruckdeschel-Hibbard, O. Ezrachi, and L. Gerstman. 1977. The Psychosocial Problems of Cancer Patients: A Retrospective Study. Paper presented at the meeting of the American Psychological Association, San Francisco, September 1977.

Heinrich, R.L., and C.C. Schag. 1985. Stress and Activity Management: Group Treatment for Cancer Patients and Spouses. *Journal of Consulting and Clinical Psychology* 53:439–446.

Kastenbaum, R.J. 1969. Death and Bereavement in Later Life. In A.H. Kutscher, ed., *Death and Bereavement*. Springfield, Ill: Charles C. Thomas, pp. 28–54.

Lazare, A. 1979. Unresolved Grief. In A. Lazare, ed., *Outpatient Psychiatry: Diagnosis and Treatment*. Baltimore: Williams & Wilkins, pp. 498–512.

McCollum, A.T., and A.H. Schwartz. 1972. Social Work and the Mourning Parent. *Social Work* 17:25–36.

May, R. 1977. *The Meaning of Anxiety*, rev. ed. New York: W.W. Norton.

Pattison, E.M., ed. 1977. *The Experience of Dying*. Englewood Cliffs, N.J.: Prentice-Hall.

Rando, T.A. 1984. *Grief, Dying, and Death: Clinical Interventions for Caregivers*. Champaign, Ill.: Research Press.

Volkart, E.H. (with collaboration of S.T. Michael). 1957. Bereavement and Mental Health. In A. Leighton, J. Clausen, and R. Wilson, eds., *Explorations in Social Psychiatry*. New York: Basic Books, pp. 281–304.

Weisman, A. 1972. *On Dying and Denying: A Psychiatric Study of Terminality*. New York: Behavioral Publications.

8

Anticipatory Grief, Meditation, and the Dying Process

Hulen S. Kornfeld
Richard W. Boerstler

I n this chapter we will provide a special relaxation method as a practical technique that may be used by anyone at any time. This procedure may be especially useful to those who are dying. It is simply a process in which a helper stays beside the person who is wishing to relax, and, by making a sound in concert with the subject's exhalation, assists the subject in "letting go." Although this method is based on meditative principles, the participants need never have meditated before. In fact, they may only think of the practice as a stress-reduction exercise. Nevertheless, both the subject and the assistant may expect to experience reduced tension and a sense of peace as they share this simple communion.

A meditative process is particularly useful in working with terminally ill patients because it may help to stabilize certain vital signs through autonomic nervous system response. This method, which we call comeditation, is especially useful because it is taught to the patient's significant others. While the patient's loved ones are engaged in a positive caring act with the patient, they, as well as the patient, will benefit from the effects with more calmed bodies and minds.

Some people achieve this level of rest almost naturally. In fact, one of us (Kornfeld) became interested in exploring meditative practices after realizing that certain patients were able to handle severe metastatic pain through quiet withdrawal periods that augmented medication. Anyone who has worked with cancer patients may recall several personally inspiring episodes in which the victims prevailed over most aggravations, becoming, in fact, the comforter.

On becoming successful in learning to endure their physical symptoms and to deal with the people they had to depend on, these patients would sometimes say they had learned to rest, or they were "giving the medicine a chance to work." Often, they were unaware of changes that observers had noticed in their behavior. Sometimes "God" and "prayer" were a part of the explanation, but often the person would be known to be agnostic.

When Kornfeld's inquiry began about ten years ago, few used the term "meditation," but often these special patients had actually found their own meditative practices. Each of these persons experienced helplessness, severe pain, and prolonged physical wasting. Through their inward turning these torments were transformed into actualization experiences leading to spiritual growth. This spiritual growth, documented by caregivers as "acceptance of dying," is remembered as a special gentleness that allowed the dying person to transcend the daily strains.

Although cultural and private emotional patterns are reflected in crisis situations, these special people demonstrated unexpected inner strength. The different responses of various patients with clinically similar organ and nerve involvement suggest that a clinical diagnosis reveals only a small part of the treatable client. Thoughts cause physical reactions that initiate a progression of mental unrest and additional related biological symptoms. Each person dealing with any serious illness must work through anger, despair, frustration, and anxiety—the various stages explained by Kübler-Ross (1969) and many other psychiatric researchers. Although this grief pattern may lead to overwhelming depression with fear, regret, a sense of profound loss, and physical suffering, it may also lead to emotional maturity, encouraging compassion and heightened awareness. Commonly, grief work touches both extremes. The question that was the foundation of this study changed from "What has aided these persons to come to terms with their fate?" to "How can a caregiver help those who struggle with pain and fear to reduce their discomforts and anxieties so they might also be eased?"

The other author (Boerstler) had pursued meditation through various religious teachings when he learned that a certain group of Tibetian lamas were devoted to assisting other lamas, who were dying, by making a special sound in unison with the sick lama's exhalation. In Boston, The Clearlight Society, led by Patricia Shelton, offered the practice, with certain restrictions, to the chronic and terminally ill. When Boerstler discovered that even persons who were undisciplined could achieve profound emotional calming when using this method in linking the mind and body, he determined to make the process available to everyone who was interested. He began by publishing his booket, *Letting Go* (1982).

Spiritual Aspects of Meditation

In meditation the mind is clear. When the mind is as open as the sky, whisplike clouds may float by but they may be quickly brushed aside. The German-born Lama A. Govinda said, "The conviction that something in us survives death does not make us immortal unless we know what it is that survives and that we are capable of identifying ourselves with it" (1976, p. 221).

The concept, "letting go," refers to relinquishing self-concern and will in order to experience pure consciousness. The term "yoga" is not a mysterious, esoteric practice; it means simply "to yoke," that is, to link the mind and body because unifying the conscious and unconscious requires discipline. Active thinking or random thoughts create chatter. Most of the world's religions have developed several similar practices to elicit this state of total awareness. Kneeling, chanting, touching rosary beads, and singing are kindred aids.

This reminds us of a patient who said, "I bet you're going to try to teach me some kind of meditation. I'm too old for anything new like that." Our reply was, "Are you too old to pray?" Religious artifacts were throughout the house, so, not surprisingly, he answered, "Of course not, I've prayed all my eighty-six years." He didn't see the connection.

His eyes widened as we continued, "Remember there are two kinds of prayer. There is the petitionary prayer that is associated with specific needs; this may be thought of as giving God a shopping list. The other form of prayer is a kind of listening; the mind is open and the body is prepared for spiritual communion."

In petitionary prayer, sometimes the worshiper acquires a feeling of relaxation as troubles are passed on to God. But there is a feeling of betrayal when requests are not answered and circumstances become worse. Anxiety intensifies as the petitioner tries to say the right things and set up a favorable bargain. The second form is the prayerfulness of the mystics. Spiritual leaders throughout history and of all religions have tried to guide their disciples in discovering this process of release from anxiety to awareness of the inner consciousness. It is the meaning, or actualization, that Frankl (1963) discovered exceeds hopelessness and heinous suffering. It is the peacefulness that "passes all understanding." All philosophies are at home in this transcendence.

Biological Phenomena

None of us, of course, can promise our clients that comeditation will give them enlightenment; that is, an individual growth process. We can, however, offer anyone a method to relax that will augment both physical and emotional comfort. The success of many chronic pain-control clinics, of the natural childbirth methods, and of certain hypertension programs are due to incorporating the teaching of meditative or controlled breathing practices with specifically related medical supervision.

Selye (1956) began to publish studies interrelating stress and body response in 1936. He discovered a "general adaptation syndrome," that is, biological manifestations evidenced by hormonal changes and organic responses when physical or perceptual strain is experienced. Meditation was shown to modify organic responses associated with the autonomic nervous system by Benson in

The Relaxation Response (1975). The Meninger Foundation in Topeka, Kansas, led by Elmer Green, specifically researched Indian yogis' physiological changes electronically to gather data on conscious training affecting the autonomic nervous system. Blood pressure and respiration drop with deep meditation; pulse rate may or may not slow depending on the meditator's intent and training.

The most significant correlation in the mind–body response is the relationship between breathing and thinking. Imagine your own reactions if you were suddenly surprised by someone, *now*, entering the room with a gun aimed at you. Your response would include a quick and deep intake of breath intiated by a pull near the umbilicus. This is automatic behavior resulting from stimulation of the solar plexus, a large aggregation of nerves and ganglia in the abdomen.

The increased mental and physical demands of defense cause faster breathing. When the respiratory intake is increased, awareness and anxious thinking increases, the heart rate speeds up, and tension is felt throughout the body. As relaxation occurs, mental activity slows down; respiration, which might have been rapid and shallow during fright, becomes slower and deeper during withdrawal. Anxious breathing, instead of providing oxygen to the lower parts of the lungs, is rapid and ineffective, thereby increasing metabolic imbalance and emotional agitation. For these reasons, instruction in deep, relaxed, diaphragmatic breathing is a component of responsible respiratory therapy.

Many medical advances have occurred through understanding the chemical–electrical complexities of living cells. The gate-control theory of pain perception, in which Melzack and Wall (1982) proposed that signals of hurt could be modified or blocked, was developed in 1965. Recently, the electron microscope and new techniques have allowed researchers to discover hundreds of peptides (minute, naturally produced, neural-endocrine proteins) that affect the reaction to pain stimuli, thought processes, and the interaction of the various organs. Today's scientists are proving that our bodies are equipped not only to warn us of danger, but to modify our agonies if we will just allow ourselves to learn how. Specific relaxation techniques modify a person's perception of pain, it appears, by the release of endorphins stimulated by descending impulses within the central nervous system. Norepinepherine, an excitatory hormone (a catecholemine), is repressed during relaxation; serotonin, another catecholamine with an inhibitory effect on the nerve pathways, contributes to relaxation.

More defined studies on the limbic system and the bicameral brain seem to be leading to greater understanding of the biochemical pathways to altered states of consciousness. Serious inquiry into near-death experiences has shown that many people have had mental events when vital signs were malfunctioning. As testimony from those who believe they have had a religious experience would support, these findings may actually lead to the recognition of the biospiritual being. This has been called the new frontier, an awareness of a world within as vast as the universe without.

Regardless of any philosophic theory, consider these facts: (1) our bodies produce mind-altering substances, such as opiate-type peptices; (2) sometimes we envision archetypal experiences, especially when the body is toxic; (3) meditative techniques enhance pain suppression and mood stability; and (4) Jungian, humanistic, and transpersonal psychotherapies effectively use meditative techniques to elicit edifying insights through spontaneous imagery. Combining this growing body of knowledge and methodology to assist those who are dying, or in physical distress, to control their own sensations and mental experiences is a contemporary caregiving practice. Comedization is an effective vehicle.

Important Questions

As professionals who are concerned about the many aspects of terminal illnesses, we recognize that "letting go" is a psychological as well as a physiological process. The caregiver who is fearful of death cannot easily accept a client's dying. Our program addresses questions necessary for anyone working with seriously ill patients and their families to consider. Particularly, think of these three questions as you develop your own attitudes regarding death:

1. What is "a good death?"
2. What are the fundamental needs of the dying person?
3. If your own consciousness is to become part of the universe at the time of transformation, in which state do you want your consciousness to be?

Most of us believe that, if we could choose, we would prefer to die suddenly without the awareness of pain. When we have watched people we have loved wasting away, consuming their own bodies because they cannot retain foods, fearing interrupted nights and confused days, we are enraged that someone we care about must suffer such indignities. Yet, this period of suffering promotes necessary activities directed toward issues that need to be resolved. These components of anticipatory grief are essential: physical distress, feelings of helplessness, anger, and despair. These lead to touching and nurturing and to making preparations aimed at reducing one's loneliness and confusion; resolution includes elements of withdrawal.

As nurse, doctor, therapist, cleric, or family member, none of us can know what is a better way to die for another. In fact, not even the person who is dying knows all of the factors relating to his or her life and death and their influence on others. Hospice management has come to signify the care of symptoms, including the relief of pain, maintaining consciousness, and allowing death to occur almost unobtrusively. But these goals are not recognized, even by the medical community, as ideals.

For instance, one of our patients and his family were unable to resolve their bid for control with the doctor before the patient's death. A reformed alcoholic, he had cancer with liver metastasis and the symptoms of toxic encephalopathy (mental disturbances because the liver is not able to metabolize certain circulatory products such as ammonia). It had been many years since his last drink, but in his illness he became wild at night, fighting everyone who came near, pulling off his clothes while shouting obscenities. Even when calm, he was more childish and forgetful than at his worst times twenty years before. He would settle down in the day, but his wife was fearful and his son had to work. The most dreadful aspect of the situation, however, was that the family was reliving their painful early years, a time they wanted to forget. The wife cried for fear that her husband's worst character would be predominate in their memory.

The visiting nurse asked the doctor to prescribe lactulose to try to reduce the ammonia being built up in the colon, as is typical in such conditions. The doctor refused to listen to any arguments about the patient's behavior or the family's feelings because he knew that these symptoms were the prelude to a hepatic coma. This physician maintained that mental confusion and loss of consciousness was nature's way of helping the patient avoid the reality of his illness. To the doctor, that was good. Before this had happened, however, we had worked with the patient and family: they had wanted to manage together and to strengthen their bonds. The patient died in the hospital, reinforcing the doctor's belief that a former alcoholic did not have the courage for a conscious death.

We contend that it is the patient and family who should determine what their needs are within the course of the illness. We also contend that caregivers have the responsibility to try to meet these needs while providing care with the tools that are available. When the suffering seems prolonged, there are often psychological factors requiring resolution. As long as there is life, there is work that can be done; for example, mending bridges and recognizing the gentle stranger within. But, even when we think we know a better way, our own goals must not become confused with our client's abilities.

Recognition of Needs

When we ask hospice students to list those things that are needed by the average person (themselves), the list is basically the same as the list they create for a person who is dying. The fundamental categories fit Maslow's hierarchy of needs (1954): (1) physiological necessities; (2) safety; (3) love; (4) self-esteem; and (5) actualization. As certain personal priorities vary in day-to-day life, the emphasis shifts according to the situation, but no quality is ever lost.

The one anticipating death may express fear of pain, or of the unknown, or of abandonment. For some the thought of their own family life without them seems inconceivable; they may become absorbed in planning future events. Commonly, minor occurrences absorb the day, significant symptoms await the doctor's direction, and private thoughts are guarded to protect others. Some patients and families use the wonderful elixir, hope, to deny the warning period granted by the sickness, rather than recognizing this gift of time for preparation. Although the task of caregiver is to provide an atmosphere in which the patient, and those who are close, may explore the anxieties that might be attended to, and use the waiting time for resolving losses and feelings, often conversation is nonproductive and tiring.

A time to review personal values when death is imminent means being surrounded by whatever seems important. Whether it be the comfort of an old chair or the warmth of a favorite pet, there is actualization potential in these significant continuations in living. The person who is dying may have few choices. Although many decisions may not be harmonious with views that others have of the situation, the patient's autonomy is precious. As the patient's network affirms the patient's personhood, self-esteem is maintained. Meeting the special physical–medical needs as well is an important, but secondary, task. In recognizing the interconnection between anxiety and physiological symptoms, it is important to identify the source of the anxieties. Most dying persons who understand the caregiver's intent will opt for the safety measure when it is appropriate. Rather than contradicting the "letting go" concept, emphasizing the patient's needs allows the realization of goodness, as an opening to the higher self.

Because of the complex problems intertwined for each person, hospice literature stresses the concept of the patient–family unit as well as the multifaceted approach. The latter is recognized as the four aspects of human support: the physiological, the psychological, the social, and the spiritual. Through the multidisciplinary team approach each aspect of care is represented by a specialist whose expertise is shifted to concerns about that particular family. Yet, even in these discussions, too often the interrelationship of each element to the whole is overlooked. Techniques and attitudes to facilitate melding these many aspects of the individual and his network are necessary.

The Continuum

If consciousness is a transpersonal experience that is the link between the mundane and the eternal, then looking at the transcience of all things is also a way of recognizing eternal continuation. We remind you of the advances in modern physics that have proven that nothing is static. The ancient Hindu concept of the god Shiva, whose continuous dance represents the endless cycles of change, closely parallels the discoveries of the behavior of subatomic particles and the theories of relativity. Just as none of us is the infant our mothers fed, tomorrow the cells of our bodies and the thoughts we have at this moment will have been modified also. We will be affected by what we experience today, as a table is affected by a hammer, or a blow, or a polishing cloth. But, the atoms making up an apparently solid table are also moving and changing; otherwise, it could not be affected by the hammer or the polishing cloth.

Govinda wrote:

> Life means giving and taking; exchange, transformation. It is breathing in and breathing out. It is not taking possession of anything but a taking part in everything that comes in touch with us. . . . He who opposes this process will die the slow death of rigidity; ne will be expelled and rejected from all that lives, like dead matter from a living organism. Death is a deficiency of the faculty of transformation.
>
> In acceptance of this definition of Death, we must see that we are really talking about life! To live, we must go through continual change, which might be called continual death. Thus, we are really courting change when we refuse to accept it. We enjoy a waterfall or a cloud formation—in spite of its impermanence: the changing forms heighten our delight (1976, pp. 182–183).

Another metaphor is to compare a life to an ocean wave. The form changes, but the elements comprising the water remain the same wherever they are; and the body of ocean, of which the water is always a part, continues. When we are unaccepting of our changes, or frightened by the unknown, it is because we are so absorbed with the component that we identify as "I," and psychologists call "ego." There are those who have claimed that by letting go of their attachments, moment by moment, even torture has been transcended. Those who practice yogic defiance of painful situations, such as walking over hot coals or lying on a bed of nails, respond to sensation in a normal way when not in a meditative state. They identify a me-ness that is beyond the physical self, and an awareness of being that is greater than the body.

The Comeditation Method

Our first experience working together teaching *comeditation* to a patient involved a fifty-year-old man who felt disillusioned by petitionary prayer. He had an affectionate relationship with his wife, but they were both disturbed that he would be leaving two young children. He was dying of cancer of the lung complicated by congestive heart failure. He was receiving intravenous medications for the pooling fluids and faulty heart action, but his perspiring skin was ashen and his respirations were forty-eight a minute. His attention was already on the fact that breathing was difficult. We asked him to try to relax his body and flow with the exhalations only.

By encouraging him to push out the old air, we were using a respiratory therapeutic approach to clear his lower lungs to receive as much oxygen (by nasal cannula already in place) as he could. We made a sound in coordination with each exhalation, urging him to focus on the sound. As he listened, his thoughts became slower and his respirations became slower and deeper, as well. Within twenty minutes his respirations were below thirty, his skin was white and drying, and his face appeared restful. The second session later that evening helped him to reduce his respirations from forty-two a minute to twenty-two, a normal working rate. This more efficient breathing pattern was more comfortable. In control, he was able to send gentle thoughts as his last words to his children. His wife worked with him through the night when his breath became irregular. She felt she was helping because he seemed to become more at ease, even as he died.

The process begins with a willing subject assuming a supported position. The demonstration plan may be used by anyone at any time. If the person is comfortable flat on the back, it is easier to relax. If the person must have the head up, be certain that the spine is as straight as possible and use pillows to prop the body and to prevent extremities from dangling freely or pressing on other body parts. The assistant must review the procedure to be used with the subject because no surprises should occur during the session. Also, they must identify some signal (such as raising the nearest thumb) for the meditator to communicate that the assistant should stop if the subject wishes.

The procedure begins with a muscle relaxation period. Because death often overtakes the body from the lower extremity, we start with "The toes and feet are relaxing," and suggest that the part said may be wiggled or contracted to identify between tightness and relaxation. Continue on up the body, making specific reference to each part:

"The calves and knees are relaxing."

"The thighs and hips are relaxing."

"The spine and pelvis are relaxing."

"The muscles of the abdomen and stomach are relaxing."

"The muscles of the heart and chest are relaxing."

"The muscles of the shoulders are relaxing."

"The muscles of the scalp are relaxing."

"The muscles of the forehead are relaxing."

"The muscles between the eyebrows are relaxing" (repeat 3 times).

"The muscles of the eyes and nose are relaxing."

"The muscles of the cheeks and jowls are relaxing."

"The muscles of the neck are relaxing."

"The muscles of the right arm are relaxing and all tension is leaving the fingertips of the right hand."

"The muscles of the left arm are relaxing and all tension is leaving the fingertips of the left hand."

"All tension is leaving the body through the toes of the right foot."

"All remaining tension is leaving the body through the toes of the left foot."

Continue the relaxation with "Now that the body is completely relaxed, please join with me in the sound of letting go, the sound of 'Ah-hh,' as you would at the end of a hard day."

The meditator may be asked to take a deep breath and make the same sound with the comeditator for the first three to five exhalations. The assistant then paces the respiration rate with the sound of "Ah-hh." The use of words such as "just listen," "nothing else is necessary," between breaths (especially when external noises may intrude) will allow a sense of peacefulness. The meditator may later express the feeling of totality, of being cradled, or free from responsibility when the mind is clear.

The assistant watches the chest very closely, assuming a semimeditative state while making the sound of "Ah-hh" as the chest falls. Counting may be used (one to ten, and repeating) with an invitation to the subject to visualize the numbers going across and disappearing over the horizon, if the meditator wishes. The use of numbers is devoid of religious connotation or personal expectation. It allows each comeditator to breathe at his or her own pace while the sound responds to the subject's exhalations.

A more personal approach involves having the assistant say certain words that have been preselected by the subject. Favorite religious phrases, such as "The Lord is my Shepherd, I shall not want," or "Forgive us our trespasses" are often chosen. Portions of favorite hymns, poems, or songs may be used. People who love the sea often select a meditation round that visualizes the ocean and light.

Although there are similarities between guided meditations and hypnosis, the subject is always in control with this particular technique. The speed follows the subject's breath exactly, or modified by every other breath if requested; the pattern and sounds are tailored to the subject's choices. If the patient is attempting any therapeutic process during the session, the subject's thoughts leading to that variation must be discussed beforehand and the clues selected must be those that feel appropriate to the subject. If the person is tired and wishes to use the method for needed rest, we advise, before beginning, that the assistant establish with the meditator that if he or she falls asleep (identifiable by a change in breathing pattern), the assistant will quietly slip out of the room and the meditator may sleep until refreshed.

Usually, the process can be effective if about twenty minutes is set aside for the purpose. This is about the average amount of time that can be taken from routine chores and impatient visitors. Most situations will permit using the procedure at least at bedtime, although many therapists recommend relaxation be practiced every four hours, or at least four times a day. Under certain circumstances, a few people will select several hours of intermittent chanting performed by dedicated loved ones, but it is not advisable to forego caregiving activities in anticipation of imminent death.

Whenever a person does any type of deep relaxation, some time is necessary to return to normal function. In concluding the session, the comeditator should suggest that the subject direct attention to the parts of the body resting against the bed (or whatever), make a fist with the nearest hand, and open his or her eyes when he or she wishes. If the person is able, he or she should rest a few moments and get up slowly, with the assistant staying nearby to maintain the mood and to provide assistance. This is important because when blood pressure drops, a sudden change in position may cause dizziness. No more than five to ten minutes are necessary for stabilization.

Actually, comeditation is similar to processes used for centuries by nurses with patients in pain. Generations of young girls have watched older women tell the laboring mother to take a deep breath and count. The Lamaze and Leboyer methods of birthing incorporate this ancient practice of conscious breathing in their preparation for natural infant delivery. Stress reduction and relaxation techniques involve having the patient consciously relax each part of the body, then a distraction routine, which is usually related to breathing, follows. Babies and the very old sometimes lull themselves to sleep by a moanlike "Ah-hh" sound as a means of natural comfort. Chorus singing, chanting, and litanies, which can only be done on exhalation, have been a part of almost every tradition throughout history. Principles of sound sharing begin in our earliest days when a parent sways the crying infant while singing a fast ditty, slowly reducing the tempo, in response to the child's decreasing agitation, until the baby is sleeping to a lullaby. Isn't it natural that the same kind of sharing accompany the dying process as well?

In comeditation, the helper not only acts as a guide, but the relationship provides reassurance that seems to complement the subject's own energy. The important difference between comeditation and other forms of relaxation therapy is that the subject does have companionship, but the subject is actually the leader. The helper must be able to accept a very rapid, medium, or very slow breathing rate by the subject. However, the helper knows that an increase in respiration means that the subject is disturbed so that certain words should be used to nullify distractions. The helper also knows that a slowed respiration indicates that the subject is experiencing reduced anxiety and using available air more efficiently. Persons not getting enough oxygen by holding their breath will pass out and breathe involuntarily if the body is capable of breathing.

If death can be turned away, then we should use our resources to maintain precious life while encouraging the patient to adjust to changing circumstances and trials garnered with hope. However, we also must acknowledge that efforts to sustain a life may, at times, be counterproductive. If we can recognize that the patient will inevitably die, we owe that person appropriate caregiving. Caregiving should be directed toward support of the person; that is, the patient's comfort needs, his efforts to complete unfinished business, the moods associated with contemplating one's own death, and fears that might be confronted when the body's metabolism causes hallucinations that seem more real than the activities surrounding him. Participating in the reduction of effort is appropriate.

Toxic conditions are a part of the dying process. Although mental confusion is a symptom of metabolic disturbance, a quiet coma state may simply signify a diminished physical awareness. While toxicity may provide a pathway into the inner consciousness, experience suggests that the passageway contains risks. Otherwise, literature about the afterlife would contain only stories of heaven, and none of our patients would cry out from frightening dreams. As Mohammed said, "This is not why I came," so can our patients with support and guidance.

Discomforts may be abated with appropriate medication and relaxation training. One subject said, "I got a tingling in my arms and hands which suggested to me that each of my cells was present and listening too. Through co-meditation I discovered that pain is actually a concentration of feeling that can be scattered." The meditator can allow this focus to disperse by letting the pain extend outward until these feelings seem to flow in waves to the fingers and toes. A visualization may help the person work with specific pain; another manner may help the subject confront the fear in the form of a lucid dream; whereas those who are ready may approach their own transition especially reinforced by a nearby companion.

We were most gratified five years ago when our first joint patient provided evidence that we had successfully taught a nonmeditator to achieve a state of relaxation and serenity as he was dying. Our elation was tempered by the full story told by the patient's wife on our bereavement call. She had been with her husband feeling that, even as he died, they had been joined in a special energy bond. She felt peaceful as she went to the nurse's station to say that their vigilance was over and to phone the news to her family. When she returned, she was not allowed in the room because the staff was conducting a code-call resuscitation effort on her husband's body, which continued nearly an hour. The staff could not understand that their actions were the source of bitter memories for her rather than a demonstration of their care.

People trained strictly in the scientific system, in which proof requires verifiable documentation, accept only the known as real. Not much differently, those who claim their personal health habits to be "holistic," linking the power of one's mind with physical well-being, usually equate wholeness with health. Advocates of either frequently see the acceptance of death as a defeat rather than an inevitable adjustment.

It reminds us of the tale about a loved one who, on dying, was restrained on a cot in a room with barred windows and a locked door. The protector placed himself, spread-eagle fashion, across the door, shouting, "Don't you dare leave me. I love you, I cannot get along without you! You cannot leave!" But there was no choice. The essential essence of the loved one slid out, across the room, between the legs of the hysterical other, and disappeared.

Another couple also recognized the inevitability of one partner's death. The stronger one said, "I don't want you to go, I shall miss you. But if you must leave me, I will go with you to the airport up to your plane so you know I am there as you fade from my sight." We would like everyone to be able to be like this latter couple when parting is necessary. That is why we teach co-meditation in thanatology.

References

Benson, H. 1975. *The Relaxation Response.* New York: Avon Publishers.

Boerstler, R.W. 1982. *Letting Go: A Holistic and Meditative Approach to Living and Dying.* Watertown, Mass.: Associates in Thanatology.

Frankl, V. 1963. *Man's Search for Meaning.* New York: Pocket Books.

Govinda, A.L. 1976. *Creative Meditation and Multi-Dimensional Consciousness.* Wheaton, Ill.: Theosophical Publishing House.

Kübler-Ross, E. 1969. *On Death and Dying.* New York: Macmillan.

Maslow, A.H. 1954. *Motivation and Personality.* New York: Harper and Row.

Melzack, R., and P. Wall. 1982. *The Challenge of Pain.* New York: Basic Books.

Selye, H. 1956. *The Stress of Life.* New York: McGraw-Hill. (Rev. ed., 1976).

9

Creating and Therapeutically Utilizing Anticipatory Grief in Survivors of Sudden Death

Mary Elizabeth Mancini

G rief is an expected response whenever there is a significant loss. In the anticipation of a future loss, a form of normal grief can occur. This has been termed "anticipatory grief." While the threat of loss usually elicits feelings of sadness, depression, anger, and separation anxiety, this struggling to accept the reality of the impending trauma has been considered relatively easier than trying to cope with the trauma afterward when the loss is unexpected (Rando, 1984).

Fulton and Fulton (1971) noted that anticipatory grief allows for absorbing the reality of the loss gradually over time. The family has time to finish any "unfinished business" and resolve past conflicts. They can begin to change their assumptions about their life and relationships, and make plans for the future without the terminally ill person. In 1976, Lebow described six adaptational tasks that family members experiencing the impending death of a loved one must address during the process of anticipatory grieving: remaining involved with the patient, remaining separate from the patient, adapting suitably to role changes, bearing the affects of grief, coming to terms with the reality of the impending loss, and saying goodbye. Specific treatment goals and therapeutic interventions have been recommended by numerous practitioners on how to accomplish these tasks.

The basic tenets of anticipatory grief, however, do not in any way attempt to postulate that the use of the process will ameliorate the expected loss *per se*. Rando (1984), in her review of anticipatory grief, states that recent research studies demonstrate that grief following anticipated loss is no less painful than that which follows unanticipated loss. Rather, because there has been some time for preparation, the anticipated death makes less of an assault on the mourner's adaptive capacities than the unanticipated death, which more seriously compromises recovery. Rando further states that interventions based on the principle of anticipatory grief can prevent problems in mourning from developing initially; while later interventions can only try to remedy difficulties that have already occurred.

Death in the Emergency Department: A Different Event

All the recommendations and clinical interventions that have been put forth in relation to anticipatory grief have been predicated on the assumption that there is a prolonged time period to prepare the family for and assist them through the death of the terminally ill patient. There is also an implied presence of a consistent, well-trained team of caregivers who have the time and opportunity to develop a rapport with the family and assist them through the dying process. This type of comprehensive care is possible for the hospitalized patient and those with known or chronic illnesses. However, for one population, there is frequently little time for preparation or establishment of a relationship with caregivers.

For the family of sudden death victims, the loss of the loved one is unexpected and occurs without warning. Soreff (1979) listed three features he felt distinguished a patient's death in the emergency department from an expiration in the in-patient hospital setting. The major difference relates to the fact that death in the emergency department occurs without warning. In the case of the hospitalized patient, that patient, the family, and the staff usually anticipate the death and attempt to prepare for it. The second difference is seen in the relationships with caregivers. In the event of a sudden death, the patient and family rarely know the staff before the event. In contrast, the hospitalized patient and family have developed some relationship with the staff. Finally, Soreff sees the emergency department death as more likely to be the first time medical students, house officers, and nursing students encounter the loss of a patient. For these three reasons, he feels that it is mandatory to prepare the staff to deal effectively with the unexpected, sudden death. This is necessary not only for the family's benefit, but for the well-being of the staff as well.

Willis (1977) has predicted that as the environment of emergency departments become more humane and greater sensitivity to bereaved families is fostered, the bereaved family's restoration to "wholeness" will be expedited. The manner in which the health care staff meets and deals with the patient's family will become an integral factor in that family's ability to deal with the crisis at hand. Despite the fact that sudden death, by its very nature, is unexpected, there are some specific administrative issues that can be addressed and clinical techniques that health care providers can develop that maximize the benefits of anticipatory grief for the family of sudden death victims.

Administrative Issues

Caregivers become frustrated and dissatisfied when they are in unfamiliar or uncomfortable situations. Knowledge, experience, and support can decrease the likelihood of inappropriate communication patterns with patients and families. This is as true in the emergency department as on any in-patient floor.

An example of problems that develop due to the caregiver's own issues can be seen in the case of the physician who is uncomfortable with informing family members of a patient's death following a motor vehicle accident. If the physician is distressed by giving this information and feels that as few of the facts as possible should be given to the family in order to avoid the possibility of a lawsuit, the information provided may be given in a quick and brusque manner. The physician may then justify his or her actions as being the kindest way of presenting such terrible news. In reality, however, this is usually an attempt to avoid an anxiety-provoking situation.

Such an approach may actually inflate the family's sense of grief and increase their problems with adjustment. By neglecting to provide important data as to the thoroughness of the resuscitation attempts, the physician may promote the family's feeling that not everything was done for the deceased. They may then start to see the death as preventable rather than inevitable. Of course, this would have a profoundly negative impact on their grief. To avoid such unnecessary problems, there should be specific, written policies and procedures to provide guidelines to assist caregivers in communicating therapeutically with the families of sudden death victims. The basic orientation time of all personnel ought to be increased to include time to address the concepts of personal death awareness, death and dying, as well as grief and bereavement. There must be practical information and training provided to caregivers to teach them the skills of delivering bad news, facilitating healthy grief, preparing the body for viewing, and assisting the family during viewing the body of the sudden death victim.

Inconsistency in contacting families of acutely ill patients can have the adverse consequences of having a negative impact on relatives, as well as inducing stress in emergency department staff. Each hospital should have a policy on what information is to be provided, along with a procedure describing the techniques of notifying family members of sudden death victims. These need to address specific interventions with the family in order to facilitate consistency, promote clarity, prevent fears and fantasies, diminish misunderstandings, avoid the family's reckless driving to the hospital, and decrease feelings of helplessness (Robinson, 1982). Such procedures should contain carefully delineated recommendations similar to those that have been identified by Robinson. For example, he suggests that when discussing the patient's status, it is best if the caregiver avoids descriptive extremes such as precise vital signs or broad statements and nondescript phrases. Specific comments that can gauge realistic hope or potential danger should be used. Fears and fantasies can be minimized by describing the noninjured body parts. If it is truthful, the caregiver might state that the patient is "moving his arms and legs" or has a "calm face." Potential misunderstandings also may be prevented by asking for feedback from the family. Immediate corrections can be given if the feedback is inaccurate. There is a need to specifically emphasize caution to prevent reckless driving. The caregiver should advise the family member to get assistance with driving to the hospital. The family member can be made to feel helpful at this time of crisis. For instance, the caregiver can elicit from him or her a baseline medical history of the patient. This can assist in diminishing the feelings of helplessness that occur in the event of unexpected illness or trauma.

Administratively, it is imperative that there be adequate staffing in areas likely to receive sudden death victims. Staffing should be at that level that allows the caregivers involved in resuscitations time to meet with and work with families of the victims. This will enhance the family's sense of continuity of care by providing them access to the patient's direct care providers. These are the individuals who can answer specific questions about the care the patient received. By having the staff meet with the family, it also allows the staff to experience a much needed, but often missing, sense of follow-through and closure. This is an important aspect of job satisfaction and will help to prevent feelings of frustration and burnout among the staff.

The staff in an emergency department must view the unit of care as including both the patient *and* the family. Consequently, there must be adequate staff to provide for the emotional, psychological, and spiritual needs of the family as well as of the patient. If a caregiver feels that he or she has provided the very best care possible to the patient, and has supported the family in such a way that the family has been helped to understand and to start to accept the patient's death, then that caregiver has no need to feel a sense of failure. The caregiver's interventions can be seen as successful, even in the face of the patient's death.

There are other issues that administrators must consider in order to facilitate the "care of the caregiver." According to Rando (1984), the primary issue is one of support. There needs to be clear delineation of all expectations and job responsibilities. There should be training and education appropriate to the individual's roles and responsibilities, with ongoing opportunities for continuing education. Immediate, specific, nonjudgmental, and respectful feedback—both positive and negative—must be provided to the staff. The physical environment must provide the necessary space to perform appropriately the duties of the job as well as to debrief what happens on the job. Organizations must also provide support for caregivers in high stress areas through policies, such as rotating days off and allowing transfers when necessary, and through developing procedures for taking time off without requiring the caregiver to lie about being ill or experience guilt or retribution.

Clinical Issues

Historically, the clinical techniques of promoting anticipatory grief have been used in cases where there are weeks, perhaps months, to prepare the family for an expected death. However, even a few minutes can be used quite effectively to enable family members of a sudden death victim to have the time to start to deal with the unexpected event they are about to confront. In a situation involving sudden death, the goals of the caregiver's interactions and communication should be (1) to provide as much time as possible for family members to internalize the gravity of the situation; (2) to provide information in a logical and sequential manner; and (3) to assist the family in starting to accept and to cope with the finality of the situation.

There are five basic contact points that arise during the time in which the caregivers interact with the family of sudden death victims: initial notification, meeting the family, providing information, viewing the body, and concluding. These areas can be addressed in light of the components of anticipatory grief.

The telephone is the caregiver's first contact with the family and can serve as a treatment intervention. To decrease the caregiver's stress when contacting family members, Robinson (1982) has developed a telephone notification checklist. This checklist provides the caregiver with an outline of how to proceed while communicating with the family. Such a checklist can provide examples of how to elicit information from the family while initially preparing them for the information they are about to receive. Soreff (1979) recommends that during any telephone contact the staff first identify themselves. Whenever possible, the staff should avoid informing the family of the death over the telephone. Rather, the caregiver should attempt to have the family come to the emergency department and should suggest that a friend drive the family member there. Using the proper techniques, the caregiver can identify the patient, secure valuable information, locate the family, and have the family arrive at the emergency department without incident, while at the same time start the family's preparation for the crisis they are about to face.

It is imperative that an identified, well-trained person meets the family on their arrival in the emergency department. They should be brought to an isolated, quiet area away from the rest of the visitors. Immediate information will have to be provided to them related to the circumstances of the injury or illness, the condition of the patient, what interventions have been done, and what can be expected in the immediate future. This information needs to be presented in a factual and honest manner. Well-meaning remarks such as "everything will be all right" will only serve to make the reality more difficult to accept at a later point. It is the task of the caregiver to provide an honest appraisal as to expected outcome without removing all hope, if indeed hope is warranted. As Hogshead (1976) suggested in his guidelines for communicating with terminally ill patients, above all else caregivers must not say anything that is not true, for that would be the cruelest blow of all.

One of the basic concepts of anticipatory grief is that the family will have time to prepare for the ultimate death: time to adjust and orient themselves to the expected expiration. In the case of sudden death, there is no expectation of the event. Nevertheless, the use of even the few moments before announcing the death of a family member can be useful in the long-term acceptance of the death. This can be achieved by providing information to the family in small pieces. The caregiver may well know that the resuscitation effort is almost complete and that the situation is indeed hopeless. Yet, this information can be provided to the family in small incremental steps during two to three contacts over fifteen minutes. For example, in the first contact the caregiver can provide all the information discussed above, but would leave the family with the fact that "the doctors are doing everything they can." At this point, the family should have a hospital support person, not directly involved in the situation, who can stay with them. This person can reinforce the gravity of the situation and help the family start to articulate the possibility that the patient may die. Unrealistic feelings of guilt or responsibility can be corrected by this support person. On the second visit, a few minutes later, the caregiver can then present the fact that things are looking worse, that nothing appears to be working. The caregiver could also emphasize the fact that the patient is unconscious, feels no pain or whatever else would be truthful to say at this point. The family would now start to focus in on the possibility of imminent death. They might still harbor feelings of hope, but the reality of the death will come more into consciousness. Now, they will usually articulate requests for those things or persons they need for support; for example, a priest, another family member, or religious contact for the patient such as the Sacraments of the Sick. The support person can see that these things are provided. The family's desire to see the patient in an uncontrolled environment can also be handled by presenting the fact that "the doctors need to be with him now." The family will then be better prepared for having the caregiver return a few minutes later to provide the information that the patient has indeed died.

Robinson (1981) made specific recommendations on how to inform the family of the sudden death of a loved one. He believes that there are distinct strategies for preparing and delivering the news of death. He recommends that the caregiver provide an informative, chronologically ordered account of events leading up to and including the death. This information should be delivered only after the caregiver has taken the time to review all the facts. This makes the task less stressful to the caregiver and, as a result, makes it less likely that the news will elicit unnecessary confusion in the survivors.

In her work on death and dying, Kübler-Ross (1969) emphasized that, especially in cases of sudden death, if a body is not viewed it may take years longer for the survivors to complete their grief because it is difficult to realize the loved one is truly dead. In cases of sudden death, there are those caregivers who feel that they are protecting the survivors by preventing them from viewing the body in a state of disarray due to mutilation or the effects of resuscitation. This is a serious misconception, and when caregivers act on this erroneous belief, they can actually impede the requisite grief of the family and predispose them to significant long-term problems in coping with their grief.

Families are usually ill-prepared for sudden death and are unsure whether or not they should view the body. As a result, the caregiver must not wait for the family members to express a desire to see the body, for frequently they will be reluctant to ask. To assist the survivors, it is important that the caregiver verbalize permission for them to see the body if they wish. Along with this, the caregiver should offer to accompany the survivors to view the body. Some grievers will be adamant in their refusal. In these cases, the caregiver must make a professional judgment as to how much to encourage the viewing of the body. Sometimes it helps to ask the family again after a few minutes or to mention something like "I was just in with your father's body and . . .", saying something appropriate about what was seen. This gives evidence of the caregiver's acceptance of the body, helps the family acknowledge the death, and gives them permission to view the body. However, no one should be forced to view the body. The objective is to give those who are hesitant every opportunity and all the support they need to make this decision (Schultz, 1980).

Schultz described several specific steps that the caregiver can take in assisting the family to view the body. First, she recommends that the caregiver show acceptance of the body by touching it and demonstrating that it is acceptable to be in contact with it. This gives the grievers permission to touch, hold, and talk to the loved one. If indeed the body is mutilated, it will still be important for the family to see as much of it as possible. In preparation, the mutilated body parts should be covered and the other parts cleaned as much as possible and/or allowable according to medical examiner guidelines. The body should be positioned as naturally as it can be, with IV tubes and other evidences of the rescue attempt removed. The immediate environment should be straightened out as much as possible as well; for example, blood cleaned off the floor and life-sustaining equipment taken away from the body on the table. The family must first be prepared for what they are going to see. Shultz recommends that the caregiver find a portion of the body that can be shown, a part that can be touched. Family members who view the mutilated body in a controlled situation, when the caregiver has had time to prepare and support them for what they will see, are more likely to accept the sudden death as a reality.

Throughout the entire experience, caregivers should support the ventilation of feelings of grief on the parts of the family members. It will not be unusual to witness varying intensities of responses such as shock, numbness, confusion, anger, tears, disbelief, sadness, hysteria, mechanical action, or quiet withdrawal. Family members should not be restrained from expressing any of these reactions, no matter how intense, unless they appear to be a real danger to themselves or others.

Once the family has viewed the body and all necessary papers have been signed, it is time for a formal concluding process. The caregiver should review what will happen to the body, how to contact a funeral home, and should give specifics about the autopsy if there will be one. Usually, the family is then unsure if they should go. It means leaving their loved one behind and accepting that the loved one will not be going home with them. The family needs permission to leave. It may be necessary to take the family to the door of the hospital, reminding them that it is all right to call back later if there are any questions that need to be answered.

Conclusion

In conclusion, situations involving sudden death may not provide a prolonged time span in which to prepare the family for the loss of their loved one. Yet, with proper administrative supports and clinical procedures and techniques, the concept of anticipatory grief can be integrated into the care of both the survivors of sudden death and the caregivers. With these concepts in mind, caregivers can feel a sense of personal support and professional achievement even in the face of a patient's death, and the chances of early and successful completion of the family's grief will be maximized. This is indeed the goal of our interventions.

References

Fulton, R., and J. Fulton. 1971. A Psychosocial Aspect of Terminal Care: Anticipatory Grief. *Omega* 2:91–99.

Hogshead, H.P. 1976. The Art of Delivering Bad News. *Journal of the Florida Medical Association* 63:807.

Kübler-Ross, E. 1969. *On Death and Dying*. New York: Macmillan.

Lebow, G.H. 1976. Facilitating Adaptation in Anticipatory Mourning. *Social Casework* 57:458–465.

Rando, T.A. 1984. *Grief, Dying, and Death: Clinical Interventions for Caregivers*. Champaign, Ill.: Research Press.

Robinson, M.A. 1981. Informing the Family of Sudden Death. *American Family Physician* 23:115–118.

Robinson, M.A. 1982. Telephone Notification of Relatives of Emergency and Critical Care Patients. *Annals of Emergency Medicine* 11:616–618.

Schultz, C. 1980. Sudden Death Crisis: Prehospital and in the Emergency Department. *Journal of Emergency Nursing* May/June:46–50.

Soreff, M. 1979. Sudden Death in the Emergency Department: A Comprehensive Approach for Families, Emergency Medical Technicians, and Emergency Department Staff. *Critical Care Medicine* 7:321–323.

Willis, R.W. 1977. Bereavement Management in the Emergency Department. *Journal of Emergency Nursing* March/April:35–39.

Part IV
Developmental Issues in Anticipatory Grief

10

Anticipatory Grief: Strategies for the Classroom

Janice DeFrances Van Dexter

> One learns to accept the fact that no permanent return is possible to an old form of relationship; more deeply still, that there is no holding of a relationship to a single form. This is not tragedy but part of the ever-recurrent miracle of life and growth All living relationships are in process of change, of expansion, and must perpetually be building themselves new forms.
> —Anne Morrow Lindbergh, *Gift from the Sea*, p. 75

It is important to realize the impact that a teacher has on students. The teacher is not solely a technician, imparting information as a means to an end but is also an affective educator, helping the child or youth live a better life in this world. A teacher is responsible for teaching socialization skills, concepts relevant to and concerning life, and empathy to the young. Through various means of instruction and discussion, a teacher can help students become aware of the many facets of life and death—the physical, the emotional, the social, and the spiritual.

Society has a strange way of telling its children about life. Death is excluded. We think that by omission we can let children keep their innocence of life. In fact, we are keeping them from truly understanding life. Statistics indicate that one out of every six children will lose one parent through death before they reach age eighteen. A teacher must provide support and guidance for that child. When a parent or family member is suffering from a terminal illness, the teacher must deal with the child's anticipation of loss and his passage through various stages of denial, anger, and acceptance.

In this age of rapid change, educational needs are greater than ever, especially in dealing with loss. Children differ in behavior and development. They understand at different levels and have diverse perspectives, depending on their experience, environment, maturity, level of intellectual ability, coping capacity, and so forth. All children experience loss and grief. School is their natural habitat outside of the home and usually becomes the focus of displacement. Consequently, as a teacher, it is imperative to be able to recognize the signals of loss and the need for support and reassurance during the tumultuous time when the child is confronted with illness and death. His teacher needs to help him in his struggle to understand life by explaining death. Death education is crucial in providing children with the resources to live life more fully.

The educator is afforded many teachable moments with the child that pertain to life and death. It is critical to use these moments to help the child learn about death, whether for the future or to cope with it in the present. Therefore, death education must be introduced as part of the curriculum from kindergarten through high school. Simple lessons involving nature allow for a natural learning environment to discuss loss or the anticipation of loss.

This chapter is of extreme importance. Its subject is often omitted in textbooks on development or education. Frequently, it is hidden under the pretense that the child will not understand, whereas it is really the adult who cannot deal with the discussion. I hope to provide the insight and resources that will allow the educator to use his or her unique role and opportunity to deal therapeutically with the child experiencing anticipatory grief.

Although written specifically for those who interact with children in the educational setting, this chapter provides practical techniques for all who deal with the child experiencing anticipatory grief, whether in school (for example, the classroom teacher, guidance counselor, psychologist, or school nurse) or outside of school (for example, the cleric, health care provider, or recreational leader). The objectives are to (1) define anticipatory grief; (2) identify the variables influencing the child's anticipatory grief; (3) delineate the symptoms indicative of grief; (4) examine the developmental stages of bereavement; and (5) explore a variety of clinical issues and therapeutic strategies associated with treatment interventions in anticipatory grief.

Anticipatory Grief: A Definition

What is anticipatory grief? Basically, it is the process of normal mourning that occurs in anticipation of death and its consequences. Lebow (1976) defines it as "the total set of cognitive, affective, cultural and social reactions to expected death felt by the patient and family" (p. 459). The diagnosis of terminal illness abruptly confronts the child and his family with a crisis: the crisis of knowledge of death. In the face of this knowledge, there are adaptational tasks for the entire family that must be addressed.

It is important for the educator to understand the problems that arise while living with a chronically ill person: the remissions and relapses; the lengthened periods of anticipatory grief; increased financial, social, physical, and emotional pressures; long-term family disruption; progressive decline of the patient, with consequential myriad emotional responses by the family members;

longer periods of uncertainty; intensive treatment regimens and their side effects; and dilemmas about decision making and treatment choices (Rando, 1984, p. 209). With some appreciation of this list of problems, the educator can help the child recognize the many factors involved. The child also needs some understanding of the different feelings that the dying person is undergoing. Everyone is human and experiencing diverse emotions at different times. The terminal illness and its effect on the dying person will affect the entire family, each member in idiosyncratic ways.

It is a difficult task not only to support and comfort the dying patient but also to struggle to find ways to continue to live with him or her as fully as possible until death. There are many different feelings that the child experiences during the time of his loved one's illness. He undergoes feelings of helplessness, ambivalence, guilt, anger, and sadness, among others. It is a strenuous time for the child as well as for the adults involved. The child needs to understand that not only is he grieving the loved one but he is also grieving the loss of part of himself and the changes that will ensue. This is a difficult concept for an adult to comprehend, imagine how much more difficult for a child.

Variables That Influence the Child's Ability to Deal with Anticipatory Grief

Many major variables contribute to the grief experience. The educator must be aware of these in order to allow for a wide latitude in the differences in grief expression. Each child responds idiosyncratically according to such variables. Some of these are: age, development, time of loss, previous losses, support, ethnic background, self-esteem, self-worth, sex role socialization, personality differences, coping abilities, family solidarity and adjustment, family coping abilities, religion, causes and circumstances of the loss or illness, how the child is told, family allowance for grieving, and the child's ability to mourn and deal effectively with the loss (Rando, 1984).

There are also inhibitors in dealing with anticipatory grief, such as the parent or adult's inability to mourn, the lack of a caring environment for the child, confusion regarding the illness, ambivalence toward the dying person, the child's inability to put feelings into words, instability within the family unit, adolescent issues that exacerbate normal conflicts, learning problems, emotional problems, and intellectual limitations such as in the case of mental retardation (Rando, 1984). A child's resources of support and care are also affected by geographical location and the nuclear family's closeness.

A child's home environment and upbringing will bear most significantly on his ability to cope. If the child comes from a home that deals with loss openly and allows him to be part of it, he will be better able to cope. However, if a child is denied his right to grieve and is not included in the significant events with his loved one and his or her impending death, he will have more difficulty with the loss. A teacher may be able to help that child understand why he is being excluded by explaining that people deal with loss differently and then exploring some of the ways that they do so. A child's grief is strongly influenced by his family, and he has fewer resources than the adult. If he lacks support for his grief at home, his teacher may be the only one to provide it as well as to give the opportunity for legitimization and expression of grief.

A teacher may well have to consider becoming an active advocate of the child with the family and to educate the family about the child's needs at this time. Many families will reconsider their exclusion of children if they have the negative consequences explained by a caring professional, and if they have been helped to find a way to deal with explaining the situation to the child and have been supported in their ongoing attempts to assist him in coping with it.

The style of death today is such that it often takes longer for an individual to accept the death. In the past, death was closer in the sense that more people died at home, not in institutions. Also, wakes and viewings were held at home, not in funeral parlors. A child was exposed to death at an early age. Today, sadly, this exposure to death, in an environment of openness and familiarity, as well as love, is sadly missing. Progress has robbed children of these benefits that allowed them to integrate death more naturally into their lives.

As a result of these social changes, a child or adolescent may suffer his first experience of death and loss with no clear understanding and no acknowledgment of the feelings and hurt involved. This became very clear to me while teaching undergraduates. I gave them an assignment to write a timeline of their life up to the present, noting eventful experiences that they felt had a major impact on their lives and that would influence their own teaching in the future. Inevitably, the majority of the students listed their first experience with losing a loved one, a grandparent or parent, as a major turning point and a stressful time. Their understanding of how they had dealt with that loss and how they would in turn use this experience to enhance their lives will be crucial in their teaching and communication with their students when they become teachers. Interestingly enough, until that moment, many of them had not fully seen the importance of death in their lives and on their teaching.

Past successful experiences with loss and having the ability to discuss uncertainties and feelings offer positive predictions of the child's or adult's ability to cope successfully with new loss. Another factor is the time at which a recurrence of loss in a child's or adult's life transpires. If there has been insufficient time to heal from a previous loss, another shock to the system will cause more reverberations with which the mourner must deal. Although grief has no specific time table, it is clear that we all require an adequate amount of time to work out our grief. Incomplete grief leads to serious problems. It is not always the symptom but sometimes the intensity that will distinguish a child who is dealing successfully with grief from one who is not.

Symptoms Indicative of Grief

When a child or adolescent suffers a loss, his teacher and caregiver, must be able to notice the symptoms of grief. Because of more limited verbal skills, these are usually manifested through the child's behavior rather than by direct discourse. They include, among others, (1) changes from previous behaviors; (2) dropping grades; (3) a supposed lack of caring; (4) acting out, either by aggressive behavior or by being quiet and withdrawn; (5) lack of appetite; (6) depression; and (7) suicidal ideation. A teacher should be on the lookout for such symptoms. These signals should not be disregarded. If the teacher does not know how to handle them, he or she should learn to do so or at least to talk with someone who can help the child. The teacher can immediately refer the child for therapeutic services and alert the family and school personnel if there is any type of suicidal ideation. Signs of depression that can precipitate suicidal behavior, as well as indicate unresolved grief, might include (1) school truancy; (2) exaggerated or extended apathy, boredom, or inactivity; (3) subtle signs of self-destructive behavior, such as carelessness and accident proneness; (4) loss of appetite or excessive eating; (5) withdrawal from peer contact and from previously enjoyed activities; (6) academic decline; (7) recent hostile behavior, for example, arguments with parents or unruly behavior in school; and (8) substance abuse, for example, drugs and alcohol.

Developmental Issues

It is important to recognize the various stages a child may traverse during this period of bereavement. According to Kübler-Ross (1969), there are five stages that an individual passes before a death: denial, anger, bargaining, depression, and acceptance. These can be seen as well in anticipatory grief.

The time immediately after a fatal diagnosis is very critical. There are feelings of resentment, shock, anxiety, despair, and depression. A child can swing back and forth in these stages. There is not a specific timeline and children will vary in their abilities to reach the acceptance stage. In order to know how to be helpful to the child, a teacher must look at the child's framework and history of previous losses and also at his ability to deal with stress and to express his anger, sadness, and other emotions. Children grieve according to their social, developmental, and emotional context, and a child must not be denied his right to mourn in his particular way as long as it is not destructive to him or others.

Children and adolescents manifest their grief in different ways. Raphael (1983) speaks about the child resting from grief and carrying on happily with daily routines at some times, while at other times exhibiting periods of very intense emotional upset.

The grief expressed by four-to-five-month-old to two-and-one-half-year-old children is nonspecific: on-going distress in reaction to loss. The child responds to the absence of the person, especially the maternal figure. From two to five years of age, the child is bewildered, exhibits regressive behavior such as clinging and being demanding. The child feels that he will be deserted and needs to express such feelings.

From five to eight years old, there is a more cognitive understanding of the loss. At this age, the child may hide his feelings. There is a great fear of loss of control, and even though the child may grieve and privately cry deeply, there may be no overt behavior indicative of grief. The child during this age may fantasize that the dying person will not die or that this is a dream and not true. During this age, the child may try to overcompensate because he feels different from his peers.

From eight to twelve years old there is shock and denial. In terminal illness, this is very intense during the period around the diagnosis. The child is threatened by the idea of mortality now. He may resist communicating with adults. He may also try to act grown-up in an attempt to conquer the pain and sorrow of his loss and helplessness. Often, in this age group, grief goes unnoticed, especially if the child tends not to act out grief, but withdraws until, in time, he can acknowledge his sorrow and grieve.

With teenagers, the ongoing tasks of adolescence may preclude mourning from being successfully completed. The adolescent may have been rebellious and may have been trying to gain his independence when his parent was diagnosed with the terminal illness. This can activate guilt and/or resentment. The adolescent is going through typical developmental tasks, as well as emotions, which serve to heighten the anticipatory grief. He is overconcerned with the acceptance of peers and his responses to others. He may lack the knowledge of social expectations and feel alien to adults. Like adults, adolescents can conceive of the future effects of death and envision the absence of the loved one from important events to come. When an adolescent cannot grieve directly, he may exhibit it through exaggerated pseudo-adult behaviors: identification with the dying person; depression and withdrawal; sexual acting out; and care-eliciting behaviors designed not only to secure care but to release tension, self-punish, and sometimes replace the dying person (Raphael, 1983).

Treatment Interventions in Anticipatory Grief

Fulton (1967) states that the wise management of grief in children (which is equally true for adults) revolves around two major factors: (1) the encouragement and facilitation of the normal mourning process, and (2) the prevention of delayed or distorted grief responses.

This is an extremely fragile, perplexing, and insecure time. The child needs reassurance that he is loved, that he is not at fault. He may think he is being punished for being bad and that others are going to leave him. He may be fearful that he too will die soon. It is a time when a teacher can provide extra tender loving care which the child needs but may not receive from bereaved family members. I have yet to see anyone who has suffered from too much caring. If anything, we do not give enough. In the classroom, a teacher can give the child the structure and sense of control he needs, especially since the other part of his life is unsettled. The teacher should continue to enforce discipline and appropriate limits. The child will sense the caring. The teacher can provide time to talk in a comfortable setting. Day-to-day routines aid in the process of adjustment. School is the child's work.

It is important to recognize and help the child recognize that different things constitute losses. Watching a loved one die is a very difficult task. It is difficult for the child to understand the many changes he will undergo in anticipatory grief, such as when a parent can no longer walk, or a friend cannot come out to play, or he cannot have his favorite meal with his father every week. Often, individuals tend to try to hold on to the past and fight the changes.

A teacher can help the child see that people experience their grief at different times and levels of intensity. Day-to-day problems may remain unresolved when a family member is terminally ill. Parents may have trouble caring for the other family members when another one is dying. Often, they are preoccupied with the dying family member and may be exhausted, feel helpless, angry, and so forth. They may displace these negative feelings onto the child.

In terminal illness, the losses occur unpredictably in the patient and family. As the illness progresses, it will exact great energy from all involved. The child will experience sadness, anguish, confusion, and pain over these losses. A teacher can help the child identify his feelings, thereby helping to lessen his fear. He or she can talk with the child about letting his grief out a little at a time and identify the intense feelings he is experiencing and let him know that this is normal. The teacher can help the child understand that it is difficult for the child and he will feel hurt because he loves the dying person very much. Certain events will trigger off volatile and/or negative emotions. A teacher can help the child talk about his anger and disappointment, and have the child acknowledge the negative, without overlooking the positive.

The world as the child knows it has been irreparably altered. This is one of the most difficult things to accept. Changes will continue as the illness progresses, and the child must learn to cope with these changes. Often, the child may deny the illness or role changes within the family. He may put on a facade as if nothing has changed or is different, but this denial is a means of numbing him until he can deal realistically with the fact. If denial continues, there is a problem that could become pathological, and the child will need professional psychological help to confront this denial.

When a terminally ill individual cannot fulfill assigned roles and expectations within the family, there is a shift in the homostatic balance of the family.

The entire energy of the family is directed toward reestablishing balance in the system. Many unique problems may arise in the family coping with a dying family member. Disruption starts with the diagnosis and increases with the demands for family adaptation and change, which causes stress. Dealing with the death of a loved one is difficult, moreso because it is coupled with the loss of the family as it was. Remissions and relapses of the illness may bring about shifts in the feelings children and adults experience. The child must adapt to a different role as well as to the dying person's different role.

The family orients its care toward the patient, and the child often feels left out. There are role changes within the family. Often, roles are reassigned as when a father is ill and the uncle takes the son to a baseball game. The child may feel he is betraying his father by his allegiance to his uncle. He needs to be encouraged and reassured that this is okay and is not a reflection of his lack of love or loyalty to his ill father. The changes will be constant and will differ depending on the fluctuation of the illness and needs.

The family unit is a system, with each member interacting within the dynamics of this system. Each experience, every feeling, has a ripple effect on each member. Like pebbles being thrown into a pond, even the smallest can cause a ripple effect that often one cannot even see. As the family undergoes the emotional reactions that lead to increased awareness that the person is dying, each family member must learn how to live with the dying person until they have to say goodbye. There is much anxiety because of the unknown that surrounds all aspects of the illness. Individuals feel helpless. Neither the child nor the adult can change the diagnosis. No matter how much the child bargains or sacrifices in his prayers or acts—for example, giving away his prized toys to others in exchange for his mother to become healthy again—the dying person is not given a reprieve.

The child must become involved in the treatment to whatever extent possible, even if it is painful, in order to allow for finishing unfinished business and to provide him with the critical opportunity to continue to demonstrate care for the loved one. This must be done with consideration as to what degree of involvement the child can tolerate in the loved one's illness. It will help to have the child identify what he would like to do for his dying loved one and then to support him in doing it (if it is appropriate). This will be extremely significant in the ultimate resolution of his grief.

Family members experience anger, guilt, and ambivalence. Anger and hostility are frequent concomitants of terminal illness for everyone involved. Everyone gets drained both physically and emotionally. There is anger if the dying patient did not take care of him or herself, or if the illness was self-inflicted. When the child wishes someone dead (a common childhood response to frustration or anger) and then finds out that the person is dying, he will feel that his death wish was the cause of the illness. The child will feel a strong sense of guilt for this and for other feelings that are normal in those experiencing the terminal illness of a loved one. He may feel he has betrayed his loved one if he wishes he could go out and play and not have to deal with the illness or problems. The child may experience survivor guilt, especially when a sibling is dying, or may experience guilt for being healthy. He may need help and permission to forgive himself, or he may need to be provided with constructive ways to atone for his guilt. A teacher can help the child vent the guilt feelings generated by such things as name calling or fighting that occurred right before the dying person became ill. This can be done through role playing or writing. The teacher should accept the child and his feelings and reassure him that everyone feels guilt for things he should and should not have done. Self-punishment or self-defeating thoughts or behaviors must be confronted.

When a child uses coping mechanisms, for example, denial, the teacher should question if they are inappropriate at the time. Some coping mechanisms may be helpful to the child as long as they do not interfere with his ability to deal with life. Perhaps the news of his loved one's illness or critical accident is overwhelming, and the child is letting only a small amount of the devastating news filter through. A teacher once called to ask me if it was normal that a little boy was not eating much and not talking a lot after his father died. I asked how long it had been since the death. She replied ten days. His behavior was a normal response to his father's death. However, if the lack of eating and talking persists over a long period of time then it needs to be looked at carefully and dealt with.

The child needs to know that it is normal to be ambivalent. He needs to become aware of the changes that ensue because of the illness. A teacher can help the child in his ambivalence. A lingering illness or long anticipation of loss can cause a great deal of stress and confusion. Not knowing what will happen from one day to the next, the family structure changes and is in turmoil. All this causes ambivalence and a need for resolution. It is quite painful to watch a loved one suffer, and at times the child may wish the person to die and then feel guilty for such thoughts. The child can be helped by talking through these feelings and realizing that it is normal to feel this way.

The child may feel cheated and angry with those who are having a good time while he must live an altered life because of the dying loved one. He may be angry with himself for being upset or for saying something that came true. Another real feeling for the child is fear that there will be no one to take care of him. The child needs reassurance that he will be cared for and that his teacher is there to help him. He needs to know that these feelings are normal and that he is not going crazy. The family may become overprotective of the child or, in contrast, may expect too much from the child. A teacher can help by guiding the family in determining what is appropriate to expect from a child of this age under these circumstances.

The sorrow the child feels when someone he loves is dying is similar to the sadness and pain the adults feel. However, the child does not always have the resources or experiences in living that an adult has. He may be unable to consistently and effectively relate his feelings and put them in proper perspective, and he may try to camouflage those feelings that are too painful to show. He might feel that it is not right to cry and lose control, that he must be a big boy now. The child must be helped to experience these intense feelings and to realize that they are in response to the love that he has for the dying person. The child needs to be helped to continue to interact as much as possible with the dying person, despite the continued loss and suffering. By being supportive and providing means for venting feelings and sorrow, we can assist the child to deal with the impending death in a way that provides some hope in that there is still life. We must not underestimate the child's ability to understand the dying process on some level, nor underestimate his sensitivity.

Like the adult, the child also needs to have time out, a respite from mourning. He should be encouraged to take time for himself, to go out and play with his friends, or to do something he enjoys. Caring for the dying person can be exhausting due to constant trips to the hospital or late night vigils at home. Physically, the child needs to replenish himself and benefits from good physical exercise, sufficient rest, and nutritional intake. Emotionally, the child is being drained due to the stress and anxiety surrounding the dying person. When her mother was dying of cancer, Sally remarked that she was exhausted emotionally as well as physically. It was so hard . . . the hardest thing she did in her life.

The child, as do other family members, feels helpless during this strenuous time of indefinite pain and duration. Like other family members, he is called on not only to give some measure of support to the dying person but to continue to live with the dying loved one and still be connected even while saying goodbye. There are many variables to consider. However, we all have strengths within us if we allow ourselves to be honest with our feelings. An educator can help the child or adolescent honestly identify his feelings, deal with them, and then use them to cope constructively with the experience.

Caregiver Posture

A child has a resilience that can help him through the pain of loss. Albeit painful, a healthy child can deal with loss. The teacher must help the child to rely on his inner strength and innocence so he can continue to have hope. In his innocence, a child has the key ingredient of hope, which will give him and others around him the strength to endure and live again.

After my own suffering of a personal tragedy, a dear sweet boy came to me. His mother died when he was seven, his father was diagnosed as a manic-depressive and hospitalized, and the boy had recently undergone open heart surgery and was placed in a child-care facility. He already had multiple experiences with loss. He walked with me one afternoon and gave me hope and guidance. His loss of words was natural, not hesitant or discomforting. He acknowledged that it really hurt to lose someone you love, and he wished he could change what had happened to me but could not. He handed me, in all simplicity, the Xeroxed picture that he had of his mother and wrote that he understood my pain. His sincerity was uplifting and has never left me. As caregivers, we must allow for the bonding and strength of children, letting them extend their empathy and caring. They need to feel a part of the treatment. They need to feel that they can give, too. Most important is their need to trust significant others in being honest about their loved one.

It is important for a child to feel that the teacher has some sense of control in his or her understanding of life. The teacher can acknowledge that he or she does not have all the answers but at the same time must also impart a sense of security to the child. A teacher needs to be a pillar for him during this tumultuous time. Just having someone say "I know it's hard for you" can provide comfort. The teacher must let the child know that he or she can be with him during this time to look at those mysteries that cannot be solved and that, although he or she cannot take away the pain, he or she will be there by his side. It is most difficult to see someone you care about and love in pain because you are unable to take it away or seemingly help them. Many times, people, in their feelings of inadequacy and helplessness, freeze in their actions and walk away. The teacher should not walk away. Taking time with the child at lunch or taking a walk with him may help him feel the teacher's support and encouragement. A teacher can let the child know he will still be taken care of. Children need to feel secure in order to grieve, otherwise they will be frightened and will stop their grief process. A teacher must teach the child to feel his sense of importance in this universe as a human being. An affective teacher must encourage the development of a positive self-concept and provide encouragement and positive reinforcement to the child to help him build his self-worth. A teacher must not protect the child from the reality of life but must help him to be stronger to deal with it.

As caregiver, it is important that a teacher has his or her own self-awareness regarding loss and death. In that self-awareness, he or she must comprehend the loss, or anticipation of loss, by identifying the impact that it has on his or her life and his or her means of dealing with it. A true educator can learn from an experience and develop it into a repertoire of skills for dealing with a new situation. A teacher's limits and strengths in dealing with loss will be reflected in the ability to handle—not necessarily have the answers to—questions about life, loss, and death. Finally, as caregivers, teachers must also take care of themselves both physically and emotionally. They must recognize the stress that they are under and have the energy they need to be effective.

Need for Communication with the Child

When kept in ignorance, children, like adults will rarely grow beyond the initial stage of denial and isolation. Not telling deprives little people of the peace and dignity which can be their's in the final stage of acceptance and resignation (Kavanaugh, 1977, p. 139).

To be able to discuss death or the anticipation of loss with a child, a teacher must open up both heart and mind. He or she must not ignore or suppress the child's need to talk about the confusion and the hurt. Above all, the teacher must learn to be comfortable with a child's crying and his or her inability to provide the answers to all the child's questions. An educator can provide a seemingly stable environment even through the painful experience of loss. Paradoxically, often in an attempt to save our children from pain, we are only making it more difficult for them to live.

When a family tries to keep the knowledge of a terminal illness and upcoming loss from a child, the child often can detect this through everyone's unwillingness to discuss the person's illness or answer the child's questions. He often is not allowed to participate in certain events involving the care of the dying person. These omissions deny the child the time and right to talk with the dying individual. If a child cannot fathom the reason for such secrecy and the various heightened emotions he perceives, he may become totally confused and isolated. He may feel detached and alone in his grief. He may feel responsible for the illness. Depending on the relationship with the family, a teacher may be able to discuss with the parents what the child is experiencing and how it would be helpful for them to include him in what is taking place at home.

A family member's terminal illness has brought a dramatic change to the child's life. It may be the child's first experience with loss, and he may not know that what he is going through is normal. He may feel guilty and need reassurance. A teacher should not assume he will come to him or her but should reach out to the child, and be available to him. The teacher should sit down by his side, play a game with him, ask him how things are at home, acknowledge that he or she knows it is difficult. A teacher should not impose personal feelings or ways of thinking as to how he should deal with death. Death is individual. Each loss is not measurable. A teacher should let the child know that he is understood, that it is painful and difficult, and that if he needs him or her to listen, the teacher will. A teacher should try to make contact with the child, especially one who typically is withdrawn and does not seek help. Communication is very significant. It is critically important to talk with the child and answer questions about the illness or his feelings, initiating conversations with him about his dying parent, peer, or sibling because he may be unable to begin such conversations. When a child does not want to talk, respect his right. He may search out others who have suffered a loss or may choose not to expose this painful part of his life in this environment. His teacher still may be a resource to him. A very good book for a youngster or adolescent to read is *Loss and How to Cope With It* by Joanne Bernstein. It deals with various aspects of loss and explains the symptoms and means of coping.

It is critical to recognize the importance of trust between teacher and child. If a teacher has a good relationship and rapport with the child, he or she can be a pillar of strength for him in the many moments and experiences that he will endure in his anticipatory grief. If he trusts the teacher, he will be more apt to confide in him or her and to give the opportunities to intervene in his grief. The teacher can also help the child by sharing with him, to the extent possible given his age and understanding, the different stages that the terminally ill person undergoes. Explaining these to the child will help him in understanding the dying person a little better. It is difficult for the child to understand when the dying person begins to withdraw and detach from loved ones. Often, the child may feel rejected unless he can talk about his feelings and know that this is a normal process for the dying person, despite his not liking it.

Bibliotherapy

A good means of allowing the child to deal with his feelings and discover their normalcy is to provide story books dealing with loss, illness, anticipatory grief, and death. Bibliotherapy is the directed group or individual reading of personal-growth literature. It involves reading, discussing, and answering questions written specifically at the child's level. The reader participates emotionally in the experience. According to Moses and Zaccaria (1968), the bibliotherapeutic process consists of three stages: (1) identification—the reader identifies himself with a major character in the story; (2) catharsis—as a result of this identification, there is a release of emotional or psychological tension; and (3) insight—as a result of this emotional release, the individual now can achieve new insight into his problems via the process of "working through." These stories may be only a few pages long with questions directed toward specific issues; for example, did the girl feel guilty about wanting her parent to die? What do you think she should do? Have you ever wished you could have spent more time helping your mom? Through discussion the child can reflect on the different emotions and concerns that are involved in this anticipated loss. The following is an example of bibliotherapy that deals with loss and the feelings surrounding that loss.

The Intruder

by J. DeFrances and Vincent Hetherman

He needed to be alone . . . a time to reflect upon his life and the issues he needed to confront. Girlfriend . . . school . . . life at home with his parents . . . these were all weighing down on him. He needed to sort out the mess. His only escape was the ocean. It seemed to listen when no one else cared . . . or had time.

The ocean, infinite in its size and understanding, was the best friend he possibly ever had. His older brother that always took the time to let him talk . . . to spill out all those bundled feelings.

So, it was to the ocean that he ran for his personal escape, or so he thought. As he walked on the beach in deep thought, picking up rocks to skim on the sea's face and shells to hold up to the sun, he came upon an intruder on his private world . . . of his solace territory.

Although frail and quiet, this intruder was infringing on his freedom. Who was this person to walk on his shore? Suddenly, he became owner of God's territory. He looked vehemently at this passerby only to encounter a warm, understanding smile. It seemed as though this intruder knew his thoughts or at least shared the brotherhood of the sea.

He was an old man, probably in his seventies. His veiny hands clasped a broken shell and his watery eyes glared out at the sea. Yet, each line on his face seemed to portray a warmness and sensitivity known through the wisdom of living through happy times and hardships.

The waves pounded and the gulls seemed to proclaim their meeting through shrieking cries. Perhaps it was fate that they met . . . one of those mysteries of our existence.

The man, acknowledging his disturbance, conveyed an apologetic message through his smile and nodding of his head. Something stopped the boy from walking on. He said it was all right and made way for the old man to pass. The old man smiled and asked the boy if he came to the sea often. They realized that they shared the friendship of the sea.

It was more of a shock for the boy to understand that the old man came also to share his thoughts with his comrade. It was the first time that the boy had felt and understood that the old man also had many conflicts . . . many decisions . . . many changes in his life.

They walked the shore for what seemed eternity, sharing their lives. This meeting was soon to be the foundation of a firm and sincere friendship, reinforced and developed through regular meetings. It became almost a need for both of them to walk together along the perpetual shore. One sharing his anguish and growing pains to live . . . another, living and reflecting upon a past life trying to form a reconciliation. Both the boy and the old man were growing and sharing. One offering vitality and spontaneity, another giving wisdom and experience.

One day the young man walked the beach and searched for his friend. Perhaps the timing was wrong, so he returned another day . . . another . . . his friend had disappeared.

Then the young man realized that his friend had walked his last walk with him. He had become united with the power that perpetuates the ocean. He had joined their comrade.

The young man ran and kept running until the pain caused him to cry and collapse on the sand. He was alone again. Yet, this time when he looked up there was no intruder.

But somehow, the young man felt stronger inside. He seemed to be able to face those questions with more courage and confidence. His tears now were not those of confusion but tears mourning a friendship that had left and yet, tears of joy for a love and friendship that became part of him.

And as time passed, he too walked the beach and one day met a young boy. . . .

Questions for The Intruder

1. Why did the boy in the story need to be alone?
2. Where did he go for his "personal escape"?
3. Who was the intruder?
4. Why was he called the intruder?
5. What did the boy say to the intruder?
6. What happened to the intruder?
7. What did the boy do when he realized his friend was not coming back?
8. Did he meet someone else on the beach?
9. Do you have somewhere special that you escape to?
10. Describe how you think the boy felt when he lost his friend.
11. What did he mean when he said they were tears of joy and not of confusion?

Promoting Healing

We must be careful not to judge a child's grieving by adult standards, for we all too often underestimate the capabilities of our children and youth to understand this complex facet of life. Life for children and adults is like a kaleidoscope. Each new aspect allows us to see a new dimension of life and understanding. Each new relationship adds to the patterns, becomes part of our existence, and has a impact on our lives, whether small or large.

At the 1981 Conference of the Forum for Death Education and Counseling in Boston, the web theory was presented. This theory describes a person's world, with their relationships as analogous to a network of fibers that contributes to the whole web. When there is a loss to the whole, there is a break in the structure. The entire web must be reconstructed and healed. Eventually, if the healing has taken a positive course, that section of the web will be rewoven into a new part of the whole. This is symbolic of the reinvestment of life. The other parts of the web still have part of the old that was lost, but it has changed, and continues to, in living. The web concept is also symbolic of the fragility of our lives and the significance of each person (fiber) that we meet.

Anticipatory grief can be a long road. The child will need special support and care. It is a special time to say goodbye and feel close to the loved one. The child may fear losing others he loves. He may see love as dangerous—you love someone, they die. He will fear what will happen to him. He will feel anger for there is no reason, nor is it fair, that his loved one should suffer so. Kushner (1981) puts forth the essential issue, stating that in the final analysis the question of why bad things happen to good people translates itself into some very different questions. No longer is the question why something happened, but rather asking how we will respond, and what we intend to do now that it has happened

All children experience loss and grieve. Some may appear to react and then proceed to their daily activities seemingly untouched, but this is not so. After the death, you may find the child trying to be like his dead brother. He may feel guilt for the death and crave extra reassurance. The child can do one of four things: remain attached to a fantasy of the dead person, invest his love in work or things, be frightened to invest his love in anyone, or find someone else to love. A teacher needs to encourage the risk taking in life to reinvest.

A dear friend once came to me during a time of despair. His remark was, "We can do nothing for the one who has died, only for the one who is dying because of it." We can help the child find his release of his pain through drawing, writing, singing, dancing, and so forth. As teachers and empathic human beings, we can help the child by providing hope and encourgement to take the risk of living and loving again. Just as an adult, a child or adolescent has only two choices. He can either not resolve his grief and live in guilt and denial, or he can confront his feelings of grief and learn to be more appreciative of life. If he chooses the latter, he will be stronger and have a fuller commitment to life. We must help him by guiding him to choose this commitment.

Summary of Guidelines on How to Reach and Treat the Bereaved Child within the Classroom

Recognize that children grieve. Give the child permission to mourn. Do not deny his feelings. He needs to be allowed and assisted to confront and talk about the impending loss. Allow the child to demonstrate his sorrow. Allow him to cry without shame. Do not make judgmental comments as to how he should handle this loss.

Children experience sorrow and loss. Anger, panic, denial, numbness, and physical illness are normal experiences in varying degrees. When overextended or severe, there may be a problem. Refer the child for help. Look for magical thinking involved in the child's explanation of death. Correct it and try to explain to the child what is happening.

Help the child by having him express emotions either verbally or nonverbally. Do not be afraid of the silence. If a child cannot or will not talk about his loss, respect that right. Do not force him to do so. Provide other avenues that will allow the child to express himself freely and openly. For example, encourage the child to draw what he feels, make something in clay, choreograph a dance to music, write a short story or poem, read a bibliotherapy piece concerning loss, go for a brisk run or a quiet walk, and so forth. Make sure you let him know that you are sorry and that you are there to talk to if he desires. Be truthful. Unhealthy explanations create fear and fantasy. Allow him to express as much grief as he is willing to share.

Talk with the child about the guilt that he may be feeling. Guilt is normal amid any loss, and moreso when it involves a loss where a relationship may not have been very positive. Help the child ventilate that guilt. Assure him that he is only human, and that we learn more and more as we experience life and love. A means of venting may be to write a letter of forgiveness to the dying person. Guilt may also be mitigated through altruistic efforts to help others.

Encourage the child to recognize his anger. Have him look at what it is that he could do that would be constructive in order to avoid inappropriate discharge of it.

Help the child become aware of those events and feelings that are changing. Especially in anticipatory grief, there is an ever-changing process over a period of time. Being able to talk about it will help.

Help the child break down the mourning experience into parts so that he can deal with it and assimilate it a little at a time. He must not overwhelm himself with guilt and loss.

Explain to the child that everyone experiences highs and lows during the mourning process. He is not going crazy. Try to focus on the positives.

Be cognizant of the child's developmental stage, especially adolescence with all its internal conflict. Be aware of the child's intellectual and emotional limitations. Talk clearly and at a level the child can understand.

Try to answer the child's questions regarding such matters as the medical situation, the funeral services, or different feelings he may be experiencing. Contact the family to establish a bond in order to offer them some understanding and possibly some insight as to how to help their child.

Provide as much reassurance and tender loving care as possible for the child during this time of bereavement.

Try to model appropriate grieving behavior.

Do not lecture or make decisions for the child. Help explain in concise terms so that the child can see the alternatives available to him. He needs to be given age-appropriate responsibility for his life.

Do not measure a child's loss. No loss is measurable—each one bears its own mark and pain on the individual. There is no time table for loss. Each of us takes a varying degree of time to heal. Of course, overly extended times of not dealing with the reality of death would warrant referral to counseling. Time can help heal, but only if the mourner, even if only a child, attends to the grief work that must be accomplished.

If not an appropriate role reassignment, do not tell the child or adolescent that now he must take over someone else's roles in the family; for example, the role of his mother or father. Do not burden the child with the misconception of replacement. Responsibilities may be reassigned, but only in a fashion that respects the appropriateness of the new role for the person and its congruence with other roles the person has.

Help the child develop some patience with himself and the others around him. This is a tumultuous time, filled with anxiety. Offer the child the opportunities to learn relaxation or vent his anxiety by running, exercising, talking, and so forth. Help the child not to expect "all" from himself during this time. He must try to be realistic regarding his limits and the fact that his loss will be overwhelming at times. He must learn to give himself time.

Encourage the child to take care of himself. To eat properly, get enough sleep, and exercise. His resilience will be stronger if he can take care of his physical needs. Use of substances, such as alcohol or pills, are detrimental and will only delay the grieving process.

Give the child permission to take a break from grief and spend some time with his peers. Suggest to the child to seek a network of friends. It is not easy, but assure the child it is important to invest emotional energy. Encourage him not to withdraw completely. Tell him that it is okay and he should not feel that he is betraying the dying person. If possible, encourage the child to join an appropriate support group during this painful time. Often a child will seek out others who have encountered a similar loss. It is important for them to see that life does go on. Perhaps there are other individuals the child may feel more inclined to speak with, for instance, someone who knew his loved one as a close friend. Allow the child the right and time to talk with that individual.

Recognize that in order to heal children need to have time for solitude, as well as time with friends and significant others. Help the child become aware of the need to reconstruct and reinvest one's life. It takes time to make essential adaptations to change.

Help the child put things into his life that are symbolic of life; for example, plants, music, pets, and so forth.

Utilize bibliotherapy. Suggest readings. Do not mandate. Be sensitive to see if the child is ready to deal with the topic. Look for signals of anxiety.

Give hope and encouragement. Life goes on. Encourage the child to remember the happy moments and to cherish them. No one can take away his memories.

References

Barton, D. 1977. The Family of the Dying Person. In D. Barton, ed., *Dying and Death: A Clinical Guide for Caregivers*. Baltimore: Williams & Wilkins, 59–71.

Bernstein, J. 1977. *Loss and How to Cope With it*. Boston: Houghton Mifflin.

Fulton, R. 1967. On the Dying of Death. In E. Grollman, ed., *Explaining Death to Children*. Boston: Beacon Press, pp. 31–47.

Grollman, E. ed. 1967. *Explaining Death to Children*. Boston: Beacon Press.

Kavanaugh, R. 1977. *Facing Death*. New York: Penguin Books.

Kübler-Ross, E. 1969. *On Death and Dying*. New York: Macmillan.

Kushner, H. 1981. *When Bad Things Happen to Good People*. New York: Schocken.

Lebow, G.H. 1976. Facilitating Adaptation in Anticipatory Mourning. *Social Casework* 57:458–465.

Lindbergh, A.M. 1975. *Gift from the Sea*. New York: Vintage Books.

Moses, H. and Zaccaria, J. *Facilitating Human Development through Reading: The Use of Bibliotherapy in Teaching and Counseling*. Stipes Publishing Co., 1968.

Rando, T.A. 1984. *Grief, Dying and Death: Clinical Interventions for Caregivers*. Champaign, Ill.: Research Press.

Raphael, B. 1983. *The Anatomy of Bereavement*. New York: Basic Books.

Schiff, H.S. 1977. *The Bereaved Parent*. New York: Penguin Books.

11
The Older Person's Anticipation of Her Own Death

N. Claire Kowalski

> The key for each one of us, to the relation for him between life and death is, I believe, the extent of his familiarity with death and the stage in his life at which he has become familiar with it.
> —Arnold Toynbee, *Man's Concern with Death*, p. 260.

In advanced age, life is lived with the knowledge that death is not only possible but indeed likely in the foreseeable future. The goal of this chapter is to increase understanding about older people who are approaching death. By focusing on late-life psychological development and on some experiences that are common among the elderly, a possible basis becomes apparent for the attitudes older people may express about their own deaths.

The wide range of attitudes older people have toward death is vividly illustrated in the film *Handle with Care* (1976). In it, older people of different backgrounds and functional abilities respond to questions about death. By the end of the film there is hardly any perspective that has not been given a very personal expression. Research is becoming more prevalent on the attitudes of the elderly toward death. Jeffers and Verwoerdt (1977) have summarized research on the reactions of old people to the prospect of death. Wass (1979) has provided a general discussion of death and the elderly in chapter form, and Marshall (1980) has written a book on the subject. A recent review of research on thoughts and fears of older people regarding their own deaths is found in Belsky (1984). The literature consistently indicates that, unlike younger adults, only a few elderly people admit fear of their own deaths. However, they do express considerable concern about experiences that may be associated with a lingering period of dying, such as prolonged pain, loss of functional abilities, or dependency that may inflict hardship on others.

This is a revised version of the chapter. "Perspectives on Personal Death in Senescence" by N. Claire Kowalski, published in R.S. Pacholski and C.A. Corr, eds., *New Directions in Death Education and Counseling* (Arlington, Va.: Forum for Death Education and Counseling, 1981), pp. 29–37.

Feelings of older people about their own anticipated deaths are not confined to the distress and sadness of grief. They may also include elements of fear, satisfaction, relief, acceptance, indifference, or resignation. The point is that the older person's anticipation of her death is likely to include simultaneously diverse feelings that reflect both attraction and repulsion. To be succinct, she is ambivalent.

There is general awareness that physical development peaks before middle age and that aging is accompanied by a certain amount of physical decline. However, our society often forgets that old age can represent the culmination of some aspects of psychological development. In old age, the individual embodies the physiological–psychological–social–spiritual effects of every preceding stage. She has the potential for whatever particular perspective, feeling, or state of mind that requires the accumulation of extended time and experience. Some societies consider wisdom to be possible only in old age. Simone deBeauvoir (1973) states, "One has to reach a certain age . . . in order to have accumulated experience, a knowledge that cannot be communicated because it is not abstract—that has to be lived" (p. 165).

Diversity within the older population cannot be overemphasized. No two older people will have exactly the same health, personality, economic situation, or social relationships. Neither will they be spiritually identical. Race, ethnicity, and religious affiliation, or lack thereof, influence the beliefs each individual holds regarding the meaning of life and what may follow after death.

In order to set the stage for the discussion that follows, a hypothetical case is given to illustrate some of the situations common in the lives of older people due to aging-associated changes and the prevailing attitudes and behaviors of other persons in our society toward the elderly. An overview of the theory of psychological development in old age, relevant to attitudes toward one's own death, is presented. The effect that common late-life experiences and developmental processes may have on an older person's anticipation of her own death is illustrated by a series of questions to which one is likely to respond differently in old age than one would have earlier in life. In conclusion, some implications for practice are suggested. Throughout the chapter the female pronoun is used inclusively to refer to older persons, reflecting the fact that the elderly population is predominantly female.

The Old Person

What are some common daily experiences in the lives of frail older people? The elderly individual has frequent reminders of decline in every body system. Her skin is wrinkled, her hair thinner, and her injuries heal more slowly. Perhaps she no longer has the strength to open sealed jars or to move a chair to clean underneath. It may be difficult to climb stairs or board a public bus. Vision changes preclude driving and make walking over uneven terrain hazardous. On television and in conversation she hears most of the words but may not always comprehend the messsage. She feels the cold more, and she tires with relatively little exertion. Frequent need to urinate is inconvenient and can cause anxiety when she is away from home. Perhaps chronic arthritis has caused discomfort, which has put an end to the handiwork she once did. It may be hard to remember whether she has taken a pill and what was on her mind a minute ago. Most food tastes bland and dentures don't fit as well as they used to.

There is the inconvenience and frustration of having to depend on others for shopping and housecleaning. It is also discouraging to need the visiting nurse who perhaps calls her by her first name and makes her feel like a naughty child. She wishes that her doctor would do more than just prescribe medication, saying that at her age she must expect health problems. There are some humiliating moments like those at the restaurant, when instead of taking her order the waitress asked her daughter, "And what will your mother have?"

Sometimes she worries that she may fall and never walk again, or suffer a stroke, or become incontinent, or senile and be a burden to those she loves. She has seen those things happen to several friends. A number of those she loved are already dead and loneliness for them cannot be removed even by the dear relatives on whom she now depends. Money carefully saved for retirement has dwindled with inflation, medical expenses, and in imprudent investment for a useless arthritis cure. She cannot afford to keep her small house much longer, but the thought of leaving it is dreadful. It's nice to fantasize that one of her three children might move back to live with her. Yet, she knows deep inside that that is out of the question, for it would completely disrupt their work and family responsibilities. Furthermore, each one already helps in many ways, and she doesn't want to impose on them.

Our older friend is also aware that, in spite of everything, her declining life is precious. It is the only life she has and to lose it would be to lose everything she knows.

Theories of Psychological Development

At this point, attention turns from common experiences in old age to theories concerning psychosocial development in later life. Some of these theories compliment each other and some offer different perspectives on what may be the same process. Be that as it may, psychological development in later life influences attitudes toward personal death. Theories considered here indicate what some of the influences may be.

According to continuity theory and personality theory, individuals age in ways that are predictable from their personality structure, their earlier patterns of coping and adaptation, and their expectations. However, research has also indicated a shift from active mastery of the environment in midlife to a more passive adaptation and compliance as one ages. With aging, adults also show greater "interiority," that is, they attend less to the external environment and more to their own inner lives (Neugarten, 1972). Disengagement theory, Erikson's stage of late adulthood, the life review, and awareness of finitude are theoretical formulations discussed below that indicate the desirability of self-attention in later life. Each of these theories is compatible with the increasing interiority that accompanies aging.

Disengagement theory is prominent in social gerontology. It indicates that a mutual withdrawal, a letting go of the aging individual and her society each from the other, is functional and satisfying to both (Cummings and Henry, 1961). Although disengagement theory has generated much criticism, it does seem appropriate to apply to those of advanced years who are approaching death (Kalish, 1972). In this final phase of life, disengagement may indeed be a developmental task in preparation for death, which is the ultimate disengagement. It is not unusual to find a frail older person reluctant to take part in an activity or a relationship she once enjoyed and that others urge her to try again. Having withdrawn from some part of life and achieved closure already, she may be unwilling to repeat the process.

Erikson (1963) has postulated specific developmental stages of life and has indicated the identity-related crisis faced by the individual at each stage. The outcome of the eighth, and final, stage of which he writes includes elements of both integrity and despair, with one or the other predominating for each person. According to Erikson's theory, the challenge of later adulthood is to culminate the journey through life by accepting and integrating all one has been with the future reality of one's not being. This is to say that fulfillment of all earlier developmental tasks can lead to acceptance of death in old age as a fitting closure to life. On the other hand, failure to attain a positive outcome of successive developmental tasks make the achievement of late-life integrity unlikely. In such a case, the result is both despair and fear of death, for death in these circumstances ends all possibility of achieving the resolution that constitutes fulfillment.

Butler (1963) has put forward the life review as a psychological process of later life prompted by the realization that one is vulnerable to death. We know that in later life memory is apt to touch distant events that have not been recalled for years. The life review consists of bringing to mind and interrelating events and experiences from one's whole history in an attempt to discover the meaning of one's life. When such meaning emerges, the result is a dimension of wisdom and serenity in the personality. If, however, one finds no acceptable meaning in what has gone before, the outcome may be despondency. An illustration of this is provided by a long-term resident of a state mental hospital who wrote the following while he was participating in a program of deinstitutionalization designed to prepare older people to move into the community.

I am 65 years of age, have spent most of my life here in _____.
If I were to go out of this place, I would not know how to act in other
peoples places. I am old now and have given up hopes of ever going
out in the world and to enjoy life again.

A psychological concept relating to late life, which has received less attention than it may merit, is "awareness of finitude." Developed by Marshall (1975),
who attributes it originally to J.M.A. Munnichs (1966), awareness of finitude
refers to an individual's gut-level realization that she herself will actually die
one day and that the lifetime remaining to her is limited. Although awareness
of finetude is age-related, age cannot be substituted as a measure for it. Marshall's research shows that awareness of finitude is also associated with the death
age of one's parents and with one's health as self-reported. Thus, those persons who have already outlived the age at which their parents died, estimate
fewer years remaining for themselves than do persons who have not reached
the death age of both their parents. So, too, persons who rate their health as
fair, poor, or recently changed for the worse, estimate shorter life expectancy
than those who rate their health more highly. Achievement of awareness of
finitude contrasts with a hopeless resignation to death. Instead, it can lead to
what Marshall (1980) terms "legitimation of biography," a process whereby concerns about the significance of earlier life events are worked out and the person is freed so she can involve herself fully in the present. She no longer needs
either to deny the past or to be burdened by it.

In order to illustrate what may be observed in a frail older person who
has apparently been successful in completing the psychological development
referred to in the theories discussed, the following excerpts are drawn from
a writeup by *Washington Post* journalist Kenneth Turan (1977) about the author
Henry Miller.

> Henry Miller is old. Nearly 86 and physically infirm. "I have so many ailments,"
> he says, "it would take an almanac to list them." It doesn't seem possible. . . .
>
> His enormous good humor, barely containable in printed words, his
> breathless zest for every aspect of existence, for the sexual side especially but
> really for everything—the scroungers, the lice, the roaches, the prostitutes with
> wooden legs—it all roars out of his books, a primeval blur of activity. . . .
> Where could growing old possibly fit in?
>
> "Well, I wouldn't recommend it," Miller says, somehow managing to look
> impishly attractive in a blue terrycloth bathrobe over pinkish pajamas and white
> orthopedic shoes. "The time when you begin to fall apart, it's something I
> never calculated on. Up to five years ago, I was riding bicycles, swimming,
> playing Ping-Pong all day. . . ."
>
> Yet despite tiring easily now, despite having to move around with a walker,
> despite losing the sight in one eye and the hearing in one ear, Henry Miller
> continues to astound. "From the neck up I'm all right," is how he puts it in
> his gravelly Brooklyn voice.

(The author reports a lengthy interview replete with life review type incidents, then continues.)

> Henry Miller knows he doesn't act or sound very old, but his ailments allow him no delusions about his lifespan. "My first operation, five years ago, that put me in touch with death. I never thought about it till then."
> "I don't fear it, sometimes I feel it's time I ought to be there. . . ." He has lived a happy life, all in all, Miller thinks now, despite the bad parts.*

A concept that has received relatively little attention may help explain the apparent rarity of acute anxiety about death among the elderly despite their nearness to it. It has been suggested that "freeze" be viewed as a type of emergency reaction in response to chronic stress, just as fight and flight are responses to acute danger (Jarvik and Russell, 1979). The freeze response does not represent hopelessness or withdrawal but rather is characterized by relative inactivity, energy conservation, and calm awareness. Jarvik and Russell cite closeness to death as a chronic stressor in old age, and they say that the most adaptive response is acceptance and contemplation.

The word "freeze" suggests a cryogenic suspension and complete immobility. Therefore, in this chapter the term "flow" is used to express much the same meaning as the concept proposed by Jarvik and Russell, but without implying noninvolvement or intertia. A flow response denotes the passive participation observable in many declining elderly persons. It can be thought of as being and trusting rather than doing. In contrast to flow, an active response to stress would demand more of an old person's limited energy and could add to the distress of the individual. It could be hypothesized that the older person who is able to flow instead of either fighting or withdrawing, increases her chance for survival. She neither wears herself out by using more physical–psychological strength than is required to cope with chronic stressors, nor does she give up by adopting an attitude of hopelessness associated with shortened life expectancy.

Selecting particular aspects of the foregoing theories, the person in advanced old age may be characterized as disengaged from most active social roles and attending more to her own inner life than to the external environment. By this time, and without her realizing it, an awareness of finitude has prompted her to undertake the self-examination of the life review and the final identity crisis described by Erikson (1963). She has completed these in ways that may or may not be comfortable for her. She also knows on a deeper-than-cognitive level that her own earthly life will end within a limited time. Her adaptation to the stresses that accompany old age is congruent with her life-long personality pattern. This adaptation may be to fight for as long a life possible, or it may be to adjust to aging-related changes by flowing in rhythm with her reality, or to withdraw from life and make no resistance to death, or even to escape into

---

*Reprinted with permission from the *Washington Post*, November 25, 1977.

symptoms of senility as a defense against thoughts of death she finds unacceptable.

Questions Illustrating Age-Associated Perspectives

The following exercise is proposed to suggest possible effects of physiological–psychological–social–spiritual experiences and processes of aging on attitudes toward personal death. Questions are posed and reasons for their responses are suggested that are compatible with the experience of old age. The questions raise issues relevant to the values one may give to both quantity and quality of life according to one's experience and to the stage in life one presently occupies. The reader is invited to compare his own responses with those an older person might make. Answers are likely to indicate some of the things that give meaning and value to life. Ambivalence will probably be evident.

"Are more than half the people you have loved already dead?" The older person has lost many of those to whom she has been closest. It is likely that she is widowed and has outlived a number of friends and relatives of her cohort. We all have some desire to be with our peers, sharing their experience. This may be so even when being with them means crossing the boundary of death. Reunion with predecessors may be attractive to those who believe this happens after death.

"Can you move around without pain; walking, driving and traveling easily to where you want to be?" Many older people are not independently mobile. They may not be able to drive or use public transport. Some need a cane, walker, or wheelchair. When this is the case, the range of choices for where one can go, what one can do, and who one can be with is severely limited.

"Have you sufficient strength and energy to take care of yourself, to work, to be useful to others, and to enjoy recreational activities all during a single day?" People who are frail must plan carefully to be able to accomplish anything outside of their daily routines. Much of their limited energy may be required to cope with degenerative changes going on within their bodies.

"How often must others take care of you? When this happens is it likely to be for a limited time?" Chronic illness, so common in old age, may mean an ongoing need for care. It has been the lifelong role of many older women to take care of others. These women are likely to have difficulty adjusting to dependency, which is the antithesis of the nurturing role that may be central to their identity and self-esteem.

"Are you a financial, physical, or emotional burden to your relatives? If so, is the situation temporary?" Family resources of one sort or another may become

depleted when a member needs ongoing care. That a family voluntarily chooses to use its resources this way does not alter the fact that what is expended on one member is not available for another. The elderly recipient knows that her special needs are likely to continue until the end of her life. The allocation of resources in families with a frail older member is likely to be a source of ambivalence and perhaps also of conflict.

"Does your future appear long enough so that you can postpone some of what you want to a later time?" An older person must take the opportunity for gratification today, since by tomorrow her ability or resources may be gone. Moreover, whatever has not been achieved by old age probably will not ever be. If the individual is left in despair over what will never be, she may become chronically depressed and vulnerable to all that is associated with depression.

"Does your environment allow frequent experience and expression of sexuality?" We are sexual beings all our lives and to be acknowledged as such by others can be the spice of life. However, much behavior toward older people, especially those who need long-term care, implies that they are sexless. The predominance of females in the older population, and also among caregivers, means that many older women have little opportunity for male companionship. Moreover, those older people who do not live independently may have very little privacy afforded them.

"When you are lonely, can you get in touch with people you enjoy, or move into situations where you may make new friends? Is your loneliness really grief for someone already lost through death? What control can you exercise to maintain a relationship that is important to you?" With advancing years people tend to have less ability to visit others, so they tend to become dependent on those who may or may not come to them. Older people often hesitate to form close attachments with peers that they know they may soon lose through death or relocation or with younger people they expect will not stay around long. We hear of many losses in old age besides relationships. The problem is perhaps not only the losses themselves, but also that the older person may be in a situation where there is no possibility for her to find substitutes for what is lost, whether that be friends, activities, possessions, or familiar surroundings.

"How often do you experience success, or new independence, or achievement?" Although these experiences are less common in old age than earlier in life, there can be real satisfaction in being able to manage self-care, tend a few plants, or do a small service for an ailing friend.

"What potential accomplishments lie ahead of you in the areas of career, family, productivity, artistic expression, and so on?" This question really is, "What do you have to look forward to?" and the answer is different in old age from what it was earlier. It has been said that having something to look forward to is what makes life worth living. It is possible that toward the end of

life some people may find something to look forward to in death, be that relief or reward. For example, there is a story about one elderly woman who told her minister that she was looking forward to reunion with her husband following death. When he asked which husband she was referring to, since she had outlived three, she smiled and replied, "The fourth one." Parenthetically, glib though it may be, this anecdote also serves to illustrate that older people may use humor very effectively as a means of coping with reality. Humor also has the added benefits of eliciting positive responses from others and providing a momentary sense of accomplishment.

"Have you a full range of lifetime experience that gives the possibility for meaning and completeness in your life?" Of course, length of life alone does not automatically bring positive integration. However, the person of advanced years has greater potential for such fulfillment than a younger person has.

"Did you experience the death of someone close to you before your adult years? Did you take part in a funeral or share family grieving while you were a child?" Today's elders grew up during a time when families were larger and mortality rates higher than they are today. It was also a time when a greater portion of deaths occurred at home and funerals often took place from home. All of this means that today's elderly are more likely than succeeding cohorts to have shared some experience of death while they were young. The unknown tends to be more frightening than the known, and exposure to death at an early age within the security of the family may mitigate some of the mystery and fear death holds.

"When you are ill, is it expected that you will recover and regain your former level of functioning? Is your physical pain acute and likely to dissipate or chronic and likely to remain with you the rest of your life?" Old age is a period of decline. Following an illness, the younger person is more likely than the older to regain her former capabilities. During any illness, the patient, the family, and the caregivers all have expectations about whether the patient will recover or die. Exactly how these expectations affect the probability of survival is open to speculation. It is apparent, however, that expectations will be related to the age of the patient. The older patient is considered more likely to die than the younger and at times may be expected to do so while the younger person with the same diagnosis is expected to survive.

"In conversation do you refer easily to your own death?" Anyone who works with the elderly knows that this is fairly common behavior for them. Thinking and talking casually about death in daily life may be a way of preparing for death.

"How many years represent the lifetime to which you think a person is entitled?" The older person is the one most likely to have reached or exceeded that age, whether one considers it to be the biblical three score and ten or some other figure.

"How much longer do you expect to live?" Many old people tell us that they have already lived longer than they expected or that they are ready to die whenever the time comes. Some who grieve the circumstances in which they presently exist express the desire for death to come without further delay.

A second quotation from Simone deBeauvoir, this one when she was 71 years of age, states some of her attitudes, which are compatible with the foregoing discussion.

> But I have come to see that [dying] is not only something inevitable but will happen to me before long. I keep before me that fact that it is utterly useless to rant and rave against the void. Death is not much of a conversationalist. He won't answer. Neither is he an enemy one can vanquish. Besides, so many people close to my heart have died—some very close—that death has become quite familiar to me. He is a part of my life. The thought that I too shall follow in sleep no longer frightens me. I really have no intention of living on until I'm in my nineties to be confronted with advanced age and all its deficiencies. (Thomasma, 1984, p. 525).

Implications for Clinical Practice

It is important to be aware that, like all of us, the elderly are living until the very moment of death and that they share the same human needs we all have. Moreover, the old person's life has value regardless of its quality, simply because there is no substitute for that life. Whatever else it may mean, death always means loss for the older person and for those bereaved by her death. The practitioner who keeps these three points in mind when relating to older people and their families is respecting human dignity.

Ambivalence toward life and death can be expected in older people. Among the many factors contributing to this ambivalence, which practitioners may wish to explore with clients, are awareness of the coming loss, realization that marked improvement is unlikely, and a variety of individual influences. In a particular case, individual factors might be the cost of ongoing care, the stress of prolonged disability or of seeing a loved one in such a state, unfinished business, or feelings about the unacceptability of death on the part of either the old person or those who will survive her. Knowing the age at which the older person's parents died and what significant losses she has already borne can contribute to understanding the basis of her attitudes toward her own mortality.

Diversity among people is maintained throughout life and, despite aging-associated changes, each older person is a unique individual. What an older person says may correspond with reality and our perception of her or it may not. Whatever the case, it is appropriate to believe what she tells us as being her experience interpreted according to her values, her developmental stage, and her state of mental health. It is also appropriate, within ethical limits, to support the response pattern of fight, flight, or flow that she exhibits and, at the same time, help her be aware of alternate actions or attitudes that could represent effective ways of coping. The fight response may result in problematic confrontations with family or caregivers. Yet, struggle toward a goal can give meaning to life at any age. In old age, the flight pattern may be expressed as depression or symptoms of senility. Since it is disheartening for anyone to spend time with those who are unresponsive, depressed behavior on the part of an older person may result in avoidance of her by family and caregivers. Whatever can be done to share among a number of people the burden of caring for a depressed older person can help reduce the strain on any one individual and also provide more of the attention the older person needs. The flow response deserves support because it appears to be an effective adaptation to aging-related stresses. However, there is also the possibility that the older person who flows with her reality may be undemanding and can be overlooked by those around her who are busy. In fact, the older person who displays a flowing response is the one who deserves recognition of her attitudinal achievement in the face of aging-related difficulties. She may also be the one who, unlike her depressed sister, is able to hear any praise that comes her way and to draw strength from it for the future.

Family and friends of older people sometimes need to be reminded that reminiscence is a healthy process. Whoever will listen and encourage the recounting of memories may be facilitating life review and the legitimation of biography. Sometimes it is possible for a listener to acknowledge achievements an older person has taken for granted. If this interpretation rings true, the older person may go on to integrate pieces of her history more positively than she had previously done. Family members may also be reminded that anything that adds even a little to the quality of life today for an older person is valuable.

It has been said that as we age we grow more like ourselves. Unless affected by disease, there tends to be continuity of personality and it is unrealistic to hope for marked attitudinal change in an older person even in the face of death. However, it is usual to become more self-centered with age, and very late in life disengagement is likely.

Younger adults are often uncomfortable with reference to death. They may deny or cut short what an older relative says on this subject. Difficulty in conversation about death is more apt to be related to the developmental stage of the younger adult than to a problem of the older person. When most of one's old friends are among the dead, death itself may begin to seem as much friend as foe. Knowing this may help younger persons tolerate death-related remarks even though they may not personally agree with what an older person expresses.

Conclusion

In conclusion, it is worth noting that age does provide some preparation for death. Physically, an older person has frequent reminders of decline from her body. Socially, some of her cohorts are already dead. Psychologically, she has a gut-level knowledge that her life will soon end. She also has the length of life experience, which is a necessary, although not sufficient, condition for the resolution of all of life's developmental issues. Positive resolution of these issues may lead her to regard her death as the appropriate ending of her life. How common this attitude is among the elderly is not known. However, it seems reasonable to suggest that of all the stages of life only old age holds the potential for acceptance of personal death as appropriate. Even in this ideal case, the death of a fulfilled older person still represents loss.

References

Belsky, J. 1984. *The Psychology of Aging: Theory, Research and Practice.* Monterey, Calif.: Brook/Cole.

Butler, R.N. 1963. The Life Review: An Interpretation of Reminiscence in the Aged. *Psychiatry* 26:65–76.

Cummings, E. and W. Henry. 1961. *Growing Old: The Process of Disengagement.* New York: Basic Books.

deBeauvoir, S. 1973. *The Coming of Age.* New York: Warner.

Erikson, E. 1963. *Childhood and Society.* 2nd ed. New York: W.W. Norton.

Handle With Care, 16mm film. Berkeley, Calif.: Berkeley Public Library, 1976.

Jarvik, L.F., and D. Russell. 1979. Anxiety, Aging and the Third Emergency Reaction. *Journal of Gerontology* 34:197–200.

Jeffers, F.C., and A. Verwoerdt. 1977. How the Old Face Death. In E.W. Busse and E. Pfeiffer, eds., *Behavior and Adaptation in Late Life.* 2nd ed. Boston: Little, Brown, pp. 142–157.

Kalish, R.A. 1972. Of Social Values and the Dying: A Defense of Disengagement. *Family Coordinator* 21:81–94.

Marshall, V.W. 1980. *Last Chapters: A Sociology of Aging and Dying.* Monterey, Calif.: Brooks/Cole.

Marshall, V.W. 1975. Age and Awareness of Finitude in Developmental Gerontology. *Omega* 6:113–129.

Munnichs, J.M.A. 1966. *Old Age and Finitude.* New York: Basel & Karger.

Neugarten, B.L. 1972. Personality and the Aging Process. *The Gerontologist* 12:9–15.

Thomasma, D.C. 1984. Ethical Judgments of Quality of Life in the Case of the Aged. *Journal of the American Geriatrics Society* 32:525.

Toynbee, A.J. 1968. *Man's Concern with Death.* New York: McGraw-Hill.

Turan, K. 1977. Henry Miller Pushes His Lust for Life into Face of Death. *The Washington Post,* 25 November.

Wass, H. 1979. Death and the Elderly. In H. Wass, ed., *Dying: Facing the Facts.* Washington, D.C.: Hemisphere Publishing, pp. 182–207.

12
Anticipating the Death of an Elderly Parent

N. Claire Kowalski

Thh two main thrusts of this chapter are to suggest some meanings death
may have for adult children anticipating the death of an elderly parent
because of aging-associated changes they observe and to explore the
reactions of these adult chldren. An explanation of terms, relevant demographic
facts, and research findings are presented by way of introduction. Illustrative
material is drawn from the anonymous writing of a middle-aged daughter of
a frail, dependent mother. In keeping with this illustration, the female pronoun is used throughout this chapter to refer to both the adult child and the
aging parent, each of whom, of course, may be of either sex. In fact, an adult
child is likely to have a longer period of concern and responsibility for an aging mother than father. There are several reasons for this. Widowhood, which
means the loss of companionship and care a spouse usually provides, is the
lot of more women than men because of longer female life expectancy and
the tendency for the wife to be the younger partner in the marriage. In 1982
elderly women, meaning those sixty-five and over, outnumbered elderly men
three to two. Among the very old, those eighty-five and over, there were only
forty-two men per hundred women (U.S. Senate, Special Committee on Aging, 1984). The age-adjusted mortality rate, which fell 26 percent for elderly
American males between 1940 and 1980, dropped a remarkable 48 percent
for elderly females during that same period (U.S. Senate, Special Committee
on Aging, 1983). Moreover, women are more likely than men to be restricted
in their capacity to take care of themselves (Shanas, 1980).

The man in the street will say that old people are likely to die, whereas
the thanatologist states that mortality rates are highest among those of most
advanced age. The important point is that the death of an old person is never
entirely unexpected even if the imminence of the death has seemed unlikely
or has been denied.

The author wishes to thank J. Eugene Knott for helpful comments during the preparation of this
manuscript.

During this century, life expectancy in the United States has increased from approximately forty-seven to seventy years for males and from forty-nine to almost seventy-eight years for females Today, the very old constitute the fastest growing segment of the U.S. population. Four-fifths of those over sixty-five years of age have one or more living children, about half have great-grandchildren, and one in ten has a child who is already over sixty-five (U.S. Senate, Special Committee on Aging, 1984). Three-quarters of those elderly who have surviving children saw at least one of them during the week prior to a national survey in 1975, and only 11 percent had not seen a child for a month or more (Shanas, 1979). All of this indicates that ours is a society with many older members who have frequent contact with their descendents. We are also a society in which more than two-thirds of the deaths that occur are deaths of people sixty-five years of age or older (Weeks, 1984).

Considering the above, one can go on to observe that the death of a parent is probably the form of bereavement of close kin most common during adult life. Technological and medical developments have brought our society to the point where parents are likely to live out their lives without the sad task of burying a child. By the same token, the most likely scenario is that today's young and working-age people will be bereaved of their parents during their later adult years. Multiple chronic conditions are common among the elderly (U.S. Senate, Special Committee on Aging, 1983), and death often follows a period of decline and increasing dependency. During this time the adult child is confronted by both the inevitable approaching death of the parent and also by any losses of functioning, cognition, or ability the parent may exhibit day by day. If these losses occur, children have cause to grieve the tragic "partial deaths" of their living parents before their final demise.

In this chapter, the term "anticipatory grief" is reserved for those instances where the sad and painful connotation of grief is needed. The term "anticipation" does not indicate any quality of feeling but means only to look forward or to foresee and provide for beforehand. It is noteworthy that anticipatory grief focuses both on the one who will die and on the one who remains. To the extent that the adult child empathizes or identifies with the aging parent, the child's anticipatory grief is for what the parent is losing bit by bit and eventually in toto. To the extent that the adult child perceives his own loss of relationship, services, satisfaction of dependency needs, and so on as due to the declining capacities and eventual death of the parent, his anticipatory grief is for himself.

Shanas (1979) reports that the family is the primary basis of security for adults in later life. Research also confirms that the family is the major caretaker for the sick older person. Moreover, nine out of ten older people who were surveyed said that in a health crisis the person other than spouse that they would turn to would be a child (Shanas and Maddox, 1976). Next to the spouse, an adult daughter is the most likely person to be the primary caregiver for an older person at home. A recent study of families in the Cleveland, Ohio, area who were providing home care for elderly members found that the spouse was the primary caregiver in 50 percent of the cases, a daughter in 41 percent, a son in 4.5 percent, and a daughter-in-law in 4 percent (Poulshock and Deimling, 1984). Placing an older relative in an institution is generally the last resort of families who have already done a great deal to meet the extensive needs of the frail older member (Brody, 1977). Also, contrary to popular belief, the family generally continues to remain involved even when an older family member is institutionalized (York and Caslyn, 1977).

Applying these observations, the scenario mentioned earlier becomes one in which many adults can expect at some point in time to experience an extended period during which they are concerned about one or both of their older parents and to anticipate their parents' eventual deaths. A number of daughters and a few sons will be primary caregivers for parents who require long-term care. Many more adult children will contribute to the social, psychological, and economic support of their aging parents without becoming primary caregivers. Whatever the case, every adult child has life-long emotional bonds with the parents. These bonds are the basis for a wide range of feelings associated with the anticipation of parental death.

In recent years, workshops and self-help groups have been begun for families of frail older persons. Increased attention also is being given to home care of the elderly. However, little has been written to date about the impact of parental death in midlife. Perhaps this is because our society considers death in old age appropriate and not worthy of particular notice or grief. Perhaps this topic is avoided as too threatening by middle-aged adults who are themselves the research investigators and at the same time those likely to experience parental death. At least this was the reason suggested by Kimmel in 1974 when he reported being unable to find any research on the effects of parental death on middle-aged persons. Since then several relevant works have appeared, the most noteworthy being that by Moss and Moss (1983–1984). The reader is referred to that article for a discussion of the bonds between children in their thirties and forties and their active, independent parents, and also for themes the authors suggest may occur when these children suffer the death of a parent.

This chapter focuses on the period of anticipatory grief when the condition of a parent indicates that death is definitely possible, though not necessarily imminent. The adult child considered here is likely to be between forty and seventy years of age.

Meanings of Parental Death

Before considering some of the meanings the anticipated death of a parent may have, a brief review of social and developmental situations common to children of elderly parents is in order. First of all, we live in a society where the dominant value system promotes preserving and prolonging life and, at the same time, views the death of an older person as acceptable and timely.

As life expectancy continues to increase, so does the average age of the children of the elderly. Many of these children are facing their own aging-related issues. These may include health concerns, the retirement of self or spouse, or widowhood. Women, in particular, are apt to find themselves torn between the needs of husband, children, or grandchildren, on the one hand, and the needs of aging parents on the other. Adult children sometimes delay relocation or travel, sometimes for years, in order to stay near an aging parent.

If a parent becomes increasingly dependent, there is the stress of role adjustment for both parent and child. Contrary to the implication of the popular term "role reversal," the adjusted relationship is not a direct role exchange. Rather, it represents a dependency shift within the context of a relationship that has evolved under the influence of shared experiences and interaction over many years. The original parent–child relationship started without such influence.

An adult child is unlikely to experience the death of a parent as timely or appropriate no matter when it occurs. This is illustrated in the following selection from pieces written by a middle-aged daughter during the five years preceding the death of her long-widowed mother at age eighty-three.

Parents

One gone too soon:
My love would have him stay
to culminate those tasks so well begun,
to draw the interest of invested years,
to know the grandson who resembles him.
Oh, would that you had stayed.

One lingering too long:
My love would have her go
beyond the memory which touches only years gone by,
beyond the fear of that which is,
beyond the need for other hands to wash and comb and feed
    as she once did for me.
God speed that you may go.

The death of any relative reminds us of our own mortality. Beyond this, the death has particular meaning for each bereaved person according to the category of relationship, be that parent, child, or spouse, and also according to idiosyncratic factors. These idiosyncratic factors also influence the particular perspective any individual will have on the meanings of death suggested here, all of which stem from the adult child–older parent relationship. For example, the middle-aged child, who for several years has taken time and energy from a career to devote to the needs of an aging parent, may have predominant feelings either of satisfaction, or achievement, or resentment as death approaches. Another child of the same parent may experience feelings of guilt or regret associated with living far from the parent and seeing her infrequently. Both children may interpret the parent's aging and death as portentous of their own future course.

Before discussing various meanings adult children may ascribe to parental death, it is worth noting that a death affects relationships between bereaved survivors. In this case, attention is focused on the relationship between adult siblings during a time of anticipatory grief for a common parent. Siblings develop strong feelings toward each other as they mature within the close physical and emotional confines of a family. These feelings are likely to include elements of affection, envy, admiration, distrust, security, competition, and just about every other affect. When siblings become adults most leave home and live apart. They have less day-to-day interaction than they did when they lived under the same roof. Hence, there is less pressure to face any unresolved issues between them. If the approaching death of a parent increases interaction between adult siblings, feelings that have receded may once again emerge forcefully. Unresolved sibling conflicts may be re-engaged and emotions from years gone by may be displaced onto interaction around present concerns. One sibling may hold unverbalized expectations of another, expectations that are unimportant until a crisis occurs requiring joint participation in decision making. The increasing dependency of a parent is stressful to most adult children. It may be a crisis that evokes aspects of early sibling relationships, for better or for worse. In other words, there may be either increased cooperation or increased conflict between siblings at this time. Whatever the case, the outcome for sibling relationships will be influenced by the particular conditions of the parent's decline and death and also by the quality of preexisting sibling relationships.

Meanings of parental death, which will now be suggested and discussed, are being orphaned, becoming the oldest generation, coming into one's own, changing roles, a pattern for one's own aging, relief, and ending the opportunity to complete unfinished business. These possible meanings have aspects that are both threatening and promising. Therefore, it is no wonder that the anticipation of the death of a parent elicits ambivalent feelings.

At the point when the second parent dies, the child, regardless of age, becomes an orphan. On a primitive level the adult child may feel, "The one who was omnipotent in my childhood is dying. The one who has known me all my life will be no more. The love I could always depend on is dissolving. I'm being let down, deserted. My roots are shaking." Nearly always the parents are the ones who satisfy dependency needs of the young child. These parents may continue to represent security symbolically to the independent adult child. Those adults for whom parental approval has been critical to self-esteem are vulnerable to feeling threatened as they see their parents age and move toward death.

When the second parent dies, the adult child becomes not only an orphan, but also a member of the oldest generation. This generation is the next in line to die. There is no longer a buffer generation between the self and death. Parental death may signify to the adult child that she herself is now "old." If her attitude toward old age is negative, this could be a personal crisis and mark the point at which she begins to decline. She may adopt a set of self-expectations congruent with her disparaging ideas of what it is like to be old. The result may be that she begins setting and never exceeding modest goals far below her potential or magnifying her minor health problems.

On the other hand, parental death can also mean that the adult child has at last come into her own. She can claim her inheritance. She can express herself as she wishes without risking parental disapproval. She can reach her potential. She can fill roles of power and influence that have been vacated. In those cultures and families where older members have the highest social or economic status, the role of elder can be very desirable. Also, in some cultures and families, nothing less than the death of an elder can release younger members from obligations they may find onerous.

Related to "coming into one's own" are the changes in role that parental death may mean for the adult child. Without a parent, is one stripped of the daughter or son role? It has already been implied that the death of a parent may be the occasion for a change in role relative to one's siblings. Oriental societies have definite rules indicating responsibilities according to generation, sex, and birth order. In our own more open society, the death of a parent can precipitate changes in relationships that are not predetermined or planned. A time of parental decline is likely to be stressful for all family members. If this period is extended, it is also a time of potential conflict between siblings who may hold different opinions on their respective roles in the care of the parent, the terms of the will, or funeral arrangements. There may be the issue of which sibling will assume responsibilities that the parent is relinquishing either during illness or at death, or indeed whether roles, such as the convenor of family gatherings, will be filled at all.

"The way my parent ages and dies is the way I, too, am likely to go." This thought, conscious or not, is practically inevitable, especially in regard to the parent of the same sex. It springs from family identification and the understanding of hereditary influences. The relationship with parents is one of the longest and closest in the lives of most people and parents are usually the first role models children observe. Intentionally or not, parents model roles, attitudes, and the living of developmental stages that lie ahead for the child. There is no reason to suppose that the way in which parents age and die is any less a model for their children than are other parts of their living. Moreover, our expectations of longevity are tied to family history. We hear people speak with satisfaction of coming from long-lived families or talk with bravado of expecting to be dead by a relatively young age as their parents were.

A death that comes at the end of a long period of illness and functional loss brings relief for the bereaved survivors. They are no longer called on to watch a sad decline or to see that required personal care is provided. Children of older people who display increasing functional loss are likely to both anticipate and experience a sense of relief when death finally comes. The desire for relief is evident in "Mother's Day Wish," one of the daughter's writings reproduced below.

Death inevitably ends the possibility of completing any unfinished business in a relationship. When it happens that cognitive abilities of an aging parent wane, the chance of working out agreements, exchanging confidences, asking and giving forgiveness, or speaking of feelings may all end or be obviated long before death arrives. In such cases, the adult child may hope and strive to complete his or her agenda with a parent during a time when it is no longer possible to do so. The parent's physical presence may become a tantalizing reminder of that which is unattainable, and death may mean hopelessness for it will end all possibility of achieving that for which the child yearns. Realization that opportunities have been lost beyond recall can come sharply and unexpectedly to the child of divorce or to any adult child who is confronted by a parent's proximity to death when the two meet after a long separation. In such cases, agenda of which the child had hardly been aware may become painfully apparent to her at the very time when the parent no longer has the ability to take an active part in their relationship.

It follows from the above that an important task for the child of a cognitively impaired older parent is to relate to the parent as she is now. This means accepting the fact that any unsatisfactory aspects of the parent–child relationship will not be resolved through their interaction, since such is beyond the present ability of the parent. This leaves the child with the task of working through her own feelings and coming to terms with unfinished aspects of the relationship without participation by the parent. An understanding friend or counselor may be of help. A therapist might employ the Gestalt technique of the empty chair with the child playing the roles of both herself and parent in a parent–child conversation. By this means, the child may achieve sufficient resolution to enable her to relate with the disabled parent without clinging to unrealistic hopes. This may reduce stress for both parties.

To conclude this review of some of the meanings the anticipated death of a parent may have for adult children, it is noted that feelings that accompany the anticipation of parental death are usually mixed and can range from the extreme of elation in rare cases, through satisfaction and relief, anger, and guilt, to heaviness and sadness. Attention is now turned to a concept that may be particularly useful in understanding the reactions of children of those elderly parents who suffer a slow decline.

Partial Grief

"Partial grief" is the term Berezin (1970, 1977) gave to feelings people have during the time before an anticipated death occurs. When this time of anticipating a death is prolonged, as is the case with many older people who have multiple chronic illnesses, feelings of partial grief can be extended and intense. Berezin explains that death is the final, total loss and the decline-associated changes on the way to death are partial losses. Also, in old age, there are partial losses in the form of the threat of potential losses. In other words, there are many reminders for the older person and her family that there is a high risk that at any time she may lose the physical abilities, possessions, relationships, and resources that she now has. She may not be able to walk or may become incontinent. She may have to give up the home in which she now resides. Intimate relationships with members of her cohort may be terminated by relocation or death. Her financial resources may be exhausted by health care demands.

The feelings of grief about these partial losses, actual and threatened, constitute partial grief. The distinguishing characteristic of partial giref, according to Berezin, is that it cannot be resolved or worked through until after death occurs. Partial grief signifies a state of limbo, a bind. This is the experience of many of the people whose older parents are incapacitated physically or mentally. They cannot achieve the comfort the Bible promises to those who mourn, for they cannot mourn the partial losses that have so changed the parent they used to know until that parent dies.

In addition to being unresolvable, partial grief is also characterized by feelings of helplessness and guilt, ambivalence, depression, irrational or hostile attitudes, and the fluctuation of hope. Each of these will be discussed relative to adult children of the frail elderly.

Feelings of helplessness are not surprising because in many cases no efforts or resources are sufficient to stem the degenerative processes. Nothing can be done to reverse partial losses or to prevent those threatening to occur. Only death can do this. To place one's hope in death would seem to be the height of impotent helplessness. There may be the feeling that by thinking about death or preparing for it one is magically hastening the day of death. This comes out in another of the daughter's pieces written during an acute illness more than three years before her mother's death.

Responsibility

This morning I sat beside her bed
    and held her hand as she allowed
    and met her vacant stare
    and strove to catch the incoherent phrase whereby I
      might gain entry to hallucinated worlds
    and read aloud that she might recognize my voice and
      me.
This noon in funeral home (who's home?)
    I met a somber, dark-clad, ageless youth
    with whom I prearranged
      no vault
      no liner
      don't embalm
      a closed, cloth covered coffin made of pine.
This afternoon I spoke with priest in preparation for her last
    attendance at the church in which she was
      baptized
      confirmed
      withdrawn
      returned
    "don't eulogize
    give her the farewell she has shared for friends
    the Christian funeral."
This evening I returned to sit beside her bed
    and having buried her
    took up her hand as she allowed
    and met her vacant stare
    and strove to catch. . .

    It is often the responsibility of the adult child to provide for parental care; perhaps by becoming the primary caregiver, perhaps by having others give care, perhaps by arranging for institutionalization. When this last is the case, it is not said that the parent's condition required institutional care, but rather that the parent was "put in an institution." By implication there is a judgment on the family. This feeds the guilt feelings to which the children of frail older parents are vulnerable. Since women who are now middle-aged were socialized to be caregivers in our society, daughters may be particularly prone to feeling that they are not doing enough for a parent who needs long-term care. Guilt feelings are also nourished by the very condition of progressive decline. The gut churns at the thought that nothing the child can do will make everything better for the parent who many years before, with a kiss, had the power to make everything better for the child.

Guilt feelings are also fostered by values that say "our family has always taken care of its own." What is forgotten is that in past decades a smaller proportion of the population survived to advanced old age. Those individuals who did, usually remained able to care for their personal needs until the last weeks or months of their lives. Only recently has medical technology made years of slow decline likely. All of which means that in the past fewer families faced the prospect of extended care for an older relative.

Ambivalence is another aspect of partial grief. The adult child wants the well-being of the parent and also wants the death, which alone can terminate deterioration. Rarely is death equated with well-being. To wish someone dead is considered a curse. It is hardly acceptable to admit to oneself that one wishes a parent dead, let alone to say so openly. Some paradoxes are easier to accept than others. The adult child may accept the paradox that it is possible to be angry with someone one loves, yet she may not be able to reconcile her paradoxical wishes for both the well-being and the death of her parent. In another writing over a year before her mother's death, the daughter expresses her wish for death to come and also her bind of partial grief. Relief, anticipated with the death, is evident as well.

Mother's Day Wish

I long to mourn your death,

to be bereaved of that last earthly vestige of the precious one
who gave me birth.
Was ever soul more bound in zombie form,

immobilized between what was and is to be?
Love becomes resentment.

Will is duty-bent.
Why must your hell be mine?
I've said a thousand half goodbyes.

Be gone!
Then I shall bid a last farewell,
shall grieve the bit of grief that's left,
shall be allowed to mourn the fragmentary loss of you

I've borne so many days and months and years.
Thus may I come at last

to render heartfelt thanks for all your life.

It is easy to understand that an adult child's anger or depression may be evoked by changes in the parent, responsibility for providing care, or the impingement of the parent's needs on the child's lifestyle. If depression is seen as anger turned inward, then whether the reaction is primarily one of depression or of anger will depend in part on the personality of the child. Of course, the expresison of anger toward a parent, especially for something as involuntary and terminal as moving toward death, is not likely to be acceptable personally or socially. So it turns out that adult children who anticipate parental death may be subject to depression from situational factors and also from the partial grief they cannot yet resolve. A situation faced by some families that is likely to elicit anger, though perhaps not the direct expression of that anger, is the depletion of family resources in order to provide the care required by an older member. In such cases, the angry thought, "You're living too long to no avail. You should be dead by now." would be in the minds of some children. The words they express, however, may be the docile phrase, "I can't wish her to linger any longer."

Irrational and hostile attitudes are not uncommon among those experiencing partial grief. The adult child may become more suspicious and argumentative with those close to her. If the parent is institutionalized, the child's hostility may be directed toward physicians and staff members. It may also be that staff members are hostile to relatives. Such hostility is likely to spring from the staff members' own partial grief as a result of close relationships formed with the elderly parent during caregiving. Siblings are apt to be critical of each other's behavior and defensive regarding their own efforts. To wit, note the hostility expressed at the beginning of a lengthy writing by the daughter concerning her trip to help her mother move into an institution.

To journey—

> knitting tension into diamonds
> and venting anger on the smokers
> lest my energy burst forth
> in guilt or fear that I'd delayed too long.

While there is partial grief, hope is likely to fluctuate. The wish for improvement in the parent's condition and the desire for positive results from care and treatment are strong. At the same time, loss is clearly evident. Awareness focuses at one time on desire, at another time on reality. When a parent's death is anticipated, there may come a point where the hope of some children becomes hope for a good death. The hope of others waivers but never turns away from life.

This discussion has been limited to the partial grief of adult children. Of course, the dying parent and other relatives will each have their own partial grief.

It is possible, and indeed likely, that the partial grief of an adult child and that of an elderly parent will have different foci at any particular time. For example, the child may be grieving the patient's loss of short-term memory, whereas the parent is distressed at not being allowed to use the electric stove any longer. The inevitable incongruence of the partial grief of elderly parent and adult child can impede mutual support and communication between them. Similarly when two or more siblings are each grieving a different partial loss, or are otherwise out of syncronization with each other, misunderstanding and conflict are likely to occur.

Obviously, there are problems for adult children who experience partial grief, but what help is there for them? Berezin (1977) recommends a family conference with a psychiatrist or other professional acting as a neutral, objective, and rational resource. In this conference, the family is to be confronted with the reality of the situation, that is, the implications of the parent's diagnosis and the prognosis for what can be expected. Berezin writes that there should be a discussion of partial grief, its unresolvable aspect, and especially the feelings of helplessness that accompany it. Stress should be laid on the need for family unity and the mutual support family members can provide for each other.

Children can get assistance through self-help groups that are organized for relatives of persons with Alzheimers and related diseases, for children of older parents, and for relatives of nursing home residents. It is also helpful if an adult child has a confidante to whom she is able to express herself openly. Hearing oneself speak of a concern helps one own the problem and legitimize feelings about it. Then, too, the individual who can express concerns in drawing, writing, music, dance, or another art form has not only a cathartic outlet but also a means of getting in touch with her feelings and gaining understanding.

Conclusion

It is my observation that, regardless of anticipatory grief, several types of grief work remain for the adult child following the parent's death. There is the grief for the final, total loss of the parent. It is at the point of death that it becomes possible to begin resolving whatever partial grief has been accumulated. The bereaved child may also need to mourn the style of death if it was other than peaceful. There may be regret that one was absent at the time of death or during the parent's last lucid period. Any unsatisfactory or incomplete aspect of the parent–child relationship must be grieved. Finally, there is the meaning or meaninglessness of the time preceding death to consider. If this was a time of comfort, lucidity, and the affirmation of close bonds, the death may feel appropriate. If it was a long period of incapacity, discomfort, and the depletion of family resources, then the apparent meaninglessness of the dying time may be a difficult part of grief to resolve.

The period after a parent's death is a time for grief and also a time for redefining relationships between bereaved survivors. Siblings who have gone through a period of partial grief and are now parentless will find their sibling relationships changed as a result. Consideration of these changes, which will vary from one sibling relationship to another, is beyond the scope of this paper.

Whatever the specific aspects of an individual case, however, each child will find that the death of a parent holds meaning for her that is somewhat different from the meaning of other deaths she may have experienced previously.

References

Berezin, M.A. 1970. The Psychiatrist and the Geriatric Patient. *Journal of Geriatric Psychiatry* 4:53–64.

Berezin, M. 1977. Partial Grief for the Aged and Their Families. In E.M. Pattison, ed., *The Experience of Dying*. Englewood Cliffs, N.J.: Prentice-Hall, pp. 279–286.

Brody, E. 1977. *Long-term Care for Older People*. New York: Human Sciences Press.

Kimmel, D.C. 1974. *Adulthood and Aging*. New York: John Wiley and Sons.

Moss, M.S., and S.Z. Moss. 1983–1984. The Impact of Parental Death on Middle Aged Children. *Omega* 14:65–75.

Poulshock, S.W., and G.T. Deimling. 1984. Families Caring for Elders in Residence: Issues in the Measurement of Burden. *Journal of Gerontology* 39:230–239.

Shanas, E. 1979. Social Myth as Hypothesis: The Case of the Family Relations of Old People. *The Gerontologist* 19:3–9.

Shanas, E. 1980. Self-assessment of Physical Function: White and Black Elderly in the United States. In S.G. Haynes and M. Feinleib, eds., *Second Conference on the Epidemiology of Aging*. NIH Publication No. 80–969.

Shanas, E., and G.L. Maddox. 1976. Aging, Health and the Organization of Health Resources. In R. Binstock and E. Shanas, eds., *Handbook of Aging and the Social Sciences*. New York: Van Nostrand Reinhold, 592–618.

U.S. Senate, Special Committee on Aging. 1983. *Developments in Aging*. Vol. 1.

U.S. Senate, Special Committee on Aging in conjunction with the American Association of Retired Persons. 1984. *Aging in America: Trends and Projections*.

Weeks, J.R. 1984. *Aging: Concepts and Social Issues*. Belmont, Calif.: Wadsworth.

York, J.L., and R.J. Caslyn. 1977. Family Involvement in Nursing Homes. *The Gerontologist* 17:500–505.

Part V
Practical Considerations in Anticipatory Grief

13
Anticipatory Grief and the Prearrangement of Funerals

Howard C. Raether

> The most enduring monuments in the world, the great pyramids, were both memorials and tombs for the rulers of Egypt. Thus for nearly four thousand years, Egyptian society at every level, from the Pharaohs down to the least slave, was given over in great part to the task of preparing and caring for the dead.
>
> R. Habenstein and W.M. Lamers,
> *The History of American Funeral Directing*

During the Middle Ages, the Renaissance, and thereafter, societies, guilds, craft organizations, and fraternal groups provided burial benefits to their members. Habenstein and Lamers (1955) point out that during the Middle Ages burial clubs assisted people of the working classes, particularly guild members, to defray the heavy expenses of a funeral and to perpetuate the memory of dead friends. A quarterage was levied among the living to provide, in advance of need, third-group participation to help pay for the care and burial of the dead.

By the mid-nineteenth century, there were over two hundred burial clubs in London designed to spread the cost of burial among many. Formally organized as Friendly Societies, these groups were the forerunners of modern industrial insurance, with high rates and premiums collected weekly. Some clergy in the United States banded together for the same purpose. They founded death insurance, which for many years since has been called life insurance.

These developments involved persons and organizations other than the actual providers of postdeath activities, that is, funeral directors. However, after World War I some providers in parts of the United States started offering burial insurance. This was followed by such plans as mutual benefit associations, funeral certificate plans, funeral debentures, funeral trusts, funeral savings accounts, and legal reserve funeral insurance, to name a few. These plans have been payable in cash, credits, merchandise, and service, or combinations of each of these elements. Funeral directors, cemeteries, and other providers have been and are today directly or indirectly involved.

Another form of prearranging funerals may be found in governmental procedures and ceremonies for the funeral of a person of note, for instance, royalty, high government officials, military heroes, and others. As a specific example, the U.S. Military District of Washington maintains a manual of standard operating procedures entitled, "State and Special Military Funeral Policies and Plans." Some state and local governments have funeral guidelines for civil servants killed in line of duty. Fraternal groups, religious orders, and veterans' organizations also have prescribed rites and ceremonies.

Definitions

"Preneed" is an omnibus term that covers any and all aspects of prearranging, preplanning, or prefunding a funeral or other postdeath activity.

"Preplanning" and "prearranging" are often used synonymously. Each means a funeral arrangement made prior to need, including those in contemplation of impending death. Each involves making clear, in writing or orally, certain specifics of what is desired. It often includes naming a funeral director, spelling out some details as to a rite and/or ceremony, funeral merchandise, and method and place of final disposition. In this chapter, the term "prearranging" will be used.

"Prefunding" is taking steps to have funds for a funeral available. Some prefunding is accompanied by funeral arrangements that allow survivors some postdeath decision making. Some arrangements are very specific, to be changed only if it is impossible or difficult to follow through as originally planned. In some instances, prearranging and prefunding mandates what should not be done, for example, the body should not be cremated or the casket should not be open. Some prefunding is permitted to provide for the funeral of those seeking public assistance. The prefunding relieves a government social service agency of having the financial obligation of funeral and final disposition costs.

A "prearranger" is the person prearranging and/or prefunding his or her own funeral or that of someone else.

Some Facts and Figures

The Committee to Study Preneed of the National Funeral Directors Association (NFDA) in 1982 concluded that preneed is a way of the future affecting those in the funeral directing facet of funeral service. This determination was predicated on an expressed growing desire of segments of the public for preneed services. A resolution of the Preneed Committee was passed by the House of Delegates of NFDA, endorsing funeral directors to prearrange and/or prefund funerals. The committee felt it essential to survey the more than 13,000 members of NFDA for their opinions and practices. Some of the findings of that study (1,728 respondents or 13 percent of the membership) are

1. Over 85 percent of the respondents said prearranging and/or prefunding was increasing, with more than 75 percent indicating the greatest increase since 1979.

2. Most prefunding was in trust or bank escrow accounts. Some was in insurance or a combination of trust funds, insurance, and plans sold by third-party sellers served by funeral homes.

3. Fifty-four percent of prefunded funerals were not changed by the survivors after death occurred. When they were, more were changed in the direction of moving from something less traditional (for example, a direct disposition or funeral without the body present) to something more traditional, than vice versa. When the funeral was prearranged and changes were made from either a less than traditional or traditional funeral, these changes were to direct dispositions with or without a memorial service. There were also a few changes to a different postdeath activity. In general, the experiences of funeral directors in this study is that most changes in prearranged and/or prefunded funerals are toward the traditional funeral, that is, a public visitation and funeral with the body present and a procession to the place of final disposition.

4. Most who prefunded funerals were sixty-six to eighty years of age. Of note is the trend toward those under sixty-five to prearrange and prefund funerals.

5. The vast majority of responding funeral directors (95 percent) felt that those who prefund their funerals help the survivors. Also, 92 percent of the funeral directors felt that those who prefund benefit personally and psychologically by having done so.

6. More than half of the funeral directors (56 percent) think prefunded funerals help survivors cope with grief. Fifteen percent (15 percent) had an opposite view. Eighteen percent (18 percent) said that they did not know if prefunded funerals helped survivors, and the balance (11 percent) expressed no opinion.

There are caveats to these findings. The opinions were of funeral directors based on their experiences. They are not psychiatrists or psychologists. The findings in five and six above should be viewed with that in mind. However, notwithstanding this, funeral directors have more experience with death and its survivors than any other discipline. Consequently, their observations are worth noting because of the lack of empirical evidence relating to the feelings of those who had prearranged and/or prefunded a funeral or of their survivors.

Why Funerals are Prearranged and/or Prefunded

Most funerals are prearranged and/or prefunded for one or more reasons including:

1. To relieve the survivors of financial and other responsibilities and/or to establish parameters for funeral expenses.
2. To let survivors know what is and/or is not wanted.
3. To insure having a funeral or certain components of one because survivors may select something else.
4. To assure a surviving spouse of having the same as was selected for his or her deceased spouse.
5. To avoid potential problems because of family members being separated by age and/or distance.
6. To ease, by predeath discussion, some of the problems associated with postdeath activities, such as the funeral and final disposition of the body.
7. To prevent an unscrupulous funeral director from taking advantage at a time of stress immediately after a death.
8. To comply with and adapt to specific rites and ceremonies suggested by units of government, religious groups, and fraternal and veterans' organizations. Most times such compliance and adaptation is limited to the incidentals. There is a basic structure to these ceremonies (most of which are not prefunded) that is to be followed if they are used.

Ways to Prearrange and/or Prefund a Funeral

Most prearrangements are made and are paid for by the individual for whom they are intended. This is done in one of various ways including, but not limited to:

1. The prearranger putting in a will or on a prearrangement form or checklist what he or she desires. (However, whenever prearranging and/or prefunding is reduced to writing, including directions in a will, the person(s) who will be responsible for immediate postdeath matters *should* have a copy. The only copy for survivors *must* not be kept in a safety deposit box, which may not be opened until after the funeral when it will be too late to follow the directions and plans already made.) This written information is also often filed with the funeral home and sometimes with a church, society, bank, lawyer, or an associate. Methods to pay for the arrangements may be made avilable from one or more of the following sources either before or at need: insurance, estate funds, death benefits, government allowance, and others.

2. The prearranger making a nonspecified prefunded contract or making specific funeral and final disposition arrangements with a funeral director. The latter may or may not be covered by a contract between the arranger and the funeral director that includes the items desired, their cost, and the payment schedule.

3. Cemeteries selling grave and mausoleum spaces in advance of death, and, when the cemetery is a combination cemetery and funeral home, prearranging funerals. Funeral prefunding through the solicitation of burial or funeral insurance has also existed for years. Within the last decade, especially since the late 1970s, making preneed programs available through active, if not aggressive marketing, has intensified.

   There are still many funeral homes where preneed activity is limited to paragraphs one and two above. However, more are becoming active because of a perceived or actual market or to be competitive with those offering preneed plans by contacting those who may be interested. Some call this "prospecting," which is done by a representative of the funeral director or a third party making the original contact and completing the arrangements to be serviced by a funeral firm. This procedure involves a contract and prefunding.

4. Arrangements that follow established customs for the funeral of a person of note, sometimes made in advance with that person. Sometimes his or her spouse or other family member(s) are given an opportunity to review the manual of procedures and make certain determinations. This applies at the federal government level in the United States for state funerals. However, most times established rites and ceremonies at other governmental levels are either followed totally or disregarded. The same is true of many military funerals and other funeral services using established fraternal or religious rites. As an example, when a Masonic funeral is desired for a deceased member, the prescribed ritual is used. There can be no variations from the basic procedure.

Advice Regarding Prearranged/Prefunded Funerals

Funeral directors and others who offer preneed options are ready to assist in providing information and then to accommodate decisions made after an open and frank discussion regarding what is desired. The following factors should be considered, especially if there is going to be prefunding:

1. The effect of advance arranging on survivors.

2. The advantages and disadvantages of planning now for something that might not occur for years, with an awareness of changes that may occur that affect the decisions made and/or the funeral director and merchandise selected.

3. A funded preneed arrangement should be spelled out in a written contract. Such a contract should be explicit, while providing safeguards for the consumer and the funeral director, including portability/transferability of the contract if the person for whom the funeral is prearranged moves away from the funeral director's service area or wishes to terminate the agreement. All states except Alabama, Connecticut, Vermont, and Wyoming and the District of Columbia had preneed trust laws as 1984 ended. Therefore, the terms and conditions of prefunding should be governed by such laws.

4. Whenever prearrangements are made in written form, those responsible for immediate postdeath matters should have a copy before the death occurs in order to act in accordance with the prearrangements. Sole copies should never be kept in safety deposit boxes, in wills, or among personal papers that may not be investigated until after the funeral is over.

Anticipatory Grief and Prearranging a Funeral

The recognition and study of anticipatory grief and the growth of prearranged and/or prefunded funerals are post-World War II phenomena. They seldom have been considered together in literature as they will be in this chapter.

There is no empirical data for the average number of years between prearranging and/or prefunding and death. The lapse time generally is longer when there has been only prearrangement. In such cases, changes in original plans are more numerous. There is often a different set of circumstances when death appears to be only weeks or months off, as compared to when it appears to be years away.

Many persons are told to "get their house in order" because they are terminally ill. This is especially true in the hospice setting. Others become aware of their fate indirectly. Often, funeral plans are made as part of getting prepared for the eventual death for one or more of the following reasons: (1) the person is aware that he or she is dying; (2) making such plans leaves only the death to occur, along with doing what will make the dying person physically and mentally comfortable; and (3) the climate is right for family involvement.

Previous literature on anticipatory grief primarily has focused on survivors and their adjustment to loss. However, the dying person himself has the potential to experience anticipatory grief in relation to the expected death, with positive consequences for some and negative consequences for others.

Many terminally ill individuals are helped significantly by taking control and prearranging their own funerals. They may experience peace of mind because their funeral has been prearranged (1) in concert with the closest of their survivors; (2) as they want their funeral, not necessarily as the family would like it; or (3) to spite a member or members of their family. There are those whose acceptance of their dying and death comes easier because of prearrangement of the funeral. However, there are some terminally ill persons who are emotional while making arrangements for their own funeral. They often continue grieving in anticipation of their death, with such grief sometimes intensified because plans are made for their funeral and they feel there is nothing left for them. There are others who remain hostile because of their condition and the need to arrange plans for the inevitable. There are also some who become depressed, which could shorten their lives. Some even become suicide-prone.

When funeral arrangements are made in advance of need, with the presumption that death is weeks or months away, there is more of a likelihood of survivors being involved than when there is a prearrangement made years in advance. Family members and others often participate in the discussion when the dying patient is placed in a hospital or extended care facility. In fact, some of these facilities have an admittance requirement for at least skeletal funeral plans to be filed with them to be referred to when death occurs.

Lindemann (1944) and Fulton and Gottesman (1980) maintain that there is uncertainty whether anticipatory grief is functional or dysfunctional for the individual or the family. The context of this reference is to survivors. Its application to the individual whose death is imminent is difficult to assess. It seems that if prearranging a funeral helps a terminally ill person get his or her house in order, there could be a grieving for self that brings with it peace of mind whether or not survivors are concerned or grieving. Acceptance of death by the terminally ill patient is neither happy nor unhappy. Its being devoid of feelings is not resignation (Kübler-Ross, 1969).

Some persons, especially the elderly, prearrange and perhaps prefund their funeral not in contemplation of impending death, but because segments of society, perhaps including their children, do not regard them as consequential persons. They want, at least, to be of some consequence after death and to have a funeral for those who want to attend. Elderly prearrangers who are physically able occasionally visit the funeral director with whom they have made the prearrangement simply to check on things or to make a change or two; for example, the clergyman they wanted to officiate may have been transferred to a church in a distant city. If it is not easy for them to get about, some will ask the funeral director to visit them to review or update their plans.

In the above situations, the grief of the elderly relates more to attitudes toward them than to anticipation of their death. When death does occur, it has been observed that their children might show less emotion than when a family pet has died. This is especially true when the elderly person has been segregated from his or her family. Out of sight is often out of mind. Out of mind becomes out of heart. And, when out of heart, prearrangement of their funeral by the elderly is often appreciated by the survivors, especially if the prearranger also prefunded the service. Without such prearrangement, there might only be the disposition of the body without attendant rites and ceremonies. However, this is not universal. There are prospective survivors who want to be a part of prearranging a funeral for someone elderly. They yield to the prearranger's wishes and sometimes assume some or all the funeral costs. This is true whether or not death is contemplated in a short period of time.

According to funeral directors, regardless of whether prospective survivors were considered during the making of a prearrangement (as a spouse most generally is) and no matter what was prearranged, most survivors of a prearranged funeral feel that they were helped by doing what the deceased wanted. Also, according to funeral directors, survivors think that the prearranging and/or prefunding helped them avoid having to make difficult decisions immediately after the death.

Discussion

"Man's concern about caring for the dead [dates back] to at least 60,000 years ago" (Pine, 1975, p. 12).

"A funeral ceremony is personal in its focus and is societal in its consequences" (Mandelbaum, 1959, p. 189).

"Insofar as our funerals meet these needs as they are present in the individual's mourning the funeral is an experience of value" (Irion, 1956).

"The mourner derives psychological, social, and spiritual benefits from well-designed funerary rituals" (Rando, 1984, p. 180).

"A funeral rite is a social rite *par excellence.* Its ostensible object is the dead person, but it benefits not the dead but the living" (Firth, 1964, p. 63).

"The funeral is both socially useful and emotionally valuable. It is not only a rite for the dead, but the right of the living" (Fulton, 1967).

Many funeral directors feel that in most cases the prearranging and/or prefunding of funerals has not interfered with the rights of the living. According to funeral directors, most survivors are satisfied with the prearrangements made. Some who are not satisfied make changes to embellish or diminish what was prearranged. More embellishment than diminution is reported. Except for funerals that have been prearranged and prefunded because of an overaggressive approach, resulting in something that would not provide what was wanted, or unless there is a problem with price, it is argued that most prearrangers feel that their actions have taken a weight off their shoulders and those of the members of their immediate family. However, less than 5 percent of the funerals conducted by NFDA members in 1983 were prearranged (Pine, 1984). Some of those that were prearranged and prefunded were done over ten years earlier.

Therefore, it is difficult to compare and/or contrast dollar and other values with current funeral selections.

Research has revealed no study that would provide meaningful insights based on the experiences or opinions of prearrangers and of prospective or actual survivors in relation to anticipatory grief and prearranged funerals. However, interviews of the widows of ten slain officers of the Detroit Police Department revealed that the widows felt that the large civic funerals given these officers were appropriate tributes to their husbands for heroism and loyalty. They also felt the funerals did nothing for them, providing no emotional support. In addition, they were unimpressed by the ride in the Mayor's car and the "carnival" aspects of the ceremony (Danto, 1974). Apparently, prescribed ceremonies were followed with no adaptations that would have made them more personally meaningful to the particular survivors.

There were many adaptations prior to and during the period of the state funeral for John Fitzgerald Kennedy. His widow, Jacqueline, his brother, Robert, and other relatives, plus friends and federal government officials made decisions to meet the needs of those close to him, as well as of those of all the country to which he belonged (Manchester, 1967). A study of forty-eight adult residents of Minneapolis regarding television functions on the assassination weekend emphasized that for most respondents the funeral provided a properly dignified and ceremonious conclusion for the emotions of the weekend (Mindak and Hursh, 1965).

What if there had been no funeral to televise because the assassinated president had prearranged something different? President Kennedy was a significant figure to millions. What about a person who is significant to only a few? Does that lessen the value of the appropriate funeral for him or her?

Will children witnessing an abbreviated postdeath ceremony, or none at all, arranged before or at-need for a deceased grandparent come to the conclusion that their deaths might be treated in the same cold, callous way?

Could funeral prearranging and/or prefunding grow to the point where there would be a generation in which many persons would experience the death of loved ones, but never have an opportunity to be involved in making arrangements for a funeral because such arrangements have already been prearranged? Or, where these survivors might not be able to go to a funeral because prearrangements were for something other than a funeral?

Conclusion

Forty years ago I had negative feelings about prearranging funerals. They were intensified when prearranging was first combined with prefunding. All encompassing promotions developed. Salesmen solicited the purchase of plans for the prefunding of "packages" that included a funeral, funeral and burial merchandise, and cemetery space. Some promoters left town with the funds paid in advance. Some funeral directors comingled preneed funds with their operating cash. As a result, when death occurred there was no money for some prefunded funerals. Then, too, the prices of some plans were in excess of those for comparable at-need selections. A court said the prefunding of funerals was fraught with the danger of fraud. It still is, but now more legal safeguards exist.

State preneed trust laws, publicity of the investigation of some preneed plans by a committee of the U.S. Senate, the Association of Better Business Bureaus' pamphlet on the subject, and intrafuneral service education has resulted in legitimate plans in addition to the availability of preneed at most funeral homes and mortuaries. These developments, coupled with an apparent public desire for prearranging and/or prefunding funerals, have changed my opinion about them. However, the premises for my current position are (1) that there be greater access to prearranging and/or prefunding to meet consumer needs in addition to being a competitive tool of those who sell and/or provide preneed services; (2) that there be proper communications in offering preneed services; and (3) that there be laws and regulations enforced to protect those choosing and those offering to prearrange and/or prefund any facet of postdeath activities.

As concluded by the Institute of Medicine's Study of Health Consequences of the Stress of Bereavement, anticipatory grieving before death, as well as postdeath grieving often lasting beyond a year after death, deserve further study (Osterweis, Solomon, and Green, 1984). Such studies should seek answers to a number of questions including the following:

1. Does the prearranger of his or her own funeral experience anticipatory grief?

2. Is any function of grief changed when prospective survivors experience anticipatory grief but are not included in making plans in advance of death for the funeral of someone loved?

3. "Is any function of grief changed when prospective survivors experience anticipatory grief but are denied the opportunity to mourn through formal [funeral] roles or rituals?" (Fulton and Gottesman, 1980, p. 52).

The findings of such research could be a valuable addition to the literature on dying, death, and bereavement.

References

Danto, B.L. 1974. A Study: Bereavement and the Widows of Slain Officers. *The Police Chief* (Feb.):51–57.
Firth, R. 1964. *Elements of Social Organization*. Boston: Beacon Press.

Fulton, R. 1967. *A Compilation of Studies of Attitudes Toward Death, Funerals, and Funeral Directors.* Minneapolis: Center for Death Education and Research, University of Minnesota.

Fulton, R., and D.J. Gottesman. 1980. Anticipatory Grief: A Psychosocial Concept Reconsidered. *British Journal of Psychiatry* 137:45–54.

Habenstein, R., and W.M. Lamers. 1955. *The History of American Funeral Directing* Milwaukee: Bulfin.

Irion, P. 1956. The Funeral: An Experience of Value. Speech at the annual convention of the National Funeral Directors Association, October. Milwaukee, Wisc.

Kübler-Ross, E. 1969. *On Death and Dying.* New York: Macmillan.

Lindemann, E. 1944. Symptomatology and Management of Acute Grief. *The American Journal of Psychiatry* 101:141–148.

Manchester, W. 1967. *The Death of a President.* New York: Harper and Row.

Mandelbaum, D.G. 1959. Social Uses of Funeral Rites. In H. Feifel, ed., *The Meaning of Death.* New York: McGraw-Hill, pp. 189–217.

Mindak, W.A., and G. Hursh. 1965. Television Functions on the Assassination Weekend. In B.S. Greenberg and E.B. Parker, eds., *The Kennedy Assassination and the American Public.* Stanford, Calif.: Stanford University Press.

Osterweis, M., F. Solomon, and M. Green, 1984. eds. *Bereavement: Reactions, Consequences and Care.* A report by the Committee for the Study of Health Consequences of the Stress of Bereavement, Institute of Medicine, National Academy of Sciences. Washington, D.C.: National Academy Press.

Pine, V.R. 1975. *Caretaker of the Dead: The American Funeral Director.* New York: Irvington Publishers.

Pine, V.R. 1984. *A Statistical Abstract of Funeral Service Facts and Figures.* Milwaukee: National Funeral Directors Association.

Rando, T.A. 1984. *Grief, Dying and Death: Clinical Interventions for Caregivers.* Champaign, Ill.: Research Press.

14

Legal and Ethical Issues in Terminal Illness Care for Patients, Families, Caregivers, and Institutions

Dennis A. Robbins

Anticipatory grief is multifaceted and multidimensional. Research has repeatedly documented that what occurs during the period of anticipatory grief has a significant impact on the quality of the dying patient's remaining life as well as on the postdeath adjustment of survivors. An area in which anticipatory grief both has an impact on, and is impacted on, is in the latter stages of some terminal illnesses when questions arise about life-sustaining treatment. These concern such issues as the withholding or withdrawing of mechanical and nutritional life supports, and the legal controversies surrounding what should or should not be done and who should have the right to make such decisions. In today's terminal illnesses, which tend to be chronic in nature and result in bioethical quandaries when patient consciousness can depart long before legal death arrives, these questions are all too frequently confronted by both patient and family as part of the anticipatory grief experience. Anxieties surrounding fear of losing control, or of having the ability to help a dying loved one compromised by legal or defensive medicine tactics, are important concerns in this experience. In fact, it can shroud many of the other clinical issues. The difficulties can be exacerbated by such conflicts among family members as to what is the proper course to follow, differing opinions surrounding the propriety of a given procedure or failure to provide a procedure, as well as disparities between patient and spouse. Denial and unexamined bias also contribute to the excess baggage that can exacerbate complicated decision making and undermine adaptive capacities in this domain.

Such mechanisms as living wills, Do-Not-Resuscitate (DNR) orders in advance, durable powers of attorney, and other legal anticipatory mechanisms may preclude some of the aforementioned conflicts that can add to the already high stress inherent in the anticipatory grief experience. In the cases of irreconcilable conflict, these mechanisms may provide a reasonable vehicle by which a patient's intent can be inferred or determined by ethics committees, courts, or other designated decision-making bodies. This chapter reviews the legal dilemmas that have arisen in the care of the terminally ill and will offer some suggestions for legal protection of patient self-determination in terminal illness and insulation against liability for caregiver and institution.

Legal Problems

Some understanding of recent legal history is necessary to fully appreciate the dimensions of this area of concern. The 1976 Karen Ann Quinlan case was the first to arise in this area and attempted to address issues of removal of life supports in light of new sophisticated technology. Although few legal cases are well known to the American public, this case clearly is among them. It involved a young woman who had stopped breathing for at least two fifteen-minute periods, leaving her in what medical experts characterized as a chronic and persistent vegetative state. The decision-making questions revolved around determining the propriety of what measures ought to be taken and whether life supports ought to be removed and Karen allowed to die. The pivotal criterion to be determined was whether Karen could ever be restored to a "cognitive and sapient" life. Decision making thus pivoted on medical prognosis.

This was a particularly novel question at the time, for there was no legal precedent to provide clear guidance. New capabilities to keep people alive beyond the time that they would have otherwise died had created new problems. For example, respirators could extend life past that time when one would previously have been clinically dead, that is, heart beat and lung functioning stopped. At the time of *Quinlan,* although the technology existed, clear established legal or ethical precedent for guidance was absent.

Karen's father sought to be appointed legal guardian to make decisions over the removal or discontinuance of the respirator. In such matters, guardianship can be of two sorts—those entailing decisions involving *property* and those involving *person*. The removal of the respirator was a guardianship over person question. The New Jersey court was reluctant to grant this decision-making capacity to Karen's father given its uneasiness about what ought to be done. In attempting to address this problem, the New Jersey court decided that the way in which matters like this ought to be decided was through an ethics committee, that is, when you have controversy and it is not clear what to do, a hospital ethics committee ought to intervene to make decisions.

Quinlan offered a novel precedent by saying that the most reasonable forum for such decisions was to be the ethics committee. The appropriate forum, they agreed, was not the courts, not doctors alone, not the patient alone, not the family alone, although these could be important ingredients in the decision-making process, but ultimately the ethics committee. However, in this context, the ethics committee was an unusual aberration of an ethics committee and accordingly rather interesting because it, upon reflection, looked like little more than a medical prognosis committee. Its charge seemed to be aimed at determining the natural progression of the disease process that was expected to happen to this patient given her condition and disease.

Basically, the ethics committee, as well as the court, was concerned fundamentally with whether Karen Ann Quinlan would ever be able to assume the normal functions of thinking and living in other than a vegetative manner, that is, would she be restored to a level where she could carry on as a human being, as a person?

Although the impact of *Quinlan* was great, it was not enough to convince the Massachusetts courts that the cognitive–sapient state criteria was sufficient to address such a controversial decision. Massachusetts was uncomfortable with the *Quinlan* decision, unsure of how far its implications would extend. The Massachusetts courts were reticent to trust a group of people in some committee to be the ones making these decisions, and they believed that the weight of such questions merited court intervention. The Saikewicz case demonstrated this departure.

The Saikewicz case (1978) was that of a seventy-six-year-old incompetent man who had leukemia. The only intervention that could possibly help him was chemotherapy. He was a ward of the state who had been institutionalized at least fifty-six of the seventy-six years of his life. He was severely mentally retarded, and neither legally nor medically competent to make decisions of this sort. The Massachusetts court, in considering what to do and whether or not chemotherapy ought to be administered to this terminally ill man, looked at a number of considerations. Two considerations were addressed most carefully: one was the ethical integrity of the medical profession and the other was the state's obligation to protect life. Here was a man who was severely retarded, with a terminal illness, and the chemotherapy he required involved a great amount of discomfort, which he could not understand. The court-appointed guardian *ad litem* (appinted for purposes of arguing the case) said that, because of his condition and status, Mr. Saikewicz could not appreciate the positive possibilities of the chemotherapy, and whereas most people would be able to derive some hope, he would only experience fear and discomfort.

The Massachusetts court deviated from the cognitive and sapient life criterion of *Quinlan* and the forum for decision making was not the hospital via the ethics committee. In fact, it appeared that the probate court in Massachusetts was the forum to make this decision. The criterion around which the decision not to treat Mr. Saikewicz was made was called "substituted judgement," instead of the *Quinlan* criterion of cognitive sapient state. Self-determination or autonomy seemed to occupy less concern in the Massachusetts court than in the earlier *Quinlan* decision. This basically implied that there is a mechanism through which we can attempt to figure out what a given person would have decided were that person able to decide for himself. In this case, that meant the need to consider what Mr. Saikewicz likely would have decided were he able to make his own decision, taking into account his terminal illness, his IQ, and all other pertinent considerations. Again, the court collectively saw these reasons as grounds not to pursue the course that most individuals would normally elect.

It is important to remember that the Saikewicz case arose at the time of a climate of emerging defensive medicine, where doctors and hospitals became very much concerned about insulating against potential liability. A lot of physicians were uncomfortable with this case, and many clinicians felt that it suggested too much uncertainty. It was unclear whether any time one needed to make a decision about whether a patient should be resuscitated, one either could let them die or had to go to court before beginning resuscitation.

In an attempt to clarify the intentions of *Saikewicz*, the Dinnerstein case arose in Massachusetts. This decision attempted to amplify *Saikewicz* and reduce some of the legal and medical uncertainty that case had created. *Saikewicz* seemed to imply, among other things, that any time one had a terminally ill person, one should go to the courts. Not only is that rather cumbersome, but when one analyzes what a reasonable time frame is for decision making in a court, it is not unusual to find that a case may go on for two, three, four, or five months, sometimes even years. In fact, it is not unusual that cases are decided mootly after the patient is already dead. Time frame differences between the legal system and the medical system are so dissimilar that using the courts as a forum for decision making is most often inappropriate. There has to be some other mechanism. Some have argued that ethics committees are more appropriate to meet this need.

The Dinnerstein case attempted to say that a competent patient, or someone acting on behalf of an incompetent individual, has the right to refuse treatment. Also, they can have their wishes written on a medical chart so that in the event that they do want DNR orders or want to refuse treatment later, and they are no longer competent, their wishes will be assured. *Dinnerstein* basically argued that a competent adult, as an extension of the privacy right, has a right to refuse treatment and has the right to have his wishes be known. This also includes the right not to have intrusions performed on one's body against one's will.

With such a mechanism, there is no need to infer what the patient likely would have decided, as in *Saikewicz*, or have some ethics committee address the issue, like *Quinlan*, because the patient or his agent has already indicated his wishes and it has been documented and certified in the chart. That serves as protection for the patient and reduces ambiguity for caregivers and the institution.

Massachusetts was still uneasy with the implications of *Dinnerstein* and reticent to accept the implications it suggested. The Spring case followed to amplify this area. This case involved a dialysis patient of questionable competence. The court laid out thirteen factors that have to be followed when decisions are to be made regarding removal of life supports, specifically in this case, removal of a kidney dialysis machine.

The propriety of what should be done in this case was decided mootly after the death of the individual in question. It had gone on for approximately two years during which time this man and his family went through enormous grief and suffering. Interestingly enough, the thirteen factors suggested were not unreasonable and were, in fact, the kinds of factors normally associated with clinical judgment. However, health care professionals were looking for a clear template and introducing thirteen factors seemed to generate unnecessary complications.

Another important case followed this, *Eichner v. Dillion*, often referred to as the "Brother Fox case." Brother Fox was an eighty-six-year-old cleric. He was lifting a flower tub and suffered a hernia. During surgery, he suffered cardiac arrest and later became comatose. His religious superior, Father Eichner, attempted to gain custody, to gain decision making power over the person for purposes of having the respirator removed. To amplify an earlier distinction, although it is not unusual to offer custody or guardianship over property, that is, for signing checks or receiving money for an individual, it is much more difficult to gain power over person. Among other things, this power over person entitles a person to make decisions regarding another's life. As previously noted in *Quinlan*, Karen Ann Quinlan's father tried to get power over person. In *Saikewicz*, this was not a pertinent issue. In *Spring*, it arose because Spring's children and his wife attempted to get power over person to make the decision to have the dialysis machine removed, and the court would not allow it.

In the case of Brother Fox, Father Eicher wanted to get power to make the decision to have the respirator sustaining Brother Fox removed. In New York, a lower court set up a five-point process. This case was appealed and was reversed, arguing that having a process like that was cumbersome and that the criterion for decision making should be "any reasonable indication of patient intent." In *Dinnerstein*, that intent was charted in advance. In this case, there was no advance planning involved. Brother Fox came in for a hernia operation and ended up going into cardiac arrest. The ethics committee did not become a pertinent issue.

The *Brother Fox* reversal seemed to offer a more reasonable manner of handling such problems than most of the earlier formulations. Basically, the decision making that arises in this domain occurs between doctors and patient or between doctor and family or some other designated surrogate if the patient is incompetent. It is not necessary to invoke a legal process. One of the reasons the legal process is so often invoked is that it is assumed that the courts are impartial—more impartial than people with vested interest. However, one might ask, when it comes to decision making about what a dying family member would like, why be impartial? What you are trying to do is to determine what this person really would like. Partiality, in this domain, is a bonus—an asset. It is something good. Impartiality in this domain, is appropriate only in the absence of dependable partiality.

The Brother Fox case was written up in *The New England Journal of Medicine*, as a wonderful example of how decisions ought to be made and was heralded as being the finest decision of its kind. Interestingly, the standard before *Quinlan* was the shared decision making with the patient and family making decisions in light of some reasonable indication of patient intent. So, between *Quinlan* in 1976 and *Brother Fox* in 1981, we made a big circle and then applauded ourselves at the end, saying that after all the legal gymnastics and venturing through the thicket of liability what we ended up with was wonderful. Any reasonable indication of patient intent seems to be a good standard; it prevents a lot of problems and does not force these cases into the courts. In fairness to the legal legacy, we did gain heightened awareness and sensitivities to these issues, particularly informed consent and the right to refuse treatment, and we developed an increased appreciation of self-determination, autonomy, and related issues.

Recently, however, everything has changed in the area of removal of life supports. In July, 1983, in New Jersey, a case arose surrounding an elderly nursing home resident, Mrs. Conroy, who, among other conditions, suffered from organic brain syndrome and was accordingly incompetent. Her family wanted to have her nasogastric tube removed so that she would be allowed to die. The lower New Jersey court decided to allow removal of the nasogastric tube but was then overridden by the New Jersey Court of Appeals who argued that removal of the feeding support would constitute homicide—active euthanasia—and could neither be permitted nor tolerated.

It is important to recognize that in the medical area there are two distinctions made in other parts of law, but made in a little bit more unusual way in a medical context than in a nonmedical context. This involves the distinction between acts and omissions. In this particular case, the higher New Jersey court said, "Removal of her feeding supports would be an act that would be unacceptable." This was in July.

In October of the same year, two physicians in California were charged with homicide. Because of various complications, a patient who came in for some corrective surgery suffered severe anoxic depression, rendering him comatose. In this case, *Barber v. Superior Court of California*, the wife of the patient was told by the attending physician that he had taken some electroencephalograms, which were all flat. After receiving the wife's consent as the designated surrogate, he removed the respirator. The patient did not die. Three days later, they took out his IV feeding tubes and he died within days.

In *Barber v. Superior Court of California*, the court argued that removal of life supports on a comatose patient is an omission consistent with good medical care. As noted above, acts and omissions have different kinds of meanings in medicine and health care than they do in the nonmedical sectors of law. The California District Attorney brought homicide charges against the physicians. "Omission" usually means in medical context, "Let the disease take its natural course." If one does not do something and the disease progresses or the condition progresses on its own, that is often considered to be acceptable. In this case, removal of Mr. Barber's IV feeding tubes was an acceptable omission, part of reasonable medical care. In New Jersey, this was an act of homicide; in California, it was an acceptable omission. The New Jersey case was reversed on January 17, 1985.

The way in which we dictate what *ought* to be done by physicians is not really by what each state says but according to national standards of practice. As a professional, one has a higher responsibility to one's professional group and to the standards of that professional group in a given state. It is always assumed that those standards will exceed the minimal requirements set forth by a state, particularly if one is board certified. Transjurisdictional issues become problematic. Until New Jersey's *Conroy* reversal, one did not know what to rely on. In the New Jersey and California cases there was no clear guidance, but instead irreconcilability for over eighteen months. Still, how does someone in Nebraska or Montana know how to act?

If we accept *Barber v. Superior Court of California* as the controlling case, until recently it was unclear whether Karen Ann Quinlan could be moved from New Jersey to California and then legally be allowed to die. Some have even argued that the *Quinlan* decision itself allowed for removal of all extraordinary measures and interpreted this broadly to include feeding supports. In fact, incongruity resulted in the filing of an *amicus curiae*[1] brief that attempted to provide some clarification of this nebulous issue. Several interested parties initiated these proceedings, including former commissioners and professional staff members of the President's Commission on Ethical Issues in Biomedicine and Biomedical and Behavioral research, the American Geriatrics Society, the New Jersey Hospital Association, the New Jersey Concerned Tax Payers, the New Jersey Catholic Conference, the New Jersey Right to Die Committee, and the Concern for the Dying.

The New Jersey Supreme Court reversal noted that removal of feeding supports, as in California, was indeed consistent with existing standards of care based on the same standards as removal of respirators. New Jersey's *Conroy* has also set forth the necessary procedures and prerequisites for decision making by surrogates. Unfortunately, the issues in these cases and in related cross-state and jurisdictional matters are often not the least bit clear. This is grossly problematic, for how can health care professionals act with reasonably perceived propriety under the law? Even lawyers do not know what the result of a given case is going to be in this area. This is exacerbated by the fact that perceptions of the same data vary in the legal, as contradistinguished with the medical, field. For example, the chart is really no more than a worksheet in the medical health care context; however, when it gets to court it is a rigid document and can be the basis for insulation from or invitation to liability. Different professionals' mindsets and goals can thus create some real problems.

Cases such as that of Baby Doe further complicate this area. When we attempt to use the sophisticated criteria we have gleaned from dealing with adult cases surrounding DNRs and decisions to forego treatment and apply them to handicapped infants, a serious morass arises. The fundamental reason for this morass is our lack of consistency, or perhaps avoidance of dealing with the notions of appropriateness, reasonableness, and acceptableness across medical disciplines. Clinicians have been told that handicaps must be ignored. But, when a child presents such a cascade of problems in which his handicap *is* his medical condition, it is perverse to ignore this.

Still, however, the Health Care Finance Administration hotline for instant whistle-blowing by an interested party followed by the "Baby Doe Squads" has been modified to require only a listing of the hospital's phone number and to require signs only visible to clinicians when, and if, the hospital develops an in-house ethics committee to assist them in addressing these matters. Recent court cases have questioned the validity of the U.S. civil rights provision of 504 regarding discrimination against the handicapped as inappropriate to dictate policy in this domain. This will likely modify current policy, as much ambiguity still exists in this domain.

A recurrent question is that because we have the technical capacity to be able to do something, does this necessarily mean we should do it? A doctor's basic charge is to save life and, at the same time, not to do harm. This leads to the question of whether doing everything possible and utilizing everything one has in one's black bag armamentarium (a hospital is just a bigger black bag) is appropriate, or whether it is excessive. Can we be doing harm by doing everything that can be done?

The word "professional" comes from the Latin word "profietur" meaning "to serve." A person goes to a doctor or hospital because he needs something he cannot do for himself. He relies on the doctor or hospital personnel to do what lies in his best interest and certainly not to harm him. Need, appropriateness, and nonharm determine propriety. Just because we have capabilities at our disposal does not necessarily mean that we should use them in all cases.

A case in Massachusetts graphically depicts this. *Lane v. Candura*, which was argued in a lower court just about the same time as *Dinnerstein*, involved a woman who had a gangrenous leg. Although it was determined that if the leg was not removed she would likely die, she did not want the amputation because she then would have to rely on other people and her independence would be severely compromised. Her daughter tried to have her declared incompetent to get decision-making power to have the leg amputated in order to save her life. In their discussion, the Massachusetts court noted, "Competent individuals have the right to refuse treatment, even though it may mean their demise." Although Mrs. Candura had her leg amputated, it was not because her daughter was going to tell her what to do and override her own sense of self-determination as to what would or would not be done to her body. This underwrote the notion that society believes people basically have the right to self-determination as an extension of their right to privacy. In other words, one is protected from harmful, painful intrusions performed upon one's person by others. Consent thus provides a legal privilege that allows what, in the absence of that legal privilege, would otherwise not be tolerated. Self-determination is at the core of the issue of whether to perform invasions on one's body.

However, if we group together the feeding-removal cases with the respirator-removal cases, many problems arise. In the removal of a respirator from a person with a prognosis of hopelessness, we let the disease take its natural course by omitting further treatment. In the removal of feeding and hydration, which is a basic requirement for the sustenance of all life, we violate the natural process and their deprivation leads to starvation. Removing feeding supports may very well be indicated, but this is not equivalent to removing a respirator.

Suggestions for Protection of Patient Self-Determination

Some have argued that self-determination can be assured, and some of the frustration noted above avoided, through living wills. Fundamentally, there are two kinds of living wills, those written in "may" language and those written in "must" language. Living wills written in "may" language basically say, "If I'm in such and such a situation, and the likelihood of my being restored to a full life is low, and I go into cardiac arrest, I do not want to be resuscitated," or "I do not want any extraordinary means to be performed to save my life," or "I want to forego any treatment if I have a cancer or a stroke, or something like that." The "may" language primarily insulates the physician against the potential liability of performing a battery or against an omission that could result in death.

"Must" language is quite different. In fact the California Natural Death Act, which is one of the first living wills that has been recognized by law or by statute, says the physician must act in accordance with the living will maker's wishes. However, if acting in accordance with someone's wishes is inconsistent with the physician's ethics, that physician has an obligation to find another physician and cannot leave the patient abandoned.

There are many problems surrounding living wills. For example, if a husband wants to die in a certain way, and the wife does not want him to die in that way, she can keep the living will in a safe deposit box and no one is the wiser. In the case of a single adult, as is often the situation with elderly people, if the living will is locked up in the box or is at home under the mattress, it gives no indication of intent. However, if presented, the living will gives some indication of what this person wants. In Massachusetts, it would be helpful because we have the substituted judgment criterion. In New York, it would help because that would certainly be a reasonable indication of patient intent. So, when states like Nebraska, Iowa, Oregon, or South Carolina make decisions in this domain, they look to the precedent—to the common law precedent—of these other cases. If there is a clear sense of intent and a clear sense of what someone would have liked, then a reasonable decision usually can be reached. Unfortunately, in the New York case of Brother Fox, this failed to work. Brother Fox formerly taught medical ethics. Numerous family members said that removal of the respirator is what he would have wanted, whereas the district attorney said he had an obligation to protect life at all costs. Consequently, even with guidance, such situations still can be problematic.

Despite its lack of perfection, a living will is still a good idea because a person has a written document outlining his wishes. Talking with family members about what he would like is another important related protection to take. A copy of the living will should be given to his physician. If the doctor has the living will and makes it a part of the medical record, he has the confidence of knowing that his attending doctor, or his primary physician, has some knowledge of his intent. In this manner, the patient has some control over what is going on. Many seriously ill hospital patients are incapable of making health care decisions on their own behalf because such factors as trauma, disease, pain, medication, or old age interfere, at least temporarily, with their ability to approve or disapprove a course of treatment. The question then arises: Who is legally authorized to speak for a patient when he can no longer speak for himself? Some of the previously mentioned solutions pose the risk that the patient's own wishes will be ignored. Although a patient may have no power to avoid the onset of an incapacitating illness, he should at least be able to maintain control of the treatment. Through the technical means of an agent, a person can design his own response to his medical predicament.

A mechanism that may insure reasonable intent and secure an agent in which a patient has trust is currently being discussed in health law circles. This is the durable power of attorney,[2] which fundamentally is a document through which a person can specifically outline what he would like done given a certain occurrence, illness, condition, prognosis and so forth and/or designate specific decision-making agents with "power of person and/or property" in advance. The strength of this approach is that it offers an agent with legal ability to make decisions. Proxy decision making by an appointed agent is also more consistent with the tradition of informed consent. Although appointment of a medical agent does pose some risks of irrational decision making, overhasty findings of incapacity, and decision making that is inconsistent with the patient's wishes, these risks are no greater than those posed by living wills or proxies designated by statute.

From the patient's viewpoint, an agent would help to assure that, if incapacitated, the patient receive treatment in accordance with his own wishes. The appointment of an agent would avoid the difficulty, inherent in living wills, of trying to anticipate medical circumstances and treatment choices before the onset of an incapacitating illness. No document could possibly address the nearly infinite range of medical options that might arise. By contrast, an agent could ask questions, assess risks and costs, speak to friends and relatives of the patient, consider a variety of therapeutic options, seek the opinions of other physicians, evaluate the patient's condition and prospects for recovery—in short, engage in the same complex decision-making process that the patient himself would undertake if he were able. Thus, an agent could extend the scope of a patient's self-determination further than could a written directive by making decisions consistent with the patient's values and wishes in situations he might not have specifically foreseen.

Also, unlike a living will, the appointment of an agent would provide someone to enforce the patient's treatment preferences, to ensure that they are not disregarded or forgotten by family members or physicians. Doctors or family members may be able to ignore a living will or determine its instructions as inapplicable to the patient's actual circumstances.

Suggestions for Protection of Caregivers and Institutions

The best advice for physicians and nurses is to use the medical chart well, both to insure patient intent and insulate against liability. A common vignette of family conflict might serve to illustrate this importance. Assume for example that Mrs. Dinnerstein had two children. Also assume that Mrs. Dinnerstein has clearly said, "This is what I want," and it has not been written in the chart. One child says, "I want everything done for Mom. I don't care what it is. I want the best and most of everything." Unfortunately, those are not always equivalent. The other child says, "I want Mom to die peacefully. I don't want anything extraordinary done. Just keep her comfortable." When such disparate views cannot be resolved, one says, "That's what Mother told me she wanted." The other says, "I don't care what Mother wanted. She didn't always make the best decisions." What often happens in hospitals is that when Mother's wishes are not charted, the doctor, nurse, or institution will often take the most conservative course legally and do all that can be done. If the health care provider does do something or everything, then he only takes the chance that if there are problems he has erred toward keeping Mother alive; and that is more reversible than not doing something, which will result in avoidable death.

The primacy of decision making must rest with the patient. A patient need not sacrifice autonomy because he is incapacitated or loses consciousness. The durable power of attorney seems the best vehicle with which to capture and assure the wishes of the patient. He can designate the agent he trusts to act in his behalf. It is much better than using the courts. A judicial proceeding not only entails delay and expense, it may also prolong the physical suffering of the patient and aggravate the distress of a family already confronting the emotional and financial pressures of coping with a serious illness. Moreover, the fear of potential lawsuits tends to prompt hospitals to be overly cautious and to seek declaratory judgments even in those cases where they could safely treat or withdraw treatment with little or no risk of liability for nonconsent.

However, in the situation where a durable power of attorney has not been made, if the patient's wishes have been charted and there are irreconcilable differences among family members, there are still a few things that can be done. One is to bring in a consulting psychiatrist and have the patient declared competent (if indeed they are competent at that time) and actually write in the chart that there is conflict among family members, for example, one family member says to do everything and the other one says to do as little as possible. Then, one can write in the chart something to the effect that "Basically our responsibility as caregivers is to meet the needs of the patient. The patient says this is what she wants. We're bringing in a psychiatrist to certify that she indeed is competent and putting in the chart that this conflict exists and that our primary obligation lies with the patient." This would make it quite difficult for a court to find against the doctor who has acted in the best interests of the patient and even has taken special pains to be sure, despite familial conflict, that he has attempted to act in the best interests of the patient. This procedure may be invoked not only for an incompetent or incapacitated patient but for a competent patient as well. Some patients feel, for example, that making a particular treatment decision will cause them great distress, or they are concerned that the complexity or uncertainty of a certain disease will make them poor decision makers. In these situations, they may feel that trusted physicians or family members would be more likely to choose the treatment most in accord with their own goals and wishes.

Some physicians say dead people sue less than survivors. Although dead people can sue, that is, there are legal mechanisms to compensate survivors or someone acting on the behalf of the deceased through wrongful death suits, the likelihood is that the angered survivors will be the ones who are going to cause problems. Caretakers must then set forth that mechanism to insure the patient's rights that appears to not only provide reasonable care but optimal care.

"Do Not Feed" cases are perhaps the most complicated. Physicians, out of fear of being sued and a need to act in ways to insulate against liability, are trying for the most part to avoid these cases. They are even reluctant to do what the guidance of removal of respirator cases really offers. It is not uncommon to take five or six years to implement in the medical community what the courts have decided. Even though two major courts have provided clarification in this area, physicians are reluctant to get involved. It is a very complicated issue.

The courts are not usually the place where decisions about terminal illness should be made and certainly are not a forum of first resort. Such decisions should be made between patient and physician and, if that is not possible, between physician and family and/or the designated surrogate such as the durable agent. Failing to reach an acceptable decision here, one can then go through ethics committees—real ethics committees where there is a small interdisciplinary group trying to get at various facets of the problem while working with the family to come to a decision. This is a much more reasonable mechanism than the courts. The process of the courts is to appoint physicians and expert witnesses to provide testimony. They start the process from scratch. Why develop another process when one already exists where people are intimately involved? When it comes to making medical decisions about a loved one, intimacy is a positive factor, not a negative one, whereas impartiality is a negative factor, not a positive one. Some irreconcilable controversies, however, can only be handled in a forum such as the courts, once other mechanisms have been exhausted. However, they are the place of last resort—not first resort.

Hospitals are becoming much more sophisticated. They are now developing their own DNR protocols as contingency planning to preclude problems in this domain. However, what the hospital says ought to be the case and what is done are sometimes two separate things. The hospital is too often in a position where its main concern is not necessarily to act in the best interests of the patient but in insulating itself against liability and staying out of court. Hospitals need to realize that acting in the best interests of the patients usually is their own best insulation. Too often they fail to understand this. Legal decisions in an individual case often create unanticipated consequences that influence other domains. For example, *Barber v. Superior Court of California* implies that removal of an IV feeding tube is ordinary when someone has a prognosis of hopelessness; correlatively, putting an IV tube in someone whose prognosis is hopeless is extraordinary. Now, if a patient whose prognosis is clearly hopeless presents at the emergency department, stabilization could be potentially perceived as committing a battery when you put IV tubes in if you use the *Barber v. Superior Court of California* standard, that is, there may be no duty to stabilize and, in fact, a duty not to stabilize. What if the patient coming into the emergency department is accompanied by his trusted friend with durable power of attorney in hand, and the friend tells the emergency department that nothing must be done to extend the life of the patient? Even more problematic is the situation of the emergency medical technician or ambulance driver when faced with the same dilemma. These kinds of quandaries are readily apparent.

It is important to anticipate and prevent problems from arising during terminal illness care. The anticipatory grief experienced during a loved one's terminal illness is painful and stressful enough without adding additional problems that may compromise the dying person's wishes or later complicate the survivors' adjustment. For this reason, it becomes clear that some understanding of the guidance offered through living wills and agencies that can be construed durable powers of attorney can be helpful. This chapter is a beginning in that process of understanding.

Notes

1. *Amicus curiae* is a term that implies friendly intervention to call attention to a legal matter that has or might have escaped the court's attention.

2. A power of attorney is a written instrument by which one person (the principal) confirms his authorization of another (the agent or attorney-in-fact) to perform specified actions in his behalf. *See* Appointing a Medical Agent, *Columbia Law Review* 84:985, 1013–1014.

15

Financial Planning for the Terminally Ill: A Process for Addressing a Major Concern in Anticipatory Grief

James Blackerby
Edwin Steward

T he purpose of this chapter is to provide professional and lay people in contact with terminally ill patients with some general financial planning guidelines and considerations for those patients. We have not gone into detail about financial action to be taken regarding estate positioning, wills, or investments, for that must be specifically tailored to the individual's need by a financial professional. However, the information provided here should help the clinican recognize need and be able to provide some preliminary advice to the patient concerning how to organize and implement the necessary financial strategy.

Identifying the Need

The time before death in the terminally ill patient's life is obviously one of major emotional upheaval. Initially there is not much thought toward rational action. However, one of the major emotional concerns of the terminally ill individual is how to organize financial affairs so that the burdens on the spouse and other beneficiaries will be minimal. This requires rational thought and direction. As a consultative professional, the counselor, social worker, psychologist or psychiatrist, nurse, cleric, or physician should identify the emotional concern stemming from the need for financial assistance and help to focus attention on accomplishing results.

Due to the suddenness of the situation initially existing when an individual may learn of the illness, his financial condition will most likely be in disarray relative to future need. Lack of attention to this matter at the outset could exacerbate the emotional turmoil and complicate financial affairs at the time of death. One of the positive aspects of the catastrophic situations surrounding terminal illness is that there is time to put one's affairs in order as opposed to the situation surrounding sudden death.

The anxious questions of the terminally ill are usually ones such as, "Who will manage my affairs when I'm no longer able to?", "How can I arrange things for my spouse, who knows nothing about the business world, for the period between the time I'm 'out of it' and the time my will takes over?", or "What should I do to insure that my estate is not eaten up by taxes, with nothing left for my children?" A terminally ill person can do a great deal to assure peace of mind and a sense of security during the last phases of the illness by asking for professional help in putting financial affairs in order. Estate planning at the eleventh hour may not be ideal, but it is better than going into the time of sedatives, palliatives, and traumatic therapies with worrisome things left undone. How do members of the health services team bring the financial professionals on to the scene? Whose help do you want to make available?

To initiate a course of action, the proper financial professionals must be brought in for assistance. These professionals should be both trusted and qualified. Dealing with financial matters is a sensitive and delicate situation that can be obfuscated by less-than-sincere advisors. There have been well-documented cases of significant portions of estates disappearing as a result of "capture," where unethical financial advisors have misappropriated or absconded with funds. A trusted advisor is one with whom the individual has a long-standing relationship or one who comes from strong referrals by friends or associates. Qualified advisors are those with necessary experience and education. If you do not have direct referrals, proper advisors can be identified through various state-affiliated associations—International Association of Financial Planners for financial planners; American Bar Association for lawyers; and the American Institute for Certified Public Accountants for accountants.

The nature of assistance needed depends on the complexity of the situation, but in almost all circumstances four steps need to be accomplished:

1. Organizing the financial data.
2. Identifying saving potentials for income and estate tax purposes.
3. Formalizing the individual's financial desires through legal arrangements.
4. Implementing financial and investment action.

Typically, these steps should be accomplished as a team effort using a financial planner, attorney, and accountant. The more complex the case, the more need for the involvement of all three. In most cases, at least two advisors will be necessary to complete the process.

Data Gathering

The first step is important for creating a base for decision making and establishing an efficient process. The best advisor to use at this stage is a financial planner, who can take a comprehensive approach to the process. If one does not know of a trusted or recommended planner, then one should be sought who is a Certified Financial Planner (CFP) or a Chartered Financial Consultant (ChFC). The role of the planner will be to gather data, assess the financial and estate situation, and provide a plan of action. The planner should have an awareness of legal and tax needs as well as of appropriate investment action. From the information assembled, he or she can determine when it is appropriate to bring in the attorney and accountant. The planner should be able to identify warning signs in situations that will need special attention.

Included in the Appendix for this chapter is a method for organizing important assets and records. This form contains the type of information that will need to be identified. Heirs will need to know its location. The use of this device from the beginning of the counselor's meetings with the patient will be a very important part of the financial planning process.

Income and Estate Tax Savings

After a financial inventory is completed, the investment and estate planning needs become more apparent. It is at this juncture that a financial planner, accountant, and attorney could work together to establish a strategy for reducing taxes on income and the estate. The efforts may include (1) identifying gains and losses from stock sales and business operations to minimize final income taxes; (2) determining how charitable contributions will reduce estate and income tax; (3) reviewing pension, insurance, and annuity payout provisions for purposes of maximizing cash flow needs, minimizing taxes, and assuring long-term existence of capital; (4) establishing asset ownership, if time permits, to transfer assets from the estate; and (5) reviewing business property assets and provisions for the potential to separate them from the estate.

Formalizing Plans

The formalized plan is the individual's statement regarding wishes for distribution of the estate. At this time, the attorney reviews the current will and upgrades it to incorporate changes or necessary adjustments. The attorney will have information from the prior two steps to determine which formal plan would be most beneficial for the client.

The greater the client's assets, the more the need for detailed plans such as trust arrangements. Individuals with assets less than $500,000 in 1986 and $600,000 in 1987 and after will not be required to pay federal estate taxes. For estates larger than that, trust arrangements will be very important and significantly reduce tax burdens.

Two documents that are important for assuring continued control of the assets are a Durable Power of Attorney and a Stand-By Trust.

A Durable Power of Attorney designates a person or corporate entity (a trust company) as the patient's attorney. When the patient is incapable of managing his affairs (which is certified by two or more physicians), the attorney is empowered to place all or specified parts of the patient's property in an existing trust that is "standing by" with a trustee whom the patient has named.

The Stand-By Trust, preferably executed at the same time as the Power of Attorney, directs the trustee to take the property in trust and use the income and/or principal for the care of the patient at home, in a hospital, in a special care facility, or a nursing home as needed. It further directs the trustee to distribute the property remaining in the trust after the death of the patient to specified beneficiaries or charities without the need of going through the costs and delays of Probate Court.

With these simple arrangements a patient can decide who is to manage his affairs and see to the care of his person. The wise choice of both attorney and trustee and the selection of a charity as a beneficiary of part of the estate will prevent "capture" of a helpless patient by an unscrupulous person or persons and give the patient a sense of security and peace of mind.

Implementation

Coinciding with the structuring of the will and any trust is the positioning of liquid assets for investment purposes and establishing proper cash payouts. The closer an individual is to death, the fewer alternatives exist to make investments that will have a positive impact on the estate plan (property transferred within three years of death is included in estate value). However, there are alternatives that provide for last minute "death bed" purchases to lower estate value, such as "Flower Bonds." These are Treasury obligations that sell substantially below face value because of low interest rate. The face value of the bond is then applied to the payment of estate taxes.

Other actions that could occur at this stage include:

1. Scheduling pension, insurance, and investment payouts and identifying proper investments for such.

2. Determining if additional insurance options exist.

3. Identifying sources for all income, such as social security, veterans, and possible state payments.

4. Structuring the investment of all liquid assets so as to meet the approval of the terminally ill individual.

Summary

Upon learning that he has a terminal illness, an individual has many concerns, one of which is organizing his financial affairs so as to minimize the burden on the beneficiaries. The health professional involved with the individual can be of assistance by recognizing this concern and discussing the action that can be taken. If the financial concern is for a small estate, then the need may be merely organizational and assuring that the will is in order. A trusted financial advisor, such as a financial planner, accountant, or lawyer should be able to assist with the basic needs. If the estate need is larger, particularly above $500,000, then a team cf advisors should be used in order to maximize tax savings, assure orderly transfer of the estate, and take advantage of investment alternatives. The most important aspect is that, in any case, planning begins early so as to minimize the concerns and allow the individual to provide input on all matters.

Appendix

Document and Asset Record

To assure that all important documents and assets can be readily located, it is important to maintain an accurate record on file. Following is a method for maintaining such a record, and ensuring that the location can remain confidential.

The first part involves completion of a location index. This is a listing identifying where each document or asset may be found. Each location is identified alphabetically.

The second part involves the document and asset listing. This is a pre-established list of possible documents and assets, plus space available for additional personal items. Identify the location of the asset or document by indicating the corresponding letter for the location.

To maintain the confidentiality of the location of assets and documents, keep Part I and Part II of this record system in separate locations.

In addition to this information, a listing of people and places should be maintained with Part I. This should include your lawyer, accountant, financial planner, banker, insurance agent, and broker.

Part I

Location Index

A. Residence _____

(Address)

    A. 1   Room/File _____

    A. 2   Room/File _____

    A. 3   Room/File _____

    A. 4   Room/File _____

B. Office

    B. 1   Room/File _____

    B. 2   Room/File _____

    B. 3   Room/File _____

C. Safe Deposit Box

    # _____

    Bank _____

    Address _____

D.   Bank

    D. 1   Name/Account # _____

    D. 2   Name/Account # _____

    D. 3   Name/Account # _____

    D. 4   Name/Account # _____

E.   Investment Institution/Insurance Co.

    E. 1   Name/Account # _____

    E. 2   Name/Account # _____

    E. 3   Name/Account # _____

    E. 4   Name/Account # _____

F.   Other

    F. 1   _____

    F. 2   _____

    F. 3   _____

    F. 4   _____

Part II

Document and Asset Location List

Documents and Assets

Location
[Write in corresponding letter from Part I identifying location and room]

1.   Insurance Policies

    A.   Homeowner's   _____

    B.   Automobile   _____

    C.   Personal Liability   _____

    D.   Disability Income   _____

    E.   Life   _____

    F.   Business Policies   _____

    G.   Title   _____

    H.   Medical   _____

    I.   _____

2.   Cash and Other Securities

    A.   Cash   _____

Documents and Assets	Location

2. Cash and Other Securities (continued)
    B. Savings Passbooks _____
    C. Checkbooks _____
    D. Certificates of Deposit _____
    E. Bonds _____
    F. Mutual Fund Shares Information _____
    G. Stock Shares Information _____
    H. Money Market Funds _____
    I. _____ _____

3. Retirement (Plans)
    A. Corporate Retirement Plan _____
    B. Keogh, TSA, or IRA Plan _____
    C. Stock Option/Purchase Plans _____
    D. Annuities _____
    E. Other Plans _____
    F. _____ _____

4. Valuable Papers
    A. Birth Certificates _____
    B. Adoption Papers _____
    C. Citizenship Papers _____
    D. Passport(s) _____
    E. Tax Returns _____
    F. Financial Plan _____
    G. Military Records _____
    H. Marriage License _____
    I. Divorce/Separation Papers _____
    J. Death Certificates _____
    K. Titles _____
    L. Deeds _____
    M. _____ _____

Documents and Assets	Location

5. Collectibles
   - A. Artwork _____
   - B. Stamps _____
   - C. Coins _____
   - D. Metals _____
   - E. Precious Stones/Gems _____
   - F. _____ _____

6. Lists
   - A. Friends and Relatives _____
   - B. Credit Cards _____
   - C. Misc. Account #'s _____
   - D. Memberships _____
   - E. Valuable Possessions _____
   - F. Borrowed Possessions _____
   - G. Loaned Possessions _____
   - H. _____ _____

7. Liabilities
   - A. Mortgage(s) _____
   - B. Loans _____
   - C. Notes _____
   - D. Bills _____
   - E. _____ _____

8. Instructions
   - A. Will(s) _____
   - B. Power of Attorney _____
   - C. Burial Instructions _____
   - D. Children's Guardian Appt. _____
   - E. Special Bequests _____
   - F. Trusts _____
   - G. _____ _____

9. Miscellaneous
   - A. Safe Combinations _____

Documents and Assets	Location

9. Miscellaneous
   (continued)

    B. Rental Property Info.   _____

    C. Other Benefit Plans   _____

    D. Business Interests   _____

    E. Cancelled Checks   _____

    F. Warranties   _____

    G. Keys   _____

    H. Jewelry   _____

    I. _____   _____

    J. _____   _____

    K. _____   _____

    L. _____   _____

    M. _____   _____

    N. _____   _____

Index

Italic page numbers refer to reference entries

About the Contributors

Stanley M. Aronson, MD, is the founding dean of the Brown University Medical School. At present he is University Professor of Medical Science at Brown University. He currently holds visiting professorships at over twenty medical schools in the U.S. and abroad. He is a noted authority in the areas of neurology and neuropathology, and serves on the boards of the National Multiple Sclerosis Society, the Association of American Medical Colleges, and numerous health-related foundations.

James Blackerby is a personal financial planner with IDS Financial Services and American Express Company in Wakefield, Rhode Island. Mr. Blackerby has ten years' experience in the financial field, serving in banking, management consulting, and government finance. He has training through IDS in estate planning and is currently studying for his Certified Financial Planner Certificate. Mr. Blackerby holds a Master's in Public Administration and Finance from the University of Rhode Island.

Richard W. Boerstler, PhD, is the founder and director of Associates in Thanatology, South Yarmouth, Massachusetts. He has been a psychotherapist in private practice since 1972. His primary interest is in teaching comeditation and the "letting go" process to the dying and their families. He is the author of *Letting Go: A Holistic and Meditative Approach to Living and Dying.*

Marion A. Humphrey, RN, MA, CS, is a psychiatric nurse, clinical specialist in private practice in North Scituate, Rhode Island. She is also a thanatologist who has been extensively involved in the Hospice Movement, helping to establish several hospice groups. She specializes in offering education, consultation, and therapy services in the areas of chronic illness, grief, dying, and death.

J. Eugene Knott, PhD, is an associate professor in human development, counseling and family studies and an adjunct associate professor of psychology at the University of Rhode Island. He is a founder and past president of the Forum for

Death Education and Counseling, and is widely known for his expertise in death education. Along with numerous chapters and articles, he has coauthored *Thanatopics: A Manual of Structured Learning Experiences for Death Education.*

Hulen S. Kornfeld, RN, MA, is program coordinator at the Learning Center for Supportive Care in Lincoln, Massachusetts. She also serves as transitional counselor and comeditation instructor and lecturer at Associates in Thanatology, South Yarmouth, Massachusetts. She holds a master's degree from Beacon College in Thanatology. Since January 1982, she has been a nurse thanatologist in private practice, providing home care assessment and guidance through long-term progressive illness.

N. Claire Kowalski, MSW, is an assistant professor in the program in gerontology at the University of Rhode Island. Her research has focused on the institutional relocation of the elderly, and she has been the director of the Elderhostel Program at the University of Rhode Island. She is an active national board member in the Forum for Death Education and Counseling. Her present interest is in alternative cancer therapies.

The Reverend David M. LaGreca served for five years as staff chaplain to Hospice Care of Rhode Island. Father LaGreca spent four years as a parish priest in Lincoln and Warwick, Rhode Island. He holds a BA in philosophy, a BA in religious studies, an MA in theology, and a STB from Catholic University of Louvain in Belgium. He is presently a novice in the Society of Jesus.

Mary Elizabeth Mancini, RN, MSN, CNA, is the director of Emergency Services, Parkland Memorial Hospital, Dallas, Texas. She is an internationally known author and researcher in the area of Basic and Advanced Cardiac Life Support Training and a frequent lecturer on the psychosocial complications of trauma and intensive care. She is a member of the American Association of Critical Care Nurses and the Emergency Nurses Association.

Vanderlyn R. Pine, PhD, is a professor of sociology at the State University of New York, College at New Paltz. He holds a BA and an MA from Dartmouth College and a PhD from New York University. He is a noted lecturer on the subject of dying and death, and has been involved with counseling and research in death education. He is a member of numerous professional associations, serving on the advisory boards of the Center for Death Education and Research, the Foundation of Thanatology, the Forum for Death Education and Counseling, and the Hospice Association of Ulster County, and on the editorial boards of *Omega: The Journal of Death and Dying, Death Studies,* and *Suicide and Life Threatening Behavior.* His numerous publications include *Caretaker of the Dead: The American Funeral Director, Responding to Disaster,* and *Acute Grief* *and the Funeral.* His articles discuss such subjects as dying and death, funeral customs, social change, statistical analysis, and computerization.

Howard C. Raether, JD, has been involved in postdeath activities since 1940. He was Executive Director of the National Funeral Directors Association for 35 years. He has published widely, and is a frequent lecturer and consultant in bereavement, focusing on immediate postdeath activities. His consulting services are offered from Milwaukee, Wisconsin.

Dennis A. Robbins, PhD, MPH, is the director of the LeVine Institute on Aging in Detroit, Michigan. He writes and consults extensively on legal and ethical issues in the health care field. He has authored *Legal and Ethical Issues in Cancer Care in the United States* (1984) and *Ethical Dimensions of Clinical Medicine* (1982).

Edwin Steward is president of the Planned Giving Institute, Inc., and is a consultant to national and international voluntary organizations. He is the former Director of Trusts and Estates of White Plains Hospital Medical Center and former Director of Income Trusts and Bequests of Memorial Sloan-Kettering Cancer Center in New York. He has also worked extensively in the development and bequest area of the American Cancer Society, various colleges, and religious organizations. Mr. Steward holds a Master of Divinity degree from the Eastern Baptist Theological Seminary in Philadelphia.

Janice DeFrances Van Dexter, MA, MEd, is the educational director at Harmony Hill School, Inc., a residential and day treatment center for behaviorally disturbed youth in Rhode Island. She is an EdD candidate at Boston University in special education administration and is the Rhode Island State Coordinator for the Behaviorally Disordered on the Council for Exceptional Children.

Eugenia Wild, MA, NCC, is a counselor in private practice in Hope Valley, Rhode Island. She is a bereaved parent whose daughter died of leukemia thirteen years after diagnosis. During that time, she coauthored the *Parent's Handbook on Leukemia,* published by the American Cancer Society, and developed the position of Parent Consultant in Pediatric Oncology, at Rhode Island Hospital, providing liaison and advocacy for parents of children with cancer.

About the Editor

Therese A. Rando, PhD, is a clinical psychologist in private practice in North Scituate, Rhode Island. She is the clinical director of Therese A. Rando Associates, Ltd., a multidisciplinary team providing psychotherapy, training, and consultation in the area of mental health, specializing in loss and grief and the psychosocial care of the chronically and terminally ill. Dr. Rando holds a PhD in clinical psychology from the University of Rhode Island and has received advanced training in psychotherapy and in medical consultation-liaison psychiatry at Case Western Reserve University Medical School and University Hospitals of Cleveland. As a former consultant to the U.S. Department of Health and Human Services' Hospice Education Program for Nurses, she developed their program for training hospice nurses to cope with loss, grief, and terminal illness. She has written numerous articles and chapters pertaining to the clinical aspects of thanatology, and is the author of *Grief, Dying, and Death: Clinical Interventions for Caregivers* (Research Press, 1984) and the editor of *Parental Loss of a Child* (Research Press, 1986).